PRAISE FOR DANIEL ALLISON

A much-needed telling of the Irish 'in the beginning'... beautifully written and very accessible

— SANDY DUNLOP, BARD MYTHOLOGIES

Despite the historical remoteness of these ancient tales, Allison's telling is deeply engrossing; his exuberant style illuminates what is human and deeply relatable in material known for the lofty and the grand... friendship, love, and betrayal alike shine with realism, and moments deeply moving and beautiful arise from the text like healing herbs growing from the dark soil of the past.

— DANICA BOYCE, FAIR FOLK MEDIA

A captivating retelling where the oldest stories of Irish mythology beat to the pulse of modern fantasy. Meticulously researched and expertly paced, this book is a spellbinding testament to the enduring power of Irish myth, reimagined for a new audience. Daniel infuses the tales with true-to-life characters and real heart.

— SORCHA HEGARTY, CANDLELIT TALES

Daniel Allison is a myth walker. Bound by his love of myth and a deeply curious mind, he walks the world with one foot in the mythical and one foot in the here and now. I've no doubt he will spend the rest of his days unearthing myth and bringing it into the light of our contemporary world. This is work that we need.

— CLARE MURPHY, IRISH STORYTELLER

Irish Mythology is the perfect blend of respect for tradition, deep love for myths, and creative storytelling. This book bridges the divide between oral storytelling and written fiction with a lively style that begs to be read aloud. Epic battles, formidable heroes, powerful magic, and deep emotions create a mythic landscape that is vividly alive. If you enjoyed Neil Gaiman's *Norse Mythology*, you will love this book.

— CSENGE ZALKA, AUTHOR OF *DANCING ON THE BLADES*

Full of action, wonder and melancholy leavened by sprinklings of humour, *Irish Mythology* is an approachable, concise, and gripping read by an author who loves the stories, writes with agility, and knows what he's talking about. Highly recommended.

— LAURA SAMPSON, AUTHOR OF *ENCHANTED TALES*

A masterful merging of myth and fantasy. Allison gives the gods and goddesses such a rich, complex emotional life that you live the tales with them. He paints the picture of these otherworldly realms so vividly that you will be completely enthralled.

I was feasting with the sidhe; I danced in the Gaels' great halls; and when Lugh called the cry to battle, I had a tear in my eye. I held my breath through the battle, tasted the blood raining from the sky, and felt the piercing shriek of crows like knives in my bones. The world outside disappeared, and I became one with the ancient.

This is unlike anything I have ever read. It is a masterpiece.

— CHRISTINE KAMMERER, JOTUN
REVOLUTION

For anyone who, like myself, who has dodged the complexity of the myths in their old forms, this makes a compelling read from beginning to end. I loved it. Especially the author's depiction of the Morrigan as the powerhouse goddess and master of magic that she is.

Prepare to be bound by the spell of a good story made all the richer by the lively and lyrical telling of it. Magical writing at its finest!

— SHEENA CUNDY, AUTHOR OF *RICHES FOR WITCHES* AND SINGER WITH *MORRIGAN'S PATH*

Epic battles, shrouded otherworlds and secret sorcery... Daniel Allison's book is a gem.

— PADDY O'BRIEN, IRISH STORYTELLER

IRISH MYTHOLOGY

THE CHILDREN OF DANU

CELTIC MYTHS & LEGENDS RETOLD

DANIEL ALLISON

HOUSE
of
LEGENDS

INTRODUCTION

Irish myths are the most baffling I've come across.

They're also my favourite.

I'm not Irish myself; let's be upfront about that. I'm Scottish with a smidge of Irish blood, I grew up in Scotland and only discovered my native folklore in later life. I say folklore because other than a few precious stories, a scattering of hints, we don't have myths in Scotland. There is no pantheon of gods nor tales of how they made the world, set the sun and moon in the sky, or indulged in romantic affairs with mortals. We can assume we once had such stories, but they are lost to time.

Yet nearby, just a short sail over the Irish Sea, lies a land whose gods and myths still live. Names like Lugh, the Dagda and the Morrigan are well-known in Ireland and far beyond her shores. Most people there know at least a handful of the tales, many far more. As an oral storyteller and lover of mythology, the allure of a neighbouring land where the gods still ride the tongues of storytellers is irresistible.

But those gods can be hard work.

Part of the reason that Ireland has such a strong mythological tradition is that her myths were written down. Not by pagan bards, as you might imagine, but by Christian monks. The *Lebor Gabála Érenn*, or *Book of the Taking of Ireland* or *Book of Invasions*, was compiled by an unnamed scholar in the 11th century. A mixture of prose narrative and verse, the *Book of Invasions* documents a series of six incursions into Ireland by the people of Cesaire, the Parthalonians, the Nemedians, the Firbolgs, the Tuatha Dé Danaan and finally the Milesians or Gaels. We learn more about the Tuatha Dé Danaan in the *Cath Maige Tuired*, which is believed to date back to the 12th century. Other texts from this period tell us of the deeds of human (or half-human) heroes such as Cuchulainn and Fionn Mac Cumhaill, but as far as mythological texts go, the *Book of Invasions* and the *Cath Maige Tuired* are the primary sources.

And here our troubles begin.

Ireland's pagan myths were written down by Christians. Whoever they were, they certainly attempted to reconcile pagan stories with the Bible. Hence, we are told that the Gaels are descended from Noah, and that Cesaire discovered Ireland after setting out to escape the Flood. So right from the outset, we see that these are stories in flux.

The written stories continued to change over time (I say written because the oral telling of the tales never stopped). The fifth wave of invaders, the Tuatha Dé Danaan, fought with a race known as the Fomorians. Dáithí Ó hOgáin writes that their name meant 'underworld phantoms', but through a confusion of the Irish words *mor* (phantom) and *muir* (sea), they came to be regarded as sea-pirates. In time, the Fomorians became equated with Vikings, who harried Ireland from 795, and in 841 built the settlement that would grow into modern-day Dublin.

So anyone looking for pure, unadulterated pagan mythology in Ireland is going to be hard-pressed. Pagan and Christian mythology met in the *Book of Invasions*, and the tales went on changing as time rolled on.

But are the tales worth less because of that? Should we see them as sullied and impure, like precious stones with fault lines running through them, or as beings whose very nature is change?

The mythologist Joseph Campbell was once asked if you could make a new myth. He answered, 'Sure. But it'll take ten thousand years'. Stories in pre-literate cultures generally take a long time to settle into a particular shape. But things are different in literate cultures. We live under what has been called 'the tyranny of the written word'. A story arising in an oral culture could have innumerable variations as it travelled from one region to another, or even from one end of the world to another. Yet such authority do we give to writing that as soon as someone writes down one such iteration of a tale, that becomes 'the correct version'.

Fast-forward to the modern day. The *Book of Invasions* is available to any Irish or English-speaker with an internet connection. Written retellings of its tales for both adults and children abound. Its characters have found their way into comic books and video games, and provided inspiration for *Star*

Wars and *The Lord of the Rings*. Irish myths are all around us, hiding in plain sight. And all the while, lurking quietly in the background, is the oral tradition.

People everywhere have always told stories from memory, without reference to books. The ancient Irish were no different. We can assume that they did not all rush to bring their tellings into line with the *Book of Invasions* the moment it was completed. So might we look instead to the oral tradition for a purer strain of story?

That's the thing about oral tradition, though. Only in the very strictest of traditions will you find tales that do not have porous borders, that do not shapeshift as they cross time and space. I won't make any general claim about Irish tellers today, but I will say that the ones I know incorporate modern ideas about the myths in their tellings. They interpret characters, they invent dialogue and detail, without going so far that they alter the fundamental nature of a story.

All of this is to say that I make no claims to authority in offering this book to the world. My versions of the tales are not 'correct'. I'm simply one in a long line of storytellers who loves these tales and feels compelled to share what they love.

My way of telling these tales is characterised by a few key factors. Firstly, I'm an oral storyteller. I've been telling stories in schools, libraries, festivals and wherever they'll have me for fifteen years, and I run a storytelling school and podcast. Naturally this influences my writing style, and I tell stories orally to a wide range of audiences before writing them down. Key to my preparation for writing this book was a period spent travelling around Ireland, talking to respected storytellers and tradition-bearers, listening to them practise their art and discussing the myths with them. Wherever you might read this, I'd like you to feel that some part of you is sitting by a fire, the words of a Donegal bard mingling with the smoke.

Secondly, I'm an author of fantasy fiction. I like to flesh out characters, dig into their motivations and use detailed description to bring a scene to life. This influences how I retell oral stories. It entails regular departure from source texts, in which the innermost feelings of characters are not subject to discussion. It's more 'He did this, then she did that, then that'. Character and motivation can be inferred from events, but are highly debatable.

This brings us to a big question. How far is too far? Where lies the divide between imaginative retelling and mythically inspired fantasy?

There's no definitive answer to that. Different authors and readers will draw the line in different places. The *Book of Invasions* is not internally coherent. The stories have changed since it was written, numerous contradictory oral versions exist, and popular retellings such as Lady Gregory's *Gods and Fighting Men* have influenced the popular understanding of these stories. It would be impossible to write an accurate and internally coherent retelling of these stories. Just to discuss how Lugh or Balor or Angus felt at a given moment can be a departure. Would any modern reader wish to read a retelling that omitted such things? I doubt it.

So where is my dividing line? I try to stay on the side of retelling where possible, while acknowledging that my style bears the imprint of my own character and culture. In order to tie together the plot and provide a satisfying level of detail and characterisation, I have at times inserted original scenes, given names to unnamed characters or otherwise made my own mark on the myths. I note all major instances of this kind in the endnotes to each chapter.

One of the most important decisions I had to make was where to start. As mentioned, the *Book of Invasions* documents six waves of invasion. I chose to focus this volume on the fifth and sixth waves, those of the Tuatha Dé Danaan and the Gaels. The stories concerning the earlier invaders are extremely sparse and are often called by Dáithí Ó hOgáin 'biblical pseudo-history'.

A great deal of invention would be required on my part to bring these narratives into line with the tone of the stories told herein. On the other hand, the fifth and six waves make for an immensely rich and satisfying narrative. So I've focused on these, preceded by a brief retelling of the early invasions in the prologue. If they resonate with you, by all means seek out other versions.

Another tricky decision concerned the character I've called the Morrigan. One of the principal Tuatha Dé Danaan, she is part of a trio of goddesses known variously as the Morrigna (not a typo, that's their collective title) and the three sisters of the Morrigan. She is sometimes referred to individually as the Morrigan, but this word is also used as a title, and sometimes given in that regard to other characters. She is also sometimes known as Anand, and some tellers will use that name to distinguish her from her sisters.

I have chosen to call her the Morrigan as this is how she is best known today, and how I know her. I'm not claiming any last word; what you call her is your decision. Morgan Daimler's books are an excellent resource if you feel inspired to further acquaint yourself with the Morrigan.

Speaking of further explorations, I'd love it if you did some. My intention is that this book be a starting point. An accessible and entertaining read that keeps you turning the pages and, once you've finished, leaves you hungry to explore other tellings of these tales. When you do so, I suggest that you seek out the work of native Irish authors and storytellers. I do not wish to appropriate or take away from their work but rather to create new fans of Irish mythology, so that the stories reach new hearts and minds, and so that both the tradition and its custodians are enriched. I appreciate that others might see this differently, and I'm always open to hearing other points of view.

With all that said, it's time to let the stories speak.

A NOTE ON PRONUNCIATION

Pronunciation of Irish words can be difficult for those who don't speak the language. Rather than offering a phonetic pronunciation guide, I suggest you listen to native Irish-speakers pronouncing the names of the key characters; there are plenty of resources available online. The website Forvo is very useful in this regard.

PROLOGUE: THE EARLY INVASIONS

It began with a dream.

Cesaire dreamed that a great flood would cover the world. She spread the news far and wide, yet few of her people believed her. Dozens of women sensed the truth of her prophecy, and a few men. One of these was her father, Bith. Another was a man named Ladra; the last was a forest-dweller named Fintan.

Cesaire's faithful asked her what they should do. She told them to build boats. So they set to work and built three vessels, each big enough to hold fifty people. That done, they set out onto the ocean with Cesaire as their captain.

The flood came. It submerged all the lands of the world. Forests, hills, towns; all disappeared in a day.

Cesaire's fleet sailed the ocean-world for seven years. One ship was lost to a storm; another was torn in two on a mountain's peak. But in time the flood waters receded and Cesaire's remaining crew sighted land.

They arrived on a beautiful green island in the very west of the world. Cesaire leapt from ship to sand, becoming the first woman to set foot on the island we call Ireland. What she called it, we do not know.

Fintan was the first man to set foot on the island. Ladra followed and was injured as he leapt; a rough-edged oar tore open his thigh.

The Cesarians agreed to remain on the island and populate it. It was decided that grey-bearded Bith would be husband to sixteen women, while the more virile Fintan and Ladra would each take seventeen. They set to work and soon bawling babies were everywhere. Yet all that action was too much for old Bith. He could not keep up with the needs of his harem. He died of exhaustion, and Ladra died of his festering oar-wound soon after.

That left Fintan to satisfy everyone.

Fintan was no average man. He had bears in his belly and lightning in his blood. He could have satisfied five thousand women; he wouldn't break a sweat over fifty. Yet women weren't on his mind. More alluring to him were Ireland's moss-flanked forests, her cave-slashed hills, the whispering summon of her stormy shores. So he fled, leaving forty-nine women hopelessly horny and one woman heartbroken. That woman was Cesaire, who had loved him before they even left their homeland.

Fintan made for the hills.

There, he chose a cave.

That cave became his home.

Within a womb of stone, Fintan dreamed.

He dreamed he was a salmon. He dreamed salmon and became salmon, questing the length of every river, apprentice to their snaking paths.

Fintan became a hawk. He soared through the skies for seasons beyond count. He learnt the secret name of every star; he watched acorns grow into oaks. He filled the firmament with lilting songs long after Cesaire and her people had perished.

Fintan went on dreaming and skin-swapping. He patrolled as a stag, a bear, a bull, while centuries ambled by. His homeland was at peace; he was at peace.

A day came when that peace was broken.

PARTHALON LED THE SECOND INVASION.

He was a giant of man. Dark-haired, dense-muscled, sunbronzed; a prince. Back home, he had helped his brother attain the throne by murdering their mother and father. Their coup succeeded, but Parthalon's dark deed wrought a curse. Everything he tried his hand at was doomed to fail.

Yet Parthalon was strong of arm and will, and people follow power. He set out to escape his fate and a band of his people followed him. They wandered the whale road, landed in the Shannon estuary and saw four lakes spring up before their eyes. Clearly, they said, a sign of welcome. So they set about clearing the forests and making the island their own.

Their claim to ownership was soon challenged.

Monstrous creatures, scaly-skinned and many-eyed, rose up

out of the western sea. They approached Parthalon and gave their name as the Fomorians. If Parthalon wished to claim the land, said their captain, he would have to fight for it.

So he did. The Parthalonians fought the Fomorians in the particular way that fighting was done at that time. Each warrior fought on one leg, with one arm tied behind their back and one eye closed.

Parthalon's people won. The Fomor retreated.

More land was cleared. Villages sprung up. Harvests were gathered, feasts were held and years passed by in peace. The summer were not too hot; the winters were not too cold.

All was well.

Parthalon decided to go on a royal progress. He would visit his chief men and women across the country, see new vistas and solidify his rule. He set off and was gone for many months. He left his wife, Delgnat, at home.

During Parthalon's absence, Delgnat took a fancy to her handsome servant, Topa. She took him to her bed. When Parthalon finally returned, she put Topa aside, having sworn him to secrecy. Yet Parthalon happened to drink from a cup which Topa had drunk from, and the cup whispered the truth to him.

Parthalon confronted his wife with her infidelity.

She answered him:

Honey with a woman, milk with a cat,
Food with one generous.
Meat with a child,
A craftsman with an edged tool.

One before one earns great risk.

The woman will take the honey.
The cat will drink the milk.
The generous one will give away all the food.
The child will eat the meat,
The craftsman will lay hold of the tool.

The one with the one will always go together.

Parthalon would not accept this. He drew his dagger and sheathed it in Delgnat's chest. Yet everyone agreed that Delgnat had the right of it.

Parthalon ruled for many years, yet his curse ruled him. A devastating plague struck his people one summer, wiping them out to the last child. Wild animals wandered empty villages; corpses rotted in the markets.

So hush fell over the island again, as long-tailed Fintan stalked the forests.

NEXT CAME NEMED.

This one was a warrior, sharp-eyed and battle-hardened. He set out from his homeland with thirty-four ships, each crewed by thirty fighters. On their long journey, they spied a tower of purest gold rising out of the ocean. The sight enflamed their greed and so they changed course, approaching the tower and seeking an entrance.

As Nemed and his people searched, a great wave assaulted them. It tore through the fleet, hurling ships against the golden tower, breaking them as if they were toys.

Only one ship survived. Nemed, his wife and his four children were aboard it.

They sailed onwards. In time they too arrived at the island in the west of the world. As they stepped onto her sands, four lakes sprung up, which they took as a sign of welcome.

The Fomorians did not welcome them.

The scaled sea-dwellers rose from the waves and made war on the Nemedians. At first they fought the same half-blind, hopping, ritual battles that they had waged against Parthalon's people. But in time, such niceties were laid aside, for the Nemedians were winning every encounter. So the Fomorians attacked in greater numbers, putting aside their own rules of engagement.

They were too late. Nemed's people had already spread across the land, their population growing year on year. They held off their assailants for thousands of years, during which time the two races learnt a fierce hatred of one another.

Eventually the Fomorians spied their chance. A plague fell on the Nemedians, wiping out two-thirds of their numbers. The Fomorians acted quickly. Led by two newly allied kings named Morc and Conand, they renewed their war, slaughtering the Nemedians on the field and in their beds until only scattered parties survived.

These last few surrendered to the Fomorians. Morc and

Conand spared their lives but demanded reparations: a third of their crops, cattle and children, passing over to each successive generation.

The taxes were paid for a decade or two. But as memories of the plague receded, the tiger-hearted Nemedians grew bolder. They elected to strike again at the Fomorians, winning their freedom or dying in the attempt.

They gathered together, raised their banners and crossed the sea to Tory Island off Donegal's coast. Conand kept a fortress there, a launching point for assaults on the mainland. The Fomorian homeland was both beneath and across the sea, in a realm which only those skilled in magic could access.

The Nemedians commenced their assault. Fomorian fighters poured from Conand's fortress and so the battle began.

It seemed an even fight. But then Morc arrived from the Fomorian realm, his vast fleet rising from the dark water. The fleet raced towards Tory Island with Morc standing on the prow of his command ship, speaking words of magic.

His spell made the sea rise up, submerging the Nemedians as Conand's force retreated into the fortress. The rising of the sea happened slowly, yet the Nemedians were so addled with battle-rage that they did not spy the danger until it was too late.

All but a few of the Nemedians perished.

Some who survived returned to their homes. There they perished of plague or fell to Fomorian war bands. A few of their ships went south then east, eventually arriving on sunbaked shores where no happy fate awaited them.

The rest of the ships turned north. These Nemedians hoped that in the world's frozen north might lie hidden harbours, places no sane race would seek out. They envisioned refuges where deep study and magecraft might empower them to win the fair green isle for all time. It was a desperate hope, but they were a desperate people.

High overhead in his eagle-skin, Fintan watched them depart.

We will hear more about the Nemedians who went north. But first, the Firbolgs.

THE GROUP that turned south were in a sorry state. They lacked food, fresh water, and hope. In all senses of the word, they were defeated.

It was no way to arrive in a war-hardened land.

They came ashore in the land now known as Greece. The local people did what was always done in such instances; they enslaved the refugees. Whipped them, beat them and set them to work. Their task was to carry bags of clay from the coast to the high hills in order to make them fertile. Their masters nick-named them 'the men of the bag', which in their own tongue was pronounced 'fir bolgs'. The slaves took that name for them-selves in time, and are still known as the Firbolgs.

Hard as their lives were, the Firbolgs never forgot the land they had fled. They told stories of her round their fires at night, and began to dream and to speak of the day when they would finally break their chains and escape. But how?

At last, a man among them named Slainge formed a plan. In secret they gathered sticks and forged wicker frames.

Stretching their bags across the frames, they made coracles. Late one night, they escaped their cells, rowed out to sea and thus won their freedom.

They reached home. The Firbolgs were a changed people, hardened by years of slavery beneath the hot sun. Despite their small numbers, they managed to survive the inevitable Fomorian assaults. But they could never defeat their foes, whose numbers were so much greater. So they agreed to pay taxes to the Fomorians, and thus bought their peace. But it was a bitter one.

The Firbolgs crowned Slainge their High King. He made his seat at Tara in the east, and divided the island into four provinces: Ulster, Leinster, Munster and Connacht. The Firbolg druids made their seat at Uisnech, a central summit pregnant with magic, which some still call the fifth province.

Slainge was the first High King of the Firbolgs. Many years later, Eochaid was the last. He was High King when the Firbolgs' kindred, those who had sailed north instead of south, returned from their long sojourn at the edge of dreaming.

They returned in immense numbers.

They returned with devastating magic.

They returned as the Tuatha Dé Danaan.[1]

PART I

1

THE LANDING

From the north of the world, in a fleet of golden-prowed ships, came the Children of Danu.

The wind was ever in their favour, for their druids had power over the wind. The sea did not trouble them with storms, for their champion, Manannán, was one with the waters. He galloped before them on his white horse Enbarr, her hooves dancing over the waves.

On the prow of one ship stood the Dagda, whom many called the Good God. His fingers strummed his oaken harp, pouring joyous music into salt-sharp air. As he played, he searched the horizon for the land which would be his new home. His fingers itched to sink themselves into her soil, to plant barley and watch it grow golden beneath the sun. He would brew ale from that barley and drink it at a thousand feasts.

The Dagda's harp was imbued with magic. Its song rang out over the entire fleet, all the way to a ship upon which sat three tawny-haired women: Badb, Macha and the Morrigan. Mothers and magic-workers, both gentle and ferocious, these three were loved by the Tuatha and feared by their enemies. They caught the visions of fields and feasts riding upon the Dagda's tune and added their own.

Women screaming in childbirth.

Couples in the throes of passion.

The bones of dead Tuatha buried in peat.

Life beginning, life lived, life ending.

The Tuatha Dé Danaan were immortal. Left in peace, they would never die. But the time to come was no time of peace.

The Morrigan abruptly shifted in shape. Her eyes turned nightshade-dark; feathers sprouted from her skin; she spread her cloak wide and became a great crow. Wearing her war form, she beat her wings and rose high into the sky.

The Tuatha had passed an unimaginable span of years in the world's frozen North. They had founded their four shining, shimmering cities of Gorias, Finias, Murias and Falias. Within those walls they attained life eternal, though they could still be killed in battle. So long did they spend there, so deeply immersed in study and sorcery, that they spoke less and less often of the home they had left behind.

At first, they sang nightly of their eventual return. Centuries passed and such songs were forgotten. Memory became myth; a myth which weakened, withered and died. Instead, the once-Nemedians now dreamed and sang of Danu, the Great Mother, who had revealed herself in the visions of their druids. They forgot the name of Nemed and styled themselves the Tuatha Dé Danaan, the Children of Danu.

The Tuatha might have remained in the North had not a dream descended on their cities one night.

That night, every sidhe from kings to cowherds dreamed of a perfect island far across the sea. They dreamed of it every night for many weeks. In these dreams they wandered her shores, swam in her lakes, climbed her peaks to gaze on her green glens.

She was lovely beyond all words. Neither too rocky nor too boggy; neither too cold in winter nor too hot in summer. She sang a siren song to them, that beating green heart of a blue world, enflaming their desire until they could no longer resist her. It was clearly the will of Danu, they said, that this island become theirs.

So the sidhe set to work. They built a fleet of golden-prowed ships so vast it could carry them all. They left their homeland, taking with them their four great treasures.

The Shining Sword from Gorias.

The Spear of Victory from Finias.

The Cauldron of Plenty from Murias.

The Stone of Destiny from Falias.

Druids and warriors, bards and smiths now strained to catch sight of the Isle of Destiny, as they had already taken to calling it. They looked with pride towards the lead ship, grandest of all, its sails as white as a midwinter moon. The Morrigan circled its sails and looked down upon Nuada, High King of the Tuatha Dé Danaan.

Brown-bearded, honey-voiced, soft-smiling Nuada. A High

King adored by his people. He planned to bargain with whomever inhabited the Isle of Destiny, hoping that it could be taken without the spilling of blood. Such was his people's faith in him that many believed he would succeed, that their swords would remain sheathed.

The Morrigan shifted her shape again. She became not one crow but a host of crows, a murder of black-beaks erupting into murderous music.

She wanted the same things as Nuada. Yet it is the wisdom of the crow to see through fantasies of friendship and kindness.

There was always blood.

FINALLY A CRY WENT UP among Danu's children; the Isle of Destiny was in sight.

King Nuada turned to his chief druids.

'Manufacture a mist,' he said. 'Ensure we are not spotted.'

The druids obeyed and soon a cloud of fog enshrouded the fleet. It turned west then south, skirting the coast until the navigators spied a likely landing place.

The Tuatha came ashore in the region they would soon call Connacht. Still shielded by the druid-fog, they heaved their boats ashore and, at Nuada's command, put them to the torch.

Had it not been for the magical mist, the smoke from that blaze would have been visible all across Connacht. It would have darkened the skies of Ulster in the north and Munster in the south. The smoke would have been spied in easternmost

Leinster, where Eochaid, High King of the Firbolgs, held court at Tara.

NUADA HAD his druids maintain their spell for many days. Few armies could match the sidhe in battle, but he was not fool-hardy. He ordered his people to build and secure a shoreside camp, and only once it was complete did the druids lift the mist. The vast sidhe camp, with its high walls, sentry towers and fluttering banners, was soon spotted by local farmers and fishers.

Messengers ran to Tara with news of the invasion.

'There are thousands of them.'

'They are taller than us, and well-armed.'

'They arrived in a fog which must have been the work of powerful druids.'

Eochaid listened from his throne, a cup of ale in hand.

His mind raced, yet he did his best to appear untroubled as he surveyed his hall. Torches burned in braziers. A great fire pit ran down the centre, hounds lazing beside it while meat roasted on skewers over the flames. The tables that lined the hall were crowded with chiefs and champions, warriors and wordsmiths.

Every one of them was watching him silently, gauging his reaction to the news. He must not show fear. Fear meant weakness. To some among his chiefs, weakness in their leader meant opportunity.

Eochaid yawned, sipped his ale and said, 'Sreng. Come forward.'

Eochaid's champion rose from his seat and came to stand before the messengers. They craned their necks to look up at him, their eyes wide, taking in his oak-thick arms, his ale-barrel chest, his spear that could have skewered a bear.

'Tell me,' said Eochaid, 'did these strangers appear stronger than this man?'

'No, sire.'

Sreng looked down at them with impassive eyes. He was Eochaid's oldest friend, fiercely loyal and the finest fighter among the Firbolgs. On top of that, he was generous, forgiving, and quick with a jest. Yet Eochaid preferred his court not to know it.

Eochaid caught Sreng's eye and nodded.

Sreng's hand shot out and clasped the neck of the nearest messenger. He lifted him into the air, squeezing his neck so that his face turned bruise-purple.

'We need not fear these foreigners. The foreigners should fear the Firbolgs!' said Eochaid as the assembly laughed and bellowed their agreement, pounding their fists on the tables.

Sreng released the messenger, who collapsed to his knees as Eochaid stood.

'Sreng shall meet these incomers. He will deliver my terms, which are simple: leave now or we shall kill you all.'

THE CHIEFS of the Tuatha Dé Danaan gathered on the seashore that evening.

'The inhabitants of the Isle of Destiny have seen us,' said Nuada, 'and doubtless sent word to their king.'

'I have taken wing across the country and looked upon his hall,' said the Morrigan. 'It is called Tara. It sits upon a hill close to the eastern shore, in the province these people call Leinster. A champion has left Tara and comes our way. He is a mighty man, though his clothing is coarse and his spear strangely shaped, as with all of the natives I have spied.'

'What else have you learnt of them?' asked the Dagda, his fingers twisting his red beard.

'They call themselves the Firbolgs,' answered the Morrigan. She frowned. 'Something is afoot here which I have not yet discerned. A shadow clings to the Firbolgs. They are tough and clever, yet their houses are crudely built, their clothing poor. They have few children, even though their fields are fertile, and many of them look gaunt and underfed. Yet whatever darkness plagues them, they survive it, and are hardened by it. They will not give up their country easily.'

There was uneasy muttering at this, which Nuada interrupted.

'We shall send a champion of our own to meet this man, making clear our own strength.'

Nuada's eyes roamed his chiefs. Should he send white-cloaked Manannán? The champion must head inland; Manannán's power was tied to the sea. The Morrigan? This was a moment to demonstrate physical prowess, not magical. Oghma might be a good choice. The hawk-eyed general was both scribe and swordsman, an artist with weapons and words.

Nuada's eyes alighted on Bres.

Bres was a favourite of Nuada's. He was young, golden-haired and fair of face, quick and cunning in combat. Many among the Tuatha mistrusted him, for the identity of his father was not known. His mother had always refused to speak on the subject, thus fostering dark rumours. Some said that the boy's father was a man of another race, or even a monster. Whatever the truth, Bres' outsider status had toughened the lad. He had worked twice as hard as his peers to prove himself and rise through the ranks. Nuada liked that about him.

'Bres shall be our champion,' said Nuada, ignoring the eyerolls. 'He shall meet this brute and deliver our terms, which are as follows.

'The Children of Danu are here to stay. If the Firbolgs wish to remain on the Isle of Destiny, they must give half of it to us in peace. If they do not, we shall take all of it from them by force.'

Sharp intakes of breath met those words.

'You said you had a plan to win the island without fighting,' said Manannán. 'You did not say that your plan would win us only half the island.'

'The Isle of Destiny called to us in our dreams,' said the Dagda. 'It is her will and Danu's will that we take her. All of her.'

Diancecht the healer joined in too, and Oghma. Eventually they all fell silent and looked to the Morrigan, who had not yet spoken.

The Morrigan held her silence. She understood how things would fare.

Perhaps Nuada was playing a trick on the Firbolgs, purposefully appearing weak. Perhaps he was counting on the Firbolgs to refuse his offer. Maybe he meant to win half the island now, half of it later.

Whatever Nuada's intentions, she knew the truth. A truth as old as iron.

There would be blood.

BRES OILED HIS SPEAR, polished his armour and took the road east. It led him halfway across the country, over open moors and through tangled forests, until he spied a warrior walking towards him.

Bres and Sreng came to within six paces of one another and stopped.

Bres tried not to look impressed as he took in the sight before him. Evening sunlight shone upon the mightiest man he had ever seen. The Firbolg champion wore nothing but a kilt rudely fashioned from wolf fur; his bare chest and arms bore the scars of a thousand battles. He carried a short spear decorated with feathers and scraps of hide. As awesome a sight as this man was, Bres' eyes were drawn primarily to that spear. He was a spear fighter himself, and cared more for his weapon than for food or friendship.

Sreng looked Bres over with his warrior's eye. The lad was young but hardened, wary like a wolf cub forced to survive alone after its pack had been slaughtered. His clothing, arms and armour were exquisite, yet the lad clearly cared little for such things. His spear was what mattered to him.

Sreng held out his shield, smiling as the lad flinched and tried to cover it. Slowly he turned his shield upside down and drove its point down into the hard mud of the road. Among his people, such a move signalled a truce.

Bres guessed Sreng's purpose. After a moment, he followed suit.

'My name is Bres. I would know your name, warrior.'

'I am Sreng. My people are the Firbolgs and my king is Eochaid, who rules this island on which you have landed unbidden.'

Bres was about to retort when he realised something. Though their accents differed greatly, he and Sreng were speaking the same language. He saw that the same thought had occurred to Sreng.

Putting that aside, Bres spoke again.

'My people are the Tuatha Dé Danaan. Our king is named Nuada, and he has bid me parley with you.'

'Then do so.'

'Hear this. The Children of Danu are here to stay. Our boats are burned; there is no turning back for us. Yet we understand that this island is your home. Judging by your speech, I think our peoples must be distant kin. So we make you this offer: give us half the Isle of Destiny in peace, or we shall take all of it from you in war.'

'I do not think the outcome of such a war is certain,' said Sreng. 'For all your finery, your people have not known such hardships as we have. As metal is hardened through the pounding of the hammer, so it is with the Firbolgs.'

'Looking at you, I can believe that,' said Bres. 'I will return to Nuada and tell him of the mighty man I met.' He turned to go, but halted.

'Hesitation is a warrior's first foe,' said Sreng. 'Spit it out, lad.'

'I know it is not done to ask this,' said Bres. 'And my king would have my head for it. But I wonder... I have never seen a spear fashioned as yours is. I was thinking...'

'I have had my eye on yours too,' said Sreng. He stepped out around his shield and advanced towards Bres, his spear held out. 'Take it.'

Bres left the safety of his own shield. The two warriors exchanged spears, each marvelling at the foreign design. Bres explained that the marks on his spear shaft were ogham, a script invented by his kinsman Oghma, which imbued the blade with power. Its greater length was suited to keeping opponents at bay. Sreng's weapon drew magical strength from fur and feathers: wolf and falcon, beaver and bear. Its short length favoured quick, stabbing thrusts.

'I have a dozen such spears,' said Sreng. 'Take this one as a gift.'

Bres thanked Sreng, and gave the Firbolg his own spear in exchange.

The sun was setting. 'Time to be on our ways,' said Sreng. 'But I tell you this: if it comes to war – and I think it will – I will not seek to face you on the battlefield. If it comes to peace, I will call you friend, and we shall drink ale and practise the spear dance together.'

'I hope so,' said Bres. He retrieved his shield. 'One more thing I must ask.'

'Ask it.'

'This land is fair and fertile. Your people have dominion over it, yet many of you are scarred and lean. Why is it so?'

Sreng gave a humourless smile as he rolled his new spear between his fingers. 'If you win the war, you will find out.'[1]

2

FIRE IN THE SKY

Bres entered Nuada's tent, where the king and his chiefs awaited him. He gave an account of his meeting with Sreng and offered Sreng's spear to Nuada.

'It is a primitive design,' said Nuada. 'And you say the man's garb was primitive too. I think that should it come to a fight, we will beat these Firbolgs. When two men fight, skill counts above all, but when two armies clash, the better-armed force will nearly always win.'

The Morrigan sat between Badb and Macha. She stood and approached Nuada, her eyes fixed on the spear.

Nuada offered it to her and she took it in hand, closing her eyes.

'I can sense the spirit of the Firbolgs in this weapon,' she said. 'They are indeed fierce. They have known terrible suffering, in recent days and in days long past. Yet they have survived. Always they will fight, no matter the odds, like a rat cornered by hounds.' She opened her eyes. 'Eochaid will not accept your offer, King Nuada. The Firbolgs will fight us. We must prepare.'

All eyes turned to Nuada.

'We will prepare for battle,' said Nuada at last. 'But we will not be the ones to begin the fighting.'

Sighs of relief met Nuada's words. He ignored them.

'We should not fight here,' said Oghma. 'I have scouted the land hereabouts. If we build a fort on the Plain of Magh Nia, before Belgata Mountain, we shall be well-placed for battle.'

'Then we shall do so,' said Nuada, his tone implying the meeting was adjourned. The chiefs stood to leave.

The Morrigan handed Sreng's spear to Bres and turned to Nuada. 'I will fly to Tara again, taking my sisters with me. If Eochaid is massing an army, we shall see it.'

'Very well,' said Nuada.

'If an army is assembled, the Firbolgs have as good as struck a blow against us. Will you allow us to answer it?'

Nuada considered for a moment, then nodded. The three sisters strode out of the tent, took their crow forms and flew into the evening sky.

DAWN's red fires lit the air as King Eochaid strode across the Hill of Tara.

His general, Gann, and his chief druid, Gnathach, walked at his side. Ever since Sreng had returned from meeting the Tuatha champion, Eochaid had laboured to gather the full strength of the Firbolgs. The call had gone out swiftly and his people had answered swiftly.

Today, the Firbolgs marched.

Eochaid reached the peak of the hill and looked down upon his army.

Ten thousand fires lit the plain. The Firbolg encampment stretched all the way from Tara's gates to the far side of the Plain of Breg. Pride swelled in Eochaid's chest. Despite all his people had endured, they still reached for their swords when the battle horns blew.

'Are we ready to march?' asked Eochaid.

'The Rudra Clan are yet to arrive,' said Gann. 'We shouldn't wait for them. Best not give these Tuatha any more time to build their defences.'

'Fine.' Eochaid turned to Gnathach. 'What have you divined of their prowess with magic?'

Gnathach frowned. 'Very little. There is a veil around...' he trailed off.

'What's wrong?' said Eochaid.

Gnathach stared through Eochaid, his jaw hanging open. A bead of saliva formed at the corner of his mouth, and his eyes rolled back in his head.

A peal of thunder split the sky.

Eochaid looked up and saw dark clouds massing over the plain. The air felt charged, as if lightning might strike at any moment.

A sickening dread arose in Eochaid's gut.

Another peal of thunder, then rain began to fall.

It fell thick, hot and red.

The sky was raining blood.

Screaming broke out. Eochaid saw a tempest of fear spread like wildfire through the camp; warriors ran back and forth between the tents, crashing into one another, terrified by what could only be Tuatha magic.

Eochaid turned to Gnathach and seized his shoulder. 'This is the work of enemy druids! Oppose them!'

Eochaid drew back in horror as Gnathach turned to face him. Blood poured from the druid's eyes.

The sky filled with deathly shrieking as three enormous, black birds swooped down from the clouds. Bigger than bulls, they flew low over the camp, making a terrible wailing that brought Eochaid and everyone who heard it to their knees, clutching their skulls, screaming for the sound to stop. The wailing was every nightmare Eochaid had ever dreamed. It stole the heat from the sun and all bravery from his heart; it sawed at his skull like a poison-smeared blade.

BADB, Macha and the Morrigan descended on the Firbolg camp. They wailed as they tore open warriors with their talons, or carried them high into the air to let them fall. So stout of heart were the Firbolgs that some among them defied the screaming, hurling spears at their attackers, but none found their mark.

The battle crows now changed tactics. They flew to a hillside at the edge of the plain and resumed their original form.

Eochaid staggered to his feet, watching and waiting to see what they would unleash next.

The one in the middle, who appeared to be their leader, stepped forward and raised her arms. Eochaid shuddered as he felt a ripping in the air around him. A moment later, a great plume of fire shot down from the clouds and struck the camp. Warriors ran screaming, wreathed in flames. Another vein of fire followed, then another, then another. Tents caught light and blazes spread, filling the dawn sky with smoke.

Eochaid's army was disintegrating before his eyes. This was sorcery; only sorcery could stop it.

'Gnathach! I need you...'

Eochaid turned to see the fallen druid rising to his feet. Gnathach was chanting, his words a writhing, rocky stream in spate. Eochaid saw that other hardy druids were running up the hill to join their leader. They clustered around Gnathach as blood and fire rained from the sky.

A westerly wind blew in, carrying the crisp tang of the ocean. It scattered the blood-clouds so that shafts of light shone down on the battlefield. The Firbolgs took heart. Scores of them charged up the hillside towards the sidhe sorcerers, who donned their war forms and flew into the air. The druid wind seized them and carried them away from the camp.

For three days and nights the three sisters terrorised Tara. They took no rest and allowed their enemies no rest. After that time, their strength began to fade and they left Tara, retreating to the camp at Connacht. They found their kindred hard at work there, preparing for the battle to come.[1]

3

THE FIRST BATTLE OF MOYTURA

Two warriors faced one another, their eyes cold.

'My name is Oghma. I speak on behalf of Nuada, king of the Tuatha Dé Danaan, the mightiest race in this world. He sends respectful greetings to your king, Eochaid, and to you as his envoy.'

Oghma was dressed in the finest armour of the Tuatha. His helm was edged with gold; intricate lines of silver curled across his breastplate. The man standing opposite him was bare-chested, his trousers made from roughly stitched leather, his skin inked with intertwining images of fearsome animals.

They stood on the wind-battered Plain of Magh Nia, midway between the Tuatha camp and the Firbolg camp. The Tuatha had left their walls behind them and assembled on the field in closely packed ranks, displaying all their sparkling strength. The Firbolgs faced them in a long, loose line; they did not fight in formation as the Tuatha did. Now was not the moment of fighting; it was a moment to stand and show strength while war leaders negotiated.

'I am Gann, King Eochaid's war leader.'

'Greetings, Gann. King Nuada bade me convey these words to you.

'"An offer was made and is made again. The Children of Danu ask for half this island. If half is not given in friendship, all shall be taken by force."'

'King Eochaid has heard your offer,' answered Gann. 'He refuses it. We do not trust that you should be true to your terms; you who sent sorcerers to harry our camp before battle was joined. This island is ours. We hunt her forests, we fish her seas, we feed her soil with the flesh of our dead. Only by force of arms shall you win her.'

'Then so we shall do,' said Oghma.

'Very well. In that case, it is our custom to have a hurling contest before crossing swords. Twenty-seven of our warriors against twenty-seven of yours. The winning side chooses the rules of engagement.'

'Then gather your hurlers.'

THE TWO GENERALS returned to their leaders. The sun broke through the clouds and made of the Tuatha a sea of glittering gold.

Oghma saw Manannán roving back and forth astride Enbarr, inspecting the ranks. Badb, Macha and the Morrigan were nowhere to be seen; they would pick their moment to join the battle. Nuada and Bres commanded the centre; Oghma and the Dagda held the flanks. Manannán alone preferred to fight on horseback, roving where he willed. Though the Tuatha had crossed the sea with a small herd of horses, in was not their custom to field cavalry at that time.

One Tuatha who drew many admiring looks from his fellows was Goibniu, the master smith. He had already built a forge within the fort, but had left it to join the battle. Few Tuatha had Goibniu's strength; he could fight all day then work through the night to repair damaged swords and spears. It was a historic battle, he said, and he would not miss it.

All the Tuatha but the very young, the very old and the healers would fight. The healers were led by white-bearded Diancecht, who had ordered the digging of a well in the woods skirting Belgata Mountain. He had filled this well with herbs, speaking potent blessings over it, so that even the most grievously injured Tuatha would be made whole within its waters.

Oghma approached Nuada and conveyed his conversation with Gann.

'Blood shall be spilt then,' said Nuada. 'So be it. Pick a team of hurlers.'

TWENTY-SEVEN TUATHA FIGHTERS soon stood facing twenty-seven Firbolg fighters, each with a pile of rocks at their side. The Firbolgs roared as the first hurler in their line bent down and selected a stone.

She hurled it at the Tuatha opposite her, who stood as still as stone himself. The missile struck him in the chest and knocked him down, to wild cheering from the Firbolgs.

The first Tuatha hurler picked a smaller stone, barely a pebble. The Firbolgs jeered at his choice of weapon. Quicker than the eye could see, he threw it at his opponent, aiming for the head. The Firbolg fell down dead.

Down the line it went. A man of the Tuatha dodged his opponent's missile, disqualifying himself and earning shame that would follow like a hound at his heels. The man after him threw a rock so big that his opponent was buried under it. All the time, the cheers of both armies grew louder, their appetite for violence fiercer.

The last two hurlers took their turn. Each was struck, but each stood firm.

Those hurlers who could do so returned to their ranks, some dragging dead comrades. A few crawled back, their legs broken. But even the wounded Tuatha hurlers were gladdened, for they had won the contest. It was a good omen.

Oghma and Gann came forward and conversed again.

'You won,' said Gann. 'You may choose the manner of fighting.'

Nuada had told him exactly what to say.

'We will fight every second day, and field an equal number of fighters,' said Oghma.

Gann's mouth twisted into a snarl. 'Very well.' He turned and jogged away as Oghma breathed a sigh of relief. Nuada would be overjoyed; such terms would negate the Firbolgs' greater numbers.

It would soon be time to fight. Yet there were still words to be spoken.

FATHACH THE BARD walked out before the Firbolg army and climbed atop one of the many standing stones marking the plain.

'It is the longest day of summer,' he cried, 'yet darkened is the summer grass, where ill-fated invaders cast their shadows.

'That soil at your feet does not look like much. You walk on it without thought. You piss on it without thought.

'Yet we have bled for this land. Your grandfather's grandfathers lie in that soil, and their grandmothers, and their grandfathers. For how many generations have we held this land? How many Firbolgs have lived and died so that each of you may be born?

'So what, you might say. That is true of every people who walk the earth and fish the sea. It does not make us special. It does not mean we are fated to win this battle.

'You might also say that our enemies are better armed. That their druids can make fire rain from the sky. You might look at all that and say we are fated to die here.'

Fathach paused a moment, surveying his audience.

'To that I say: fuck fate!' Fathach thrust a fist into the sky. 'I'm going to spill some Tuatha blood today, and if I meet fate, I'll cut her throat before she can take me.'

The Firbolgs howled their approval. Meanwhile, Corpre walked out before the Tuatha Dé Danaan, climbing atop another stone pillar. He addressed Danu's children in their own style.

On the ocean floor walks an army of men
I, Corpre, am the raising of their spears.
On the farthest road rides a horse of silver,
I am his steaming breath.

I tore open the world one day
And remade it in a shape that pleased me.

I carved the sapphire in Danu's crown,
I ride the tip of her spear.
Every word I ever spoke
Is carved on my enemy's bones.

The power in the poet's words rang in the hearts of the Tuatha. Their sword arms grew stronger, their spirits more ferocious.

Corpre returned to the ranks.

Nuada looked left and right, up the line. He felt the immense power he held in that moment: to order the slaughter of thousands. It was the way of the world. It was the will of Danu. It was the will of the blessed isle herself.

Nuada drew his sword.

His front line drew their swords.

'Forward!' called Nuada, and the Children of Danu charged at the Firbolgs.

Eochaid's Firbolgs raced to meet them, each warrior eager to make the first kill.

As the Firbolgs drew closer, Nuada cried, 'Halt!'

The Tuatha halted their charge, forming tight ranks fronted by shields. The Firbolgs kept coming, then faltered as they closed in. They couldn't see a way through those ranks, but they kept coming all the same.

'Spears!' called Nuada.

The Tuatha hurled their first spears, bringing down waves of the faltering Firbolgs. Yet many Firbolgs evaded those spears. They darted and rolled past them, hurling themselves towards the Tuatha who as one brought their second spears up, forming an impenetrable forest of blades backed by a wall of shields.

So the battle began. Gradually the tight ranks of the Tuatha were broken. The Firbolgs engaged their enemies in single combat. Every Tuatha had trained for combat, but it seemed to them that the Firbolgs had not only trained, but fought. They knew tricks of evasion, attack and counter; for all their ferocity they remained relaxed and loose-limbed. A savage light gleamed in their eyes, and sometimes one or another of them would grow in size, a bestial fury seizing them and tripling their strength, so that they snapped shields with their bare hands and cut through armour as if it were butter.

The first day's fighting ended.

The armies retreated to their camps.

All night the smiths' anvils sang. Diancecht and his healers worked tirelessly at their well, using herbs and charms and healing songs on broken-bodied fighters.

THERE WAS A DAY OF REST, then battle was joined again.

Renewed by their spell-steeped wells, the Tuatha fought as if fresh to the fighting. The tiring Firbolgs were hard-pressed. They were prepared now for the Tuatha tactic of bunching together behind shields; Sreng had instructed them to leap over the Tuatha front line, or to grab hold of their opponents' spears and pull the line apart.

The fighting was desperately close. For all their superior arms and armour, the Tuatha could not match the raw ferocity of the Firbolgs. That ferocity, allied with experience and raw cunning, made them deadly opponents.

Each Tuatha chief made their mark upon the battle. Where the Tuatha line was close to breaking, Manannán would suddenly appear, scattering the Firbolgs as Enbarr galloped among them. The Dagda sang while he fought, his far-carrying songs giving heart to his comrades as he crushed Firbolg skulls with his club. And at the centre of the line, Nuada and Bres blazed like twin suns.

Nuada's sword arm was not as quick as it had once been. Yet he read his opponents with ease, parrying or evading blows before gliding in for one perfect strike. He cut down Firbolg after Firbolg with the grace of a poet's song. Bres was lightning-quick, fighting two or even three opponents at once, pairing sinuous elegance with a bloodlust that never ebbed. When Nuada tired, he looked to Bres; watching his young prodigy at work gave him strength.

The second day of fighting ended. Both sides retreated as crows descended to feast on the fallen. Goibniu removed his armour and went to his forge, there to begin his night's work, while wounded sidhe limped to the well of healing.

A day of rest, then a third day of fighting. Little was different from the second day. The Tuatha arrived replenished, with new edges on their blades and their wounds healed. Yet they still could not fight like the Firbolgs.

NUADA WALKED through the Tuatha camp that night. By moonlight it was as busy as ever; despite the respite between each battle-day, Goibniu and his smiths could not rest if they were to mend every dented blade and broken helm. Warriors rode stretchers to Diancecht's well. Some gathered to raise toasts to fallen comrades, but many more lay asleep on the ground, too weary or wounded to return to their tents.

The king of the sidhe had fought in many battles; he knew how to read the mood of a camp. This was not the camp of a winning side.

He entered the woods. There he found the Morrigan standing by a pool, gazing into its silver waters.

Nuada stood beside her.

'You smell of fear,' said the Morrigan.

'I am afraid we may lose this battle.'

'We will not.'

'If you have help to give, I ask that you give it soon.'

The Morrigan turned to Nuada and smiled.

'Peace be upon you, Nuada. On the next day of fighting, the Firbolgs shall fall.'

THE ARMIES CLASHED for the fourth time. Every fighter on both sides was beyond tired now, no matter the healing well's power, no matter the Firbolgs' hard-bred sturdiness. Warriors swung their swords like drunkards, tripped and were trampled by comrades. The heaps of bodies grew higher as all sensed the battle's end drawing near.

King Eochaid was in the thick of the fighting. He was no king by inheritance; he had risen to his rank by reddening his blade. Enemies fell like leaves before the Firbolg king, yet no one man could turn the tide of so vast a battle.

But the death of one man could.

Inspiration struck Eochaid. He spotted a pillar of stone nearby and fought his way to it. Eochaid climbed the pillar and shielded his eyes from the sun as he searched the field for his quarry.

There. The invader king. Nuada.

'Sreng!' Eochaid called out to his champion. 'To me!'

Sreng was fighting nearby. He heard Eochaid's summon, ran to the pillar and ascended it.

'That man is their king. Let us bring him down together, and this battle will end.'

Sreng growled his assent.

Eochaid and Sreng leapt from the pillar. They forged a bloody odyssey through the fighting, deadly purpose gleaming in their eyes.

Not far away, in the shadow of the trees beneath Belgata, the Morrigan spoke words of enchantment.

King Eochaid thrust his sword into a Tuatha warrior's chest. She fell to the ground, he pulled his blade free and a sudden sensation came over him.

Eochaid was desperately thirsty.

His throat was as dry as ash. Thirst slammed against him and dropped him to his knees. He needed water as desperately as a man trapped underwater needs air.

'Sreng!' he called out, speech raking his raw throat. 'Keep going! Get to Nuada! I will join you soon.'

Sreng looked baffled, but Eochaid did not stop to see if his champion assented. He turned and called out to the nearest Firbolgs, 'Firbolgs, to me! Guard your king!'

EOCHAID AND HIS SMALL, hastily formed squad slipped through the ranks.

They reached the edge of the battle. Eochaid turned to his warriors and said, 'I need to drink. Take me to the nearest river.'

'This way,' said one of the warriors.

They followed the warrior. After a while, the warrior halted and said, 'It is strange. I am sure there was a river this way before, yet I see no river before me.'

'I know of a stream that runs through the woods there,' said one woman. 'Follow me.'

So they followed the woman into the woods, but found no stream.

By this time, all of Eochaid's companions were as thirsty as he was. They gave dry, hacking coughs as they milled around in confusion. Eventually someone pointed west and said they knew of a river in that direction.

The Firbolg king and his guards moved more slowly now. Their thirst was deep and dark enough to cloud their minds and weaken their limbs. Yet onwards they limped. They found no river, so simply kept going, each reasoning that if they kept going in the same direction then surely they would reach some waterway.

They had all but forgotten the battle now. Their only thought was of water.

It was in such a state of mind that they crested a rise and saw before them the sea.

They did not despair. They did not turn back. So mad were they with thirst, brought on by the Morrigan's magic, that they croaked with joy, ran to the shore, waded into the water and bent down to drink.

Eochaid slopped up salty water in his hands. He drank and drank, not caring that it was seawater he swigged. Yet soon the salty liquid did its work. As Eochaid's mind cleared, he fell to his knees in the shallows, vomiting salt water. His vision spun; the sun was so bright that he could barely see.

Yet he could make out a figure walking slowly towards him.

Eochaid's vision returned as the spell loosened. The Firbolg king and his vomiting, retching warriors lay helpless before the Tuatha champion, Bres.

'Your reign is over, Eochaid,' said Bres.

Eochaid reached for his sword.

He could not even grasp its hilt.

Eochaid watched Bres visit each fallen Firbolg in turn. He put his sword through them without ceremony. Then he came for Eochaid, and Eochaid knew no more.

BRES RETURNED TO THE BATTLEFIELD. He vaulted atop a rock and shouted, 'King Eochaid is dead! The leader of the Firbolgs has fallen!'

In case any doubted his words, he held aloft Eochaid's head.

The nearby Tuatha heard his words, saw the severed head in his hand and cheered. They took up Bres' cry and it soon spread to the farthest reaches of the battlefield. The Firbolgs paused in their fighting, not knowing if the Tuatha spoke truly. The fires of courage in their hearts flickered.

It was in that moment that the Morrigan struck again.

She and her sisters descended from the sky as three gargantuan crows. They screeched as they swooped upon the battle, and their terror-song extinguished the courage of the Firbolgs. They fell to the ground, crying like newborns, or dropped their weapons and fled the battlefield.

The Tuatha were not merciful in that moment. They made use of the Morrigan's magic, slaughtering foes who lay prone on the earth or casting spears at their backs as they ran. The crow sisters circled the field, their midnight song unrelenting. To the Firbolgs, it seemed the sun was setting on their world. Their home was lost. All hope was lost.

Soon every Firbolg was dead, maimed or in rout.

Save for a few.

One of those was Sreng.

EOCHAID'S CHAMPION heard the news of Eochaid's death. He did not disbelieve it; his heart whispered that his dearest friend had fallen.

The crows descended.

Sreng's allies fled.

He did not.

Sreng felt that same terror they felt. Yet greater than his terror was his grief, and his soul-tearing hunger for revenge.

Sreng stalked forward, shouldering past the fleeing Firbolgs. He was a hunting wolf now, and his prey did not elude him for long.

Nuada.

The Tuatha king stood not a hundred paces ahead. He had Bres beside him, and others with the look of fierce fighters.

'Firbolgs, avenge your fallen king!' cried Sreng, charging forward.

A few who resisted the crow-song rallied to his side. They fought their way through the sidhe. Towards Nuada.

The Tuatha in their path were at ease, thinking the battle won. Sreng and his pack took them by surprise; slaying them was easy work. Sreng's force cut a red road through the ranks until Nuada was within reach.

Oghma had returned to the centre. He spotted them coming. 'To me! Protect the king!'

A circle of fighters packed in around Nuada.

Sreng and his warriors moved in on them. Swords, axes and spears clashed. Though battle had been waged for four days, the fighting was fiercest there and then, as the hardiest survivors on each side laid into one another.

Sreng was only interested in one thing. He parried a swing from his opponent and used it to move in behind the man, bringing him face to face with Nuada.

'Single combat!' he growled.

The warrior about to slip a blade into Sreng's back stayed his strike. A challenge had been given; it must be answered.

Nuada's eyes narrowed as he looked up at Sreng, who towered over him.

'Very well,' he said. 'You will soon wish you had fled like your cowardly kin.'

'You will soon wish you had not killed my king.'

Sreng drew back his spear.

'You are a younger and stronger man than I,' said Nuada. 'To make it a fair fight, you might strap one arm behind your back.'

'One on one is fair enough for me,' said Sreng, and he lunged at Nuada.

Spear against sword, Firbolg against sidhe, Sreng and Nuada fought. Nuada had his grace, his practiced eye, his serenity; Sreng was a savage storm. He seemed to grow even larger as he fought, his eyes red, the veins on his muscles bulging like blue serpents. He darted as fast as an adder; his blows carried a bear's brute strength. Cold fear crept into Nuada's heart as he was swept back, ever back, until Sreng spun his spear and brought it down on Nuada's trembling sword arm.

Sreng's spear cleaved Nuada's arm. Nuada's hand and wrist fell to the blood-soaked earth as blood spurted from the wound.

Nuada fell to his knees, clutching at his stump. He looked up at Sreng's face; the face of death.

Sreng raised his spear.

As he brought it down, Nuada cried, 'Connacht!'

Sreng paused.

'Connacht,' repeated Nuada. 'Spare me... and I will give the province of Connacht... to your people.'

Sreng took a deep breath. He wanted nothing more than to avenge Eochaid. Yet he knew what Eochaid would have him do.

'My last gift to you, my friend,' he murmured.

Sreng withdrew his spear.

'Agreed,' he said to Nuada. He grabbed Nuada's remaining hand and hauled him to his feet.

'Now get the fuck off our land.'

SO THE BATTLE ENDED. It came to be known as the First Battle of Moytura, meaning 'The First Battle of the Plain of the Pillars'.

It was not the last great battle to be fought by the sidhe.

The victors built pyres, burned their dead and sang keening

songs. When that was done, they left their camp and made their way east across the Isle of Destiny and out of Connacht, leaving the Firbolgs to make of it their home.

The Tuatha reached Tara, and celebrated as their king claimed the throne.

But Nuada was not that king.[1]

4

A NEW KING

A golden serpent of triumphant Tuatha crossed the country to Tara.

Nuada walked at the head of the procession. Bres walked beside him with Diancecht at their rear. Diancecht had treated Nuada's severed hand, which was now wrapped in bandages, no longer bleeding. Nuada had taken herbs, for the pain which he bore with a grim face as he walked. He had been offered a litter but refused it.

It was morning on the second day of their journey. The sun rose bright over green fields and empty farmsteads. Horned cattle lifted their heads to watch the army march past. Those cattle now belonged to the Tuatha.

Nuada and Bres talked as they went, remarking on the landscapes they passed through. Eventually Nuada said, 'There is something you and I must discuss.'

'What is that, sire?'

'Don't be a fool,' said Nuada. 'You know what is on my mind. You know our laws.'

'Your hand.'

Nuada nodded. 'The king must be perfect in form. An imperfect man cannot be king.'

'It is a foolish law. You are as fine a king—'

'It is not foolish! You must understand this. The king does not simply rule the land; he is the land. If there is a blemish on the king then a blemish shall blight the land. To be injured as I am, yet retain my title, would be to curse this green isle even as we gain her.'

Bres was silent.

'When we reach Tara,' continued Nuada, 'a counsel shall convene. The chiefs will elect a new king. Every chief has the right to nominate a successor. There will likely be some debate before votes are cast, but many of the chiefs will follow my lead.

'Bres, I plan to nominate you to succeed me.'

Nuada turned to watch Bres, who displayed no reaction to these words.

'I am honoured,' said Bres eventually. 'I will not say I am surprised. I know you favour me, however undeserving of that favour I may be. But I do not think I can be king.'

'Why not?'

'Because the chiefs will not accept me.'

'You speak of your lineage.'

'Yes.'

'Bres, listen to me.' Nuada clutched Bres' hand with the hand that remained to him. 'It is because of your lineage that you shall be king.' Bres looked at him, his expression puzzled.

'Do you not see? It is the doubts over your origins that made the other children scorn and exclude you. It was their cruelty that drove you to be stronger and more skilled than them.

'You have lived your life set apart from those around you. Forced to find your own way, never free to find safety in the middle of the herd. That is the life of a king. And did you not lead our forces into battle? Did you not kill the Firbolg king?'

'I did.'

'And you won the friendship of their champion. Fighting, diplomacy; you are a master of both.'

'But I do not believe I know what is best for our people.'

'Another reason why you should be king.'

Bres seemed about to argue but instead, after a long pause, he said, 'Thank you, sire.'

Nuada smiled and wrapped his arm around Bres. 'Help me along, would you? That litter is growing ever more tempting.'

They continued down the road. Nuada quietly instructed Bres while a few ranks behind them, the Dagda looked on with a grim face.

On the evening of the second day of their march, they spied the Hill of Tara.

SUNBEAMS SHONE down among the summer clouds, illuminating Tara. The hill sat at the far side of a vast plain, that they would come to know as the Plain of Breg. It was low, almost squat in in shape, with gently sloping sides leading to a wide, flat crown. Nuada could just make out the shape of a

great hall at the crown. The hill had an aura of peace and serenity, as if the coming and going of kings and queens, Firbolgs,
Tuatha and others before them were but water washing over a
river stone.

The Tuatha crossed the plain and reached Tara's perimeter
wall. The gates stood unmanned. The few Firbolgs remaining
at Tara had fled at the sight of the approaching army.

Nuada and Bres passed through the open gates. Turning to
a nearby serving man, Nuada said, 'Have the chiefs supervise
the distribution of lodging and food. At sundown they are to
join me in the hall atop the hill.' The man bowed and departed.
'Come,' Nuada whispered to Bres. 'Let us take a look at your
hall.'

THAT EVENING, resplendent in their brightest robes and jewels,
the lords of the sidhe entered the feasting hall at Tara.

Torches lined the walls, illuminating newly hung tapestries,
shields and swords. Rows of tables covered the flagstone floor
and surrounded the long central fire pit. At the rear of the hall
stood a platform. Upon it was a wooden throne draped in
animal skins, with an intricately carved bear growling from the
end of each armrest. This had been King Eochaid's throne; soon
it would belong to one of them.

The Stone of Destiny now lay beneath it. One of the four
treasures of the Tuatha Dé Danaan, it would give an ear-split-
ting shriek whenever a new king of the sidhe first sat the
throne.

Nuada stood beside it.

'Children of Danu,' he said once the chiefs were assembled and the doors closed. 'I wonder if the great cities of Gorias and Finias seem as far away to you as they do to me. Today I recall that night, sleeping in my chambers at Gorias, when I first dreamed of the Isle of Destiny. I heard her song, and a sound like the beating of a drum, and I knew that sound to be the beating of a heart. The green heart of the blue world. We all dreamed that dream, we all heard that song, and we all awoke thirsting for the Isle of Destiny.

'I, Nuada, led you here!'

Cheers filled the hall. Some Tuatha remained silent, their eyes shifting this way and that.

'It was not a land to be won without a fight,' continued Nuada. 'I, Nuada, led you in that fight.'

More cheering.

'And in that fight I nearly fell.' Nuada lowered his voice as the cheering subsided. 'Many times. But I did not fall, for at my side fought this man.'

Nuada beckoned to Bres, who mounted the dais and stood beside Nuada.

'It is because of Bres that I survived, and it is thanks to him that you survived too. For Bres it was who slaughtered King Eochaid, causing the Firbolgs to lose heart and flee the battle, even though they stood on the knife-edge of victory.

'Children of Danu, we are a warrior race. We know that a sidhe's true face reveals itself amid the blood and screams of battle. In our darkest hour, Bres proved himself the best of us. Let him lead us. Let him be king.'

Shouts of agreement rang across the hall. Some came from warriors who had fought beside Bres or been saved by his sword, others from Tuatha who trusted Nuada more than they distrusted Bres. But there were many who did not cheer.

The Dagda stepped forward.

'Children of Danu,' he said. 'There will never come a day when I do not praise Nuada. He is wise. He is just. He is skilled in swordcraft and he led us here, to this land which is already dearer to me than ale and honey. The last of our race should meet death with Nuada's name upon their lips.

'But to truly love a man, one must be willing to point out his errors. We all have a place in which we are blind, and I say our king is blind when it comes to Bres.

'I do not deny Bres' bravery. I have witnessed his prowess with sword and spear. I see, as Nuada sees, that Bres grew up apart from his peers, forced to fight hard to distinguish himself, never falling back on friends who would defend him. Nuada looks at all this and sees a man who has trained all his life to be king.

'But why did our children shun him?' asked the Dagda, pacing up and down the hall now, the mighty club upon his back gleaming in the firelight. 'Did they pick him out by chance? No. They did so for the same reason that I distrust him. Because they do not know who his father was. We do not know if his father was even a sidhe at all.'

Dark muttering met these words. A few Tuatha found their hands straying towards their swords. There were monstrous beings in the world whose very nature was mayhem and murder. Might Bres' father have been one of them?

'Hard words,' said the Dagda, silencing those who whispered. 'But now is the hour for hard words and hard truths. It is a hard truth that Nuada cannot remain king, for a blemish upon the king shall show upon the land. And another hard truth is that the spirit of the father lives in the spirit of the son.

'I know your father,' said the Dagda, pointing to Midir and then Lir, two of his allies. 'And yours, and yours. Our bards will sing all winter of their deeds, and the deeds of their mothers before them, and their fathers before them, back to the dawning of the world.

'But this one?' He turned to face Bres. 'I do not think badly of you, boy. I will sit beside you at a feast and drink deep with you. But to let you lead our people? When we have not yet broken the soil of this land with our ploughs, nor watched the oaks grow on the graves of our dead? No. I cannot accept such a risk.

'Choose another, Children of Danu,' concluded the Dagda. 'Choose Oghma.'

At a nod from the Dagda, Oghma stepped forward from the throng.

'Oghma led you in battle just as Bres did. He gave us our writing, ogham, which gives permanence to words which once only rode the breath.

'Wisdom. Strength. Beauty. Bravery. Oghma has them all. Make Oghma king.'

There was no speech-making after that; the hall erupted. Nuada and Bres stood side by side, watching the chiefs' faces redden as they argued. After a time, Nuada took his horn from its sheath and blew upon it.

The hall fell silent save for the spitting of fires.

'Does anyone else wish to nominate a king or queen?'

No answer came.

'Then we shall put it to a vote,' said Nuada. 'All those who favour Bres to be king, raise a hand.'

Nuada's gaze roved the hall, meeting the eyes of Tuatha he had known and led for hundreds of years. It took courage to meet his gaze and not raise a hand, but there were many who did so.

'All those who favour Oghma, raise a hand.'

The remaining chiefs raised their hands.

'So be it,' said Nuada. 'Bres shall be king.'

So it was that Bres mounted the dais and sat upon the throne. Nuada lifted the crown from his own head and placed it upon Bres' brow while beneath the throne, the Stone of Destiny wailed.[1]

5

THE SPOILS OF WAR

Bres refilled his cup.

The hour was late. The preceding hours had passed as expected, with much carving of meat and clashing of cups. Alliances that had been endangered when a sister backed Bres and a brother backed Oghma were reforged in the furnace of feasting. The balance of power swayed like the hull of a ship in rough seas.

Bres missed none of it.

Throughout the night the chiefs had approached him, alone or in groups, to congratulate him and swear allegiance. They followed custom and so did he, speaking courteous words as he accepted their vows. Yet he watched them with hawkish eyes as they returned to the mead benches. He saw who nodded at whom, who winked, who laughed. Not a single wink or nudge would he forget.

Even now, the sidhe dared to mock him. Even when the

crown rested upon his head, placed there by that old fool who insisted on sitting by his side, doling out advice as if Bres were a simpleton. If only Sreng had cut out Nuada's tongue as well as cutting off his hand. But then, Nuada's tongue had served Bres well; it had made him king.

They wouldn't mock him for much longer. Instead, they would pay for every insult.

'It is not just the body of the king that must be perfect,' said Nuada. 'This is what so few understand. It is his mind too. You must be ever watchful of your thoughts, my boy, catching them when they stray towards hatred, envy, cruelty. Such thoughts will manifest as boat-breaking storms, ravaging sickness, rotting crops. Let your thoughts instead be the sun that shines brightly—'

'I have some thoughts already,' interrupted Bres. 'It's time I shared them.'

Bres stood. Within moments the hall fell silent.

'Chiefs of the Children of Danu,' said Bres, his voice carrying across the hall and cutting through drink-addled minds.

'We have wet our throats and filled our bellies. You have all sworn your allegiance to me as your king.' The Tuatha responded by cheering, stamping their feet and hammering their cups on the tabletops. Whether they loved Bres or not, he was their king and they would stand together. 'As we carved up our meat, so it is time to carve up the Emerald Isle.'

Cheering again, yet more subdued. Bres' next words would decide their futures.

'Edan,' said Bres, naming one of his few childhood friends.

All eyes fell upon Edan. 'You fought bravely at Moytura. You never gave ground. Thus you shall have dominion over the south of the island, the province the Firbolgs call Munster.'

Some cheering met this, but much muttering too. Edan was a passable fighter but few felt he deserved such a gift.

'Neit. Step forward.' More muttering; Neit was an ally of Bres and, like Edan, had voted that he be king. 'You shall rule over Ulster.'

So it went. Bres brazenly rewarded every man and woman who had voted for him. To some he granted fertile land; to others he granted the stewardship of mighty rivers and mountains.

When that was done, he began on those who had voted against him. He made them servants of those whom he had rewarded, or made them the lords of bogs, moors and rocky outcrops.

As Bres spoke, he kept one eye on Nuada. It was the crowning pleasure of the evening to see understanding dawn on the old halfwit's face.

'Bres,' said Nuada eventually. 'I think you might reconsider—'

'I think you might go to bed,' said Bres, finally turning to face Nuada. 'It is late, and the sight of a cripple offends me.'

No jewel could be worth as much to Bres as the pain on Nuada's face in that moment. To break the old man's heart was not the repayment of a debt; it was simply the best of sport.

'MY GOOD FRIEND,' said Bres at last. 'Come forward.'

Oghma stepped forward. 'King Bres,' he said, his voice as cold as a frozen lake.

'Everyone in this hall is thinking the same thing. You stood against me as king, and they wait to see if I will punish you.' Bres leaned feared, grinning. 'Do you think I would do such a thing?'

'I think you will act in accordance with the nobility of your nature.'

A few drunken Tuatha couldn't help but laugh at that. The rest were fearfully silent. Oghma had given them their writing and led them in battle; they loved him dearly.

Bres' grin became a sneer. 'Artful words, as I would expect. Few Tuatha have a mind as nimble as yours. I fancy I should keep you close, so my reign can benefit from your wisdom.

'Yes, I will keep you close. Very close. Here in my hall. Would that suit you?'

'I would be honoured,' answered Oghma.

'Very good. Of course, you will need a task to occupy your mighty mind throughout the day.' Bres drummed his fingers on the arms of his throne, upon the carved bears' brows. 'I think I will have you collect firewood to warm my hall.'

Bres savoured the outrage which darkened many a face in that moment. The great Oghma, reduced to collecting firewood! Such a sight would never cease to give him joy.

'I have only one chief left to reward,' said Bres, leading back and giving an elaborate yawn. 'Would the Dagda please step forward.'

The Dagda came to stand before the throne.

'I know you spoke against me with good intentions,' said Bres. 'When you questioned my parentage, you only thought to serve our people. Is it not so?'

'It is so,' said the Dagda.

'And you shall go on serving, by building paths and walls in the fields around Tara.'

The hall fell deathly silent. Not a few sidhe fought to keep their hands from their sword hilts. Through rivalries ran through them like rot, they were united in their love for the Dagda.

'Any work which sets my hand to stone and soil shall suit me well,' said the Dagda.

'Then you had better get some rest,' said Bres. 'You begin work at sunrise, and shall labour every day until sundown.'

So started Bres' rule. His division of land and labour enraged many sidhe but none moved against him.

Nuada left early the next morning. He slipped out through a side gate in the dark, broken by the shame of Bres' betrayal and his own foolishness. He took the road west and told none where he went.

Many Tuatha besides Nuada kept away from court. Bres made a horde of enemies the night he became king, and his allies turned against him as he demanded exorbitant taxes and tribute. He asked for the milk of every white cow in the land, along with grain and gold and more besides. Soon every sidhe, from the richest to the poorest, was labouring long hours at his behest.

The Tuatha had some respite from their grief. Bres made it a habit to tour the country, sampling the milk of prize cows. Milk was his chief delight, and he obsessed over it as others did whisky and ale.

He once visited a sidhe named Nechtan. Nechtan had made a wooden cow in preparation for such a day, and filled its udders with milk mixed with his own wastewater. Bres drank it down and was ill for many days afterwards. The story spread quickly and was told nightly by many a fire.

The Children of Danu had won the land of their destiny. It should have been the best of times; instead it was a time of misery. Their king was a tyrant and their hatred of him only grew as the weeks and months passed.

They could not have guessed that their troubles were only beginning.[1]

6

A TIME OF CHAINS

It was early in winter and early in the evening when Manannán came to Tara, to visit the Dagda and see how his friend fared.

Manannán had left the Emerald Isle immediately after the Battle of Moytura. He rode west over the waves and then under the waves, building a hall for himself deep beneath the sea. At times he would leave his undersea hall and pass seasons in other places such as the Isle of Man, which still bears his name. He was of the Tuatha but apart from them, preferring to remain unentangled in their politics and bickering. But now the pull of friendship had brought him to Tara.

The Son of the Sea rode Enbarr through Tara's gates, resplendent in his glistening white armour and cloak. He dismounted and asked a serving man where he might find the Dagda. The man failed to meet Manannán's eyes as he pointed to a crude hut.

No firelight flickered in the tiny window; no smoke rose from the chimney. Manannán approached the hut and entered, stooping in the low doorway. The room was bare but for a mattress of straw, a single rough stool and the Dagda's harp standing against the wall. Manannán ran his fingers across it; it was covered in dust.

He raked the embers of the fire and sat down on the stool to wait.

Darkness fell. Sometime later, the Dagda arrived home.

Manannán was shocked by what he saw. Whenever he thought of the Dagda, he pictured him laughing his booming laugh that could fill any feasting hall, swinging his club in the thick of battle or playing the sweetest of melodies on his harp. No man of the Tuatha was so full of life as the Dagda, and none loved life so dearly.

The man standing before Manannán looked close to death.

The Dagda's red beard had thinned and fallen out in places. His arms, which could once have wrestled oaks from the earth, were thin and wasted, their grey skin sagging. His ribs showed through his ragged, stinking shirt and he stared with hollow eyes at Manannán, seeming barely to recognise him.

'You...' he said eventually.

'Yes, my friend?'

'You... should not have come here.'

'Why not?'

'I... I am ashamed for you to see me like this.' He bent to sit, as if doing so cost him great pain. Manannán jumped up from his stool and helped the Dagda onto it. 'I am ashamed that I have no food or drink to offer you.'

'There is no shame upon you,' said Manannán. 'The shame is upon Bres. I see that not only does he make you do work that is beneath you, but he starves you too.'

'This is not Bres' doing,' said the Dagda, shaking his head slowly. 'My own idiocy brought this upon me.

'You are no friend of Bres, and you keep apart from other Tuatha. You have not stopped at Bres' hall to feast and drink or listen to the tales of poets. If you had, you would have been disappointed. For all the taxes Bres places upon the Tuatha, he seems to have little gold to spend. At his feasts, he serves ale weaker than water, and bones bare of meat. Poets come expecting splendid treatment; instead Bres yawns through their songs and refuses them payment.

'Poets like to talk, of course. Word spread among them and soon few stopped at his hall. And then Corpre came to Tara.'

'I know Corpre,' said Manannán, recalling the poet's incantation at Moytura. 'Poets are a proud lot, but none are so proud as he.'

A smile cracked the Dagda's face. 'Quite so. He arrived thinking that however the other poets had been treated by Bres, it would not be so with him. He let it be known that he had composed a new song about Moytura, and that it painted Bres most heroically. He expected to be fawned over, applauded, showered with gold and silver.'

'And he was not?'

The Dagda chuckled. The sight warmed Manannán more than the hut's pitiful fire. 'No,' said the Dagda. 'He was not. Bres did not even come out to greet him when he arrived. Instead, he had a servant show Corpre to a hut even ruder than this one, with a hole in the roof and mould in the mattress. There was no wood for a fire and when Corpre asked for food, he was brought three small, dry cakes.'

'That must have pleased him,' said Manannán.

The Dagda laughed again. 'I would have loved to have seen his face. But I never saw him and neither did Bres, for he left that hour. It is said that after he passed through the gates, he turned around and said:

Without food enough to feed a mouse;
Without milk enough for a newborn calf;
Without firelight, fine speech or song;
So shall be every evening in Bres' hall.

'And so it has been,' concluded the Dagda. 'On some nights Bres' false friends sit bickering and snarling at one another. When they are absent, the hall is like a graveyard.'

'I am pleased to hear it,' said Manannán, 'and saddened too. A joyless feasting hall is a shame upon all Tuatha, even if it belongs to Bres. But you still have not told me how it is your fault that you are starved.'

'I was a fool. Do you know a poet name Cribendal?' Manannán shook his head. 'There is no reason why you would. He is petty and cruel, and his tongue is as nimble as a pregnant sow. Of all our poets, he is the only one who will stop here now. He praises Bres endlessly and so our king keeps him and tolerates his ramblings.

'Anyway. Cribendal saw me leaving the kitchens one evening with my small daily meal. He asked if he could have the best share of my food. I will not refuse any man who asks hospitality of me, so I divided up my meal as he asked.

'He has waited for me every night since then, and asked me each night for the best share of my food, knowing I will not refuse him. Thus I am starved. I would understand if this man were my enemy, but I never even had words with him before this.'

'There are always those who take pleasure in seeing the mighty brought low,' said Manannán. He paused, stroking his beard. 'But I think there is something to be done about this.' He reached into his pocket and took out three pieces of gold. 'Take these. When you are given your supper tomorrow, mix them in with your food.'

The Dagda took the gold pieces. He gave Manannán a puzzled look, then understanding dawned on his face.

'Thank you, my friend,' he said.

MANANNÁN TALKED with the Dagda a while longer before leaving Tara. He made a camp out in the forest and returned to Tara the following evening. Instead of heading for the Dagda's hut, he rode up the hill towards Bres' hall.

The hall was ablaze with light and loud with voices. Manannán entered and saw a company gathered near the foot of the throne. He pushed his way to the front and found the Dagda there. At his feet was a corpse.

'You will explain to me, labourer,' Bres said to the Dagda, 'why my chief poet is dead.'

Yes, my king,' said the Dagda. 'You must forgive me if I halt and stumble in my speech, though. I am deeply saddened by the death of such a noble and eloquent man.'

There were a few snatches of laughter before Bres said, 'Go on.'

'A moon or so ago, Cribendal met me outside the kitchens when I had just obtained my supper. He asked me for the best share of my meal. No man of the Tuatha will refuse hospitality to another, so I gave it to him, and have done so nightly ever since.'

'Then why is he dead?'

'It is most unfortunate. Yesterday evening Cribendal met me and asked for the best share of my food as usual. I gave it to him.'

'And?'

'And it just so happened that I'd mixed three gold pieces in with my food before leaving the kitchen. So when Cribendal asked for the best share of my food, I had no choice but to give him the share with the gold pieces mixed in. I suppose he must have eaten them and died.'

The hall was silent for a moment, then it erupted into laughter. It seemed that even Bres' allies thought that the Dagda had played a fine trick on Cribendal. Manannán smiled with relief. Yet how would Bres react?

Bres looked furious. He seemed about to speak when the hall fell quiet behind Manannán.

Shouts and laughter turned to whispers as the hall turned icy cold. Manannán felt a sinking sensation, as if a great blast of cold breath had blown out all the stars in the sky.

He turned and saw Tuatha moving fearfully for the walls as a cloaked and hooded figure passed through the doors.

Manannán found himself backing away too, as did the Dagda. The newcomer advanced until only the poet's corpse stood between him and Bres on the throne. No part of the stranger's face was visible beneath his hood.

Torches sputtered on the walls. All but a few died, leaving the hall wreathed in shadows.

'Who are you to enter my hall with your face hidden?' said Bres. He attempted to sound commanding but it was clear to see how he squirmed.

'A servant of your master.' The visitor's voice was as dry as a discarded serpent skin.

'I am king of the Tuatha Dé Danaan. There is no one above me.'

'I do not come from above. I come from below.'

The visitor pulled back his hood and threw off his cloak.

His skin was covered in dark green scales. An arch of lethally sharp spikes ran from his forehead to his tail, which flicked back and forth across the floor. His enormous mouth was lined with rows of glittering fangs; instead of having two eyes in his head, he had a row of eyes up the length of each forearm. They roved the hall as the Tuatha recoiled.

'I visit your hall and I speak these words on behalf of Balor, king of the Fomorians.

'Bres of the Tuatha Dé Danaan,' said the stranger in a deep, hulking voice that Manannán guessed was the voice of Balor. 'You have come to these lands unbidden. You won them from the Firbolgs by blood and slaughter. Such was your right, for your race proved stronger than theirs. Now, as your people feast in the Firbolgs' halls and farm their fields, you must take up their duties.

'The Firbolgs paid tribute to the Fomorians, for we are mightiest of all races. Since you came, no tribute has been paid. I have given you time to make yourselves at home here. But I will wait no longer.

'I, Balor, demand that you pay me tribute. I demand a third of the grain in your fields. I demand every third of your cows. I demand every third of your children, to be taken by my people as slaves.

'My emissaries will appear to your people. They will come from caves and coasts to take what must be given. This is how things shall remain, until this land is won from you or until the ending of the world.'

The Fomorian fell silent. All eyes turned to Bres.

'I... I do not accept your demands,' he said.

'In that case,' said the Fomorian in his own voice, 'we will make war upon you. We shall cover the land like a wave, and slaughter you like swine, and those who escape the slaughter shall be enslaved.'

'We won this green isle once,' said Bres. 'If need be, we shall win her again.'

The Fomorian grinned at Bres. 'I would speak with you alone,' he said.

Bres laughed. 'And why would I grant that?'

'Because your father would wish it.'

Bres turned pale.

'Clear the room,' he said.

No one moved.

'Clear the room!' Bres screamed, rising to his feet. The Tuatha reluctantly obeyed.

BRES LOOKED DOWN at the grotesque creature. The dark hall was empty save for the two of them.

'What do you know of my father?'

The Fomorian grinned. 'I do not know of him. I know him.'

He stepped closer, all of his eyes upon Bres.

'I will tell you a story.

'Your mother Eri was a beautiful woman in her day. Many dreamed of marrying her; many more dreamed of bedding her. Yet no Tuatha Dé Danaan won that prize.

'Eri lived by the sea, not far from the city of Finias. One day, she was out walking when she saw a man piloting a boat towards the shore. She saw that he was handsome. He stepped onto the sand, greeted her and gave his name as Elathan.

'Elathan spoke words that charmed Eri. They say it took no great effort on his part to win her,' the envoy said with a laugh. 'Soon they were rutting upon the sand together, your mother moaning as the surf washed over her feet.

'When Elathan was done with her, he left, promising to return... but well you know that he never did. Once with your mother was enough.'

'Why should I believe you?' asked Bres. He desperately wanted to draw his sword and cut down the creature, but even more he wanted to hear his tale. 'How do you know this Elathan?'

'Elathan is a Fomorian.'

Bres laughed. 'You will understand why I find that hard to believe.'

The Fomorian spoke a word unknown to Bres.

His shape changed. In place of the gruesome monster stood a man as handsome as Bres himself. 'We choose what shape we take,' said Balor's emissary. 'The shape of your desire or the shape of your fear. It is all the same to us.' He spoke in his own tongue again and resumed his monstrous form. 'You are one of us, Bres.'

'I am not.'

'Are you a sidhe, then? Have they ever truly accepted you? Loved you? They do not. They mock you and whisper against you. This very night, they humiliated you. Sooner or later they will find some excuse to turn on you and take your throne.

'Stand with us. With your own kind. Balor recognises you as kin. He will allow you to collect your tribute alongside that which we collect. With the might of Balor at your back, you have nothing to fear from your subjects. You will have nothing to fear ever again.'

Balor looked down at the Fomorian. It was strange to hear such honeyed words coming from a mouth so hideous. Why would the creature choose to wear such a form when he could be beautiful? Yet there was power in such a form. Power to inspire fear, and fear meant control.

If he allied with the Fomorians, every last Tuatha would fear him. Truly fear him. All their mockery would end; even the mightiest of them would grovel at his feet and fight for his favour. When they saw him as a Fomorian king, they would fear him and see his true strength.

Knowing what he now knew, he could never again hope to be one of the Tuatha. But he could belong somewhere else. He could truly belong.

'So be it,' he said. 'I acknowledge Balor as my overlord. He shall receive his tribute.'[1]

7

THE SILVER HAND

The days that followed were the darkest the Tuatha ever knew.

Bres sent out emissaries to every province of Ireland. They went from hall to farmhouse to fishing hut, announcing that new taxes of grain, cattle and child-slaves would be paid to the Fomorians. The Fomorian tax collectors came soon afterwards. They collected their due from weeping Tuatha and wherever they were refused, they returned in greater numbers, burning families out of their homes or putting them to the sword. Charred corpses hung from a hundred wayposts.

The Children of Danu were a fighting people, but Bres had already sapped their spirit with his betrayal of Nuada and his own exorbitant taxes. Few had the strength or will to resist both Bres' tax collectors and the Fomorians. Soon it was not possible to stand anywhere on the Emerald Isle without hearing the sound of weeping. Tuatha lifted starving children from their beds and carried them out into the night, never to see them again.

DURING THIS TIME a family of healers travelled the Emerald Isle. They roamed back and forth across the country, treating the sick in every settlement they passed through. These three were Diancecht, his daughter Airmed and his son Miach.

Wherever the family went, they were assured a warm welcome. Diancecht was well-known among Danu's children. He had been chief healer to Nuada and chief healer at the Battle of Moytura. Though Diancecht was justly famous, his children were also highly skilled. They worked hard and learnt much in those days, for ill health and sickness were common under the rule of Bres.

Miach and Airmed watched their father treat his patients. Everything they learned, they remembered. After several years on the roads of the Emerald Isle, there was little their father knew which they did not. This often led to trouble, for Miach regularly argued with his father over the best way to treat a patient. He dreamed up ideas for entirely new treatments, but Diancecht would not hear of them. He believed the old ways were best. Airmed had original ideas too, but she kept them to herself, or convinced Diancecht that they were his own ideas.

One day in autumn, they rounded a bend in the road and saw before them the Hill of Tara.

'Surely we are not stopping there,' said Miach. Like his father, he hated Bres with a passion.

'We are healers,' said Diancecht. 'I like Bres even less than you do, but if there are sick people upon that hill, we will help them.'

'Even Bres?'

Diancecht grimaced. 'Even Bres.'

THEY REACHED the gates of Tara. The guards bowed and let them pass. Walking among the huts and storehouses, they encountered a one-eyed man who sat nursing a cup of ale, his head hanging.

'Greetings, friend,' said Diancecht. 'We are healers. Do you know of any sick persons in need of treatment?'

'Well, there's me for a start,' said the man. 'I'm a swordsman, or I was until I lost an eye at Moytura. Now I'm no good for fighting and no good for anything. But I doubt even you, the mighty Diancecht, can help with that.'

'That is beyond even my skill,' said Diancecht. 'But I wish you well in finding a new trade to practise.'

'Forgive me, father,' said Miach. 'But I've been thinking about this particular malady and may have an idea. If we—'

'Do not deal in false hopes,' said Diancecht. 'Let us find others whom we truly can help.'

THE FAMILY FOUND lodgings and soon had a queue of patients at their door. They worked side by side until the moon was high in the sky. Finally they closed their door and lay down to sleep, exhausted.

Save for Miach.

He slipped out of his bed and into the night. At the gates, he asked the sentries where he could find the one-eyed warrior.

The warrior awoke soon afterwards to find Miach kneeling by his bed.

'I have an idea for your treatment,' said Miach. 'It has not been tried before. I think it will work but I can offer no guarantees. Would you like to proceed?'

'I'd rather be dead than never wield a sword again,' said the man. 'Try whatever you like.'

Miach grinned and left him. He returned a little while later with a cat struggling and hissing in his arms.

'Are you fond of cats?' asked Miach.

'Yes.'

'You might want to look away then.'

The warrior looked away. He heard a yowl, followed by a snapping sound, followed by silence.

'Lie on your back, close your eyes and keep still,' said Miach.

The man did as instructed. He heard snapping and tearing sounds followed by whispered prayers and blessings. Miach forced something into the man's eye socket. The warrior had a vision of roots plunging into deep, fertile soil.

'Open your eyes,' said Miach.

'You mean eye...'

The warrior opened his eyes. He had two!

He leapt up from his bed and embraced Miach. His eyes roved the room, alighting on his sword which lay in a dusty scabbard by the fireplace. He seized it and ran out of the house.

Miach followed him and watched as the man drew his sword in the moonlight. He leapt and spun across the court-yard, cutting and thrusting expertly with his blade.

'Your father may be the famous one in the family,' said the warrior, 'but I'll soon have it known that Miach is the true talent.'

Miach gave him an awkward smile. 'You'd best get some sleep. I imagine you'll want to return to the sword yard in the morning.'

'Yes.' The man frowned. 'Though I have a strange urge to spend the rest of the night hunting for mice.'

A WEEK OR SO LATER, the family left Tara. They took the road south and made camp at the edge of a woodland.

'It is good to be out of that place,' said Diancecht by the fire that evening. 'It is hard enough to see how our people suffer under Bres, but to see the man strut about wearing Nuada's crown is ten times harder. At least he wasn't sick, so we didn't have to treat him.'

'I enjoyed visiting Tara, even if were close to Bres,' said Miach. 'I discovered some interesting new remedies.'

'You watch that pride of yours,' said Diancecht. 'You think you're so clever, giving that man the eye of a cat. I hear he now spends his nights hunting mice and his days sleeping in the sun.'

'Many medicines have unintended side effects,' answered Miach. 'You taught me that.'

'I taught you everything you know! Don't forget it.'

'Please don't argue,' said Airmed.

They sat in silence for a while. No one looked happy.

'Visiting Tara and seeing Bres himself made me think,' said Airmed eventually. 'We suffer under the Fomorian yoke because Bres is king and has aligned with Balor.' She lowered her voice. 'But what if Bres were not king?'

'Clouds and castles,' said Diancecht. 'Bres is king by law, and our laws are sacred. There is nothing to be done.'

'But Bres was only made king because Nuada was no longer whole.'

'So?'

'So, what if Nuada were made whole again?'

Diancecht and Miach stared at Airmed.

'I know you two have your disagreements. But if you worked together – if we all worked together – I think we could make Nuada whole again. If he were whole, he could depose Bres and become king again.'

Miach slowly nodded. He and his sister turned to look at their father. For all his jealousy of his son's skill, and his refusal to accept new ideas, Diancecht lived to heal the sick. He loved Nuada and truly hated Bres.

'What do you have in mind?' asked Diancecht.

WEEKS LATER, in the far west of Munster, the healers halted on a clifftop and looked out towards Crow Island.

'It is a lonely place that Goibniu calls home,' said Miach, regarding the brooding hulk of dark rock.

'Crow Island is the place Bres chose for Goibniu,' said Diancecht. 'Goibniu voted for Oghma to be king. I doubt Goibniu minds, though. Smithing is a solitary craft and his temperament well suits this rock.'

'He may not be pleased to see us, then,' said Miach.

'He will be pleased when he hears what we have to say,' said Diancecht.

Airmed suppressed a smile. She and Miach had both watched their father growing steadily more excited about their plan and the possibility of dethroning Bres. It had been Miach's idea but they had agreed to pretend it was Airmed's. Diancecht would never have accepted their plan if he had known the idea originated in Miach.

The healers had traded for a small skin-boat at the last dwelling they visited, and carried it on their shoulders along the coast. As drizzling rain began to fall, they descended to the water and set out to sea. The crossing was choppy but it was only a short distance to Crow Island. Soon they stepped onto its stony shore.

They stowed their boat and set off up a narrow rocky path. It led them up the steep, treeless hill that was the island's only feature. At the brow of the hill stood a long, low building. Smoke rose from the chimney and its door stood open. Even from twenty paces away, they could feel the intense heat radiating from it. Outside the hut, a white cow grazed on the wind-scoured grass.

All three of the healers stared at the cow in wonder. She was no ordinary cow; she glowed like silver forged in the heart of the moon.

'That is the Cow of Plenty,' said Diancecht. 'Goibniu is her steward. From her udders flows all the joy and passion, all the love and plentitude which our people enjoy. If we did not have her, we would have nothing.'

'And anyone who tries to take her will meet the business end of my hammer,' said a voice from the forge's doorway.

A short, stout, hunched man emerged from the shadows. His beard was wild, his body thick with bristling black hair; he looked strong enough to shape iron with his bare hands.

'Goibniu,' said Diancecht. 'Meet my son Miach and my daughter Airmed. We do not come to Crow Island to steal. We come to give a gift, to you and all the Tuatha.'

GOIBNIU LED the healers into a chamber that preceded the forge itself. He bade them sit down and fetched cups of ale. The heat from the forge was enough to melt the wax in their ears.

'It is good to see you and to meet your children,' said Goibniu as he took a seat. 'But if you come with gifts of medicine, yours is a wasted journey. Smithing keeps a man strong; the fires of the forge burn away all impurities.' Goibniu glanced towards the forge as he spoke, as if he could not bear to be away from it for long.

'We are here to cure a sickness,' said Diancecht, 'but it is not a sickness of the body. It is a sickness that plagues all the Tuatha Dé Danaan. A sickness that sees our people grow gaunt as they give over their harvest to enemies, and send their children into slavery.'

Goibniu's eyes narrowed. 'Bres.'

Diancecht nodded grimly.

'I love him as little as you do,' said Goibniu. 'But he is our king by our own law.'

'Only because Nuada cannot be king,' said Miach, 'and that is only because Nuada is not whole. What if he were to become whole again?'

'You speak of magic,' said Goibniu.

'I speak of smithing,' said Miach, a grin breaking across his face. 'And of medicine.'

'Make a new hand for Nuada. Forge it from bronze or iron or whatever you will. Give it to us and we will take it to Nuada. We will make his new hand fit like his old hand, and the true king will be whole once more.'

'That sounds like magic to me, lad,' said Goibniu. 'Magic that cannot be done. Even the Morrigan could not undertake such a spell, much less the three of you.'

'It sounds absurd, I know,' said Diancecht. 'But my boy here has a way of looking at the world which reveals things we old ones don't see. I am often against him, for I suspect sometimes that he cares more for new discoveries than his patients' welfare. But he is truly a great healer. He is... he is better than me. If he says he can do this, he can.'

Goibniu sipped his ale as outside the west wind began to howl, spattering rain against the walls.

'Even if this plan of yours were to work,' said Goibniu, 'even if Nuada were whole again, that would not make him king. He gave up the kingship and put the crown on Bres' head himself.'

Diancecht finished his ale and wiped his mouth with his sleeve. 'I would call that a minor detail,' he said, fixing Goibniu with his gaze.

Goibniu put down his own cup. He gave Diancecht a hard look that seemed to last a century.

'So would I,' said the smith. He threw back his head and laughed. 'I'll get to work.'

GOIBNIU POINTED his guests in the direction of his sleeping quarters. They were welcome to his bed; he would not see it that night.

It turned out that no one slept on Crow Island that night, save perhaps the Cow of Plenty. Diancecht and his children lay awake, huddled together in Goibniu's bed, listening to the music of ringing metal as Goibniu worked his forge until dawn.

Finally he called for them to join him.

They rose and hurried through the house.

The great smith of the Tuatha Dé Danaan stood at the door of his furnace, drenched in sweat and with a storm-wild gleam in his eyes.

He held a hand of purest silver.

At a nod from his father, Miach stepped forward and took the hand from Goibniu.

'With this hand, Nuada will not be made whole,' said Miach. 'Nuada will be perfected.'

THE HEALERS DID NOT STAY another hour with Goibniu. He gave them each a drink of the Cow of Plenty's milk, which left them lively as boxing hares. They returned to the mainland with Nuada's silver hand wrapped in cloth, taking the coast road north. Rumour had it that Nuada now called Ulster home.

It was a long journey to Ulster, and a sad one. Winter walked the road with them, bringing maladies to every house they visited. The Tuatha had little to do during the dark season but sit by dim fires, weeping for lost children or drinking until they raged and cursed at the children remaining to them. Sickness of body and mind was everywhere.

The arrival of healers was good news to every hall and homestead, but the healers brought their own strife with them. Diancecht's praise of Miach on Crow Island was forgotten as tensions resurfaced.

'This salve will cure you in three days,' Diancecht would say to a patient.

'Take my salve and you shall be better tomorrow,' Miach would say.

It seemed to Diancecht that whatever he said, Miach contradicted him. Diancecht was regularly offered a comfortable chair to rest in while his hosts crowded around Miach, clamouring for his help. It was not easy to bear. He had long been the most esteemed healer of the Tuatha Dé Danaan, and he took every compliment Miach received as a slight upon himself.

MIDWINTER CAME AND WENT. Finally the physicians arrived on a headland in Donegal and looked down on a sandy cove.

Winter winds lashed the sea. They sprayed saltwater over an outcrop of rocks where a lone fisherman stood, holding a rod in his single hand.[1]

8

A KING REFORGED

Diancecht, Airmed and Miach found a path leading from the headland to the beach. They crossed the sands and approached the outcrop where Nuada fished. Drawing close, it seemed that he had not heard them over the shrieking wind and surging waves, so Diancecht called out to him.

Nuada did not turn.

The healers clambered over the slippery rocks until they stood behind Nuada.

'Nuada, who was king of the Tuatha Dé Danaan,' said Diancecht. 'Turn and face your friend.'

'I am not worthy of friendship,' said Nuada. He twisted to looked each of them up and down before turning back to the sea. 'I am a traitor to my race.'

'You are no traitor,' said Airmed, shouting to be heard over the wind. 'Bres is the traitor.'

'I am a traitor!' said Nuada, facing them again. 'A king cannot say "It is not my fault" or "I didn't know what would happen". I defended Bres for years against those who named him my false friend. They said I saw more of myself in the boy than was merited. They were right.'

'Fine,' said Diancecht. 'They were right. You failed in your judgement of Bres and now we all pay the price. What reason is that to give in to despair? Why follow betrayal with betrayal, in the darkest hour your people have known?'

'How can I betray the Tuatha when I am no longer one of them?' said Nuada, his fishing forgotten now. 'Why do you think I came here? This piece is no longer on the gaming board. I came here to be forgotten. I came here to die.'

'So die then,' said Miach.

Three shocked faces watched Miach unsheathe his dagger.

'We are healers,' he said. 'We understand that sometimes the only medicine is death. My father will not help you with this, but I am willing. Would you rather I pierce your heart or open your throat? Either way, I will be glad to hear an end to your whining, you weak-minded whimperer. You snivelling once-man.'

'Impudent little leech,' hissed Nuada. 'I still have one good hand. I'll take that knife and cut your throat...'

Nuada's mouth hung open as if his words had been stolen away by the wind.

He laughed. His laughter grew and grew until he was bent double. When he finally straightened up it was with a new gleam in his eyes.

'Your father told me once that medicine begins in the mind,' he said to Miach. 'I see he taught you that too. There is fight in this old hound yet.' He shook his sodden head, spraying water in every direction. 'Let's get out of this rain.'

N<small>UADA LED</small> them north over the rocks bordering the bay. They came to another cove where a hut stood beyond some sand dunes.

Nuada led them in inside. He bade them sit while he built up his driftwood fire, accepting no help.

'I found the hut empty and untended,' he said. 'It must have belonged to a fisher of the Firbolgs.'

Soon the fire was blazing. Steam rose from rain-soaked clothes, mingling with the smoke. Nuada took four herring from a barrel, skewered them and set them to cook over the flames.

They ate in silence. Nuada appeared to be deep in thought.

Finally he spoke again.

'You surely walked a long road to find me. Tell me how things fare with the sidhe.'

The healers glanced at one another.

'Things are as you must fear,' said Diancecht. 'Bres rules the Tuatha with scant care for either their wellbeing or their suffering. The Dagda builds walls around Tara and receives a pittance of food in payment. Oghma gathers wood for Bres' fire while across the country, our people sicken in body and mind as they hand over their crops, cattle and children to Bres' Fomorian masters.'

'Fomorian masters? I know nothing of this.'

Diancecht told the tale of how Bres had accepted Balor, king of a dread race known as the Fomorians, as his overlord.

'I never heard of such creatures, nor paid them taxes. I must have escaped their notice,' said Nuada. He looked at Miach. 'Your boy here is clever. He proved there is still some fight in this broken body. But what good is that against Bres and his demon masters?'

'You believed your spirit broken,' said Miach, 'and saw the lie of it in a moment. It is the same with the Tuatha. We have taken some grievous blows, yes. What of it? Were we really fool enough to believe we could win this island with one battle? We took her; now we must defend her. After that, we will likely need defend her again. The young stag routs the old to claim his herd, then clashes antlers with any newcomer who fancies his females. It is the way of the world.'

'Fine words. But how to mend the spirit of a whole race?'

'The true king is one with his land and one with his people. The Tuatha will become whole when they see you whole again.'

Nuada frowned. 'They will be waiting a long time to see that, lad.'

Miach nodded at his sister. She took from her pack a bundle of cloth and unwrapped it.

Nuada stared.

'That hand is Goibniu's work,' he said.

'It is not a hand,' said Miach. 'It is a lump of metal. My work – our work – will make of it a hand.'

Nuada looked at Diancecht, who nodded.

Even the flames of the fire and the howling wind fell quiet as they waited for Nuada's next words. Words which would decide the fate of the sidhe.

'Bres is going to need a silver head when I'm done with him,' said Nuada.

THE HEALERS BEGAN surgery that hour. They worked into the night, through the next day and into the following night. It quickly became clear to Nuada that only Miach understood what was happening, and even Miach seemed to be guided by intuition more than by any plan. He directed his father and sister to boil herbs, make compresses and recite blessings as he worked. A light shone in his eyes which Nuada recognised. It was the look of a master who had been set the ultimate test and now rose to meet it.

Diancecht and Airmed were quiet. At times they asked Miach questions but his answers made little sense to them. He seemed to have entered a realm in which words had little meaning. Airmed stole glances at her father from time to time, searching for signs that his jealousy of Miach might be resurfacing. Yet the work being done was so wondrous that Diancecht's pride and jealousy scattered like ashes before it.

Nuada did his best to follow Miach's instructions, to grit his teeth and make no sound as the wound on his wrist was opened up and teased apart. The pain was excruciating but he bore it by thinking of Bres.

DAWN ROSE on the third day since the surgery began. Miach stepped back and said to Nuada, 'Your hand is ready.'

Nuada looked down at the silver hand gleaming in the firelight. He took a deep breath, furrowed his brow and commanded the fingers to move.

Nothing happened.

'Relax,' said Airmed. 'Don't push. Allow the fingers to move.'

Nuada took another breath and closed his eyes.

One silver finger trembled.

Nuada laughed. The finger moved a little more, then its neighbour joined it, and soon the silver hand was a clenched fist.

Nuada opened his eyes. They fell upon his sword. He had buried it beneath a heap of possessions, but Diancecht had uncovered it. Nuada rose and took hold of his sword.

He left the hut and stepped out into the sunlight.

The sun had risen over the cliffs, casting long shadows across the bay. Gulls rose shrieking into the golden dawn, crying out that the king of the sidhe was whole again. Nuada thrust his sword into the sky, somehow feeling the sun's warmth on his silver hand. He roared out his joy, roared out his strength, roared to sun and sea that Nuada had returned.

He turned to face his grinning companions.

'My friends,' said Nuada, 'Let us take the road to Tara.'[1]

9

A CLOAK OF FLOWERS

Bres was sitting on his throne, examining the ale in his cup, when he noticed it was moving.

It was as if a giant lumbered across the land, making his drink dance with every crashing footstep. Had he drunk too much? Well, yes. He had taken to drinking from breakfast onwards; there was little else to do.

Bres stood to stretch and shake out his befuddlement. He realised that he really could hear the footsteps of a giant. A rhythmic pounding was shaking the whole hall. There was a sound, too, like the roaring of many voices...

Fear seized Bres and sharpened his ale-addled mind.

He descended the dais, ran to the doors of his hall and out into the open.

He stared west across the Plain of Breg.

An army bore down on Tara; an army of Tuatha Dé Danaan. They were almost upon Tara's gates, and at the head of the army...

No. It couldn't be.

'Get down there!' Bres shouted to a pair of guards who stood nearby. 'Man the gate! Stop them from entering!'

The guards looked at one another. 'I think we'd rather stay here, sire,' said one.

Bres drew his sword.

The guards drew theirs.

Bres turned back to the approaching army. His own guards were opening the gates! The army was entering Tara. That roar which he had heard was the sound of cheering. It grew deafening as Tara's occupants ran to greet the invaders, lending their own voices to the din.

Traitors! Traitors, all of them. And now the army of betrayers was winding its way up the hill. There was no mistaking him now; Nuada led the procession, holding a sword in a hand he should not have.

Bres sheathed his sword and retreated into his hall. He slammed the doors shut, pushed chairs up against them then returned to his throne.

The doors crashed open. Nuada entered.

'Stop there! I am king and I order you to stop!'

Nuada strode across the hall, his eyes fixed on Bres as Tuatha poured in behind him. He mounted the dais. Bres leapt up and edged away from him, keeping the throne between them. He drew his sword once more; it trembled in his hand.

'Where did you... that hand is not yours!' said Bres. 'You are not whole!'

'This throne is not yours. I am taking it back, Bres.' Nuada rounded the throne, advancing on Bres who backed away, slipped and fell to the ground.

Nuada flipped his sword in his hand. The blade now faced downwards, towards Bres' heart.

'You cannot take the throne from me! I am king by law. You put the crown on my head yourself.'

'I call that,' said Nuada, 'a minor detail.'

He held his sword high.

'Mercy,' sobbed Bres. 'I beg mercy.'

Nuada hesitated. The hall was full of Tuatha; more entered by the moment. There was Bodb Dearg, who had fought at his side at Moytura. There was Corpre, his bard eyes recording every moment. The Dagda and Oghma looked on impassively; two lords whom Bres had made his slaves. The three sisters of the Morrigan had arrived on crow wings and now stood in woman shape, watching him with six inscrutable eyes.

In this moment his new reign began. What lesson would he teach his people? Revenge or restraint? Mercy or murder?

Sometimes it was best to put a sick dog down. To do so took a certain kind of strength. It was easy for weakness to masquerade as gentleness.

He turned back to Bres. Fear and hatred mingled in the young man's eyes. It would be better for the Tuatha if this one died.

Yet Nuada had loved Bres. Loved him like a son.

Bres saw the doubt in Nuada's eyes. 'I have made mistakes,' he said, 'but I always loved you. I loved you like a father.'

'Lies,' said Nuada. 'You love no one but yourself. All the same,' he said as he sheathed his sword, 'I will show you mercy.

'Bres, you are banished. Leave now. Leave this hall, leave this island. Any sidhe who sees your face seven days from now may blacken their blade with your blood.

'Go. Go now!'

Bres leapt up at Nuada's shout. He threw the crown onto the floor and elbowed his way through the throng to the doors. He ran from Tara and did not look back.

Inside the hall, Nuada turned to the assembled Tuatha.

'I made the darkest of errors when I gave that man a crown,' he said. 'I shall not be so foolish again, if you would once more call me king.'

The assembly answered with a roar of joy. Nuada sat upon the throne and beneath him, the Stone of Destiny shrieked, its deafening call echoing back and forth across the hall. Many would remark later that the stone's sharp shrieking sounded joyful to their ears.

The cheering grew wilder as the Dagda mounted the dais, retrieved the crown and placed it upon Nuada's head. Food, drink and musicians were sent for. Drums soon beat in the hall atop Tara, where every throat was now full of song. Pipes sang on the hilltops from Munster to Ulster as the news spread, fast as an eagle on the wing, that Bres had left Tara and Nuada reigned again.

As for Bres, he travelled quickly too. He went north, keeping to the dense woods and shadowed places. He knew a place where he would find sanctuary.

ON THE NINTH night after Nuada returned to Tara, Diancecht sat alone in a corner of the high hall.

It was the time of the night for tale-telling. The foremost Tuatha poets were present, yet none of them spoke a word. The only voice anyone wanted to hear was that of Miach.

Nuada had been called on nightly to tell the tale of his silver hand. The king did his best to be gracious, highlighting the roles played by Goibniu, Diancecht and Airmed in making him whole again. Yet his eyes shone and his voice quickened when he spoke of Miach. How Miach had revealed his sleeping strength; how Miach worked such wonders that he did not know if Miach practised medicine or magic. The crowd would roar their approval and Miach would be called on to share his side of the tale.

As he did now. Yet again.

'We came to a headland. In the bay beyond I spied a man fishing on salt-spattered rocks. Even at that distance I recognised our true king...'

Miach was always careful to acknowledge his father's teachings. But a smile crept across his face when he spoke of his own endeavours, betraying his self-satisfaction. He offered praise as a king did, aggrandising himself by deigning to recognise those beneath him. Well, he might fool the toadies who gathered at his feet, but he didn't fool his own father. All the boy had done was take Diancecht's lessons and go a few steps further. Diancecht had done the hard work.

There had been a time when all the Tuatha knew that. Songs were once sung of Diancecht, of how his herbs and hymns could make a brackish pool into a well of healing. He had done so at Moytura, healing half the sidhe who now fawned over Miach. Yet when did he last hear those songs?

So went Diancecht's thoughts as he drank alone and refilled his cup.

Finally. The boy had stopped talking. Women were crowding around him, tossing their hair.

Enough.

Diancecht rose and went to where Airmed sat conversing with another healer. 'Tell your brother to gather his things and meet us at the gates,' he told her. 'We're leaving.'

THE HEALERS GATHERED at the gates soon afterwards.

'What is the matter with you?' said Miach. 'It's the middle of the night—'

'Yes, it is. A time when a healer should be resting. Instead you carouse and prattle with drunkards.'

'You were at the feast too!'

'To keep an eye on you. I did not like what I saw. The moon is out; it is a good night for herb-gathering. Come.'

Diancecht turned and passed through the gates. Miach met his sister's look, shook his head wearily and followed.

They took the road east towards the coast. The moon was so bright that its light served as well as daylight. The road wound its way among farms, fields and patches of forest, where moonlit leaves shone like silver.

'It is too long since we passed this way,' said Diancecht as they walked. 'The people here have lived close to Bres, and likely suffered all the more for it.'

His children did not respond.

They walked on in silence. Cold air cleared the fog of feasting from their heads. Eventually they came to a dense woodland and stopped at a ford within its bounds.

'I remember this place,' said Diancecht. 'Many herbs grow here, especially now as spring dawns. The return of Nuada will give all the plants a new vigour. We will camp here and gather nightly until the full moon has passed.'

The silence between them stretched on as they went through their well-established routine of collecting wood and water, kindling their fire and laying out sleeping rolls. Once their camp was established they went their separate ways, hunting for those herbs which were most potent if picked by moonlight. Diancecht covered the forest on one side of the river, Airmed the other, while Miach searched along the riverbanks.

Normally Miach loved night-walking. He liked to be awake when other people were asleep, to glimpse a silent-swooping owl or a badger emerging for the evening. He would quieten his mind and search for plants with his ears as well as his eyes. Every plant sang a subtle song which grew louder beneath the full moon; he loved to become still and tune his ears towards their rapture.

But not tonight.

Anger filled Miach's mind, drowning out the music of the

night. He walked heavily, snapping twigs and stumbling over roots. Forest animals fled before him, calling out warnings. He walked alone but for the spectre of his rage.

Why could Diancecht not accept that Miach had outdone him? Why could he not celebrate with the rest of their race that Bres was deposed and Nuada returned? Any other man would burn with pride to see his son accomplish such a thing. But not him. Diancecht could only be proud of Diancecht. He could not bear to be second best, and was too weak to even admit that to himself.

Perhaps the time had come to part ways. Miach and Airmed could leave their father to travel alone, doing things his own way. It would be a blessed relief to be free of his sulking resentment. Airmed was so full of ideas, yet she held herself back for fear of their father's disapproval. What marvels could they achieve if they worked together, free from interference?

As Miach's mind turned, he sensed the song of the plants take on a different tone. They seemed to be reaching out to him, as if there was some urgent news he must hear. But he was in no mood to listen. Not tonight.

He was done with Diancecht. The thought of spending even one more day with him was unbearable. Besides, their father was old. It was past time he gave up the wandering life to attend some lord in his hall. Miach and Airmed had nothing left to learn from him.

'You'll wake the dead, walking like that.'

Miach leapt at the sound of his father's voice. He turned to see Diancecht strolling up the riverbank towards him, passing beneath a weeping willow whose branches caressed the cool air.

'Herb-gathering should be done with quiet body and quiet mind. Otherwise the plants will cease their moon-song and lose their power.'

'I know,' said Miach, his voice flat.

'Of course you do,' said Diancecht. 'You know everything, don't you? I've never known a healer with so much pride.'

'Really? Not even, say, yourself?'

Diancecht smiled and shook his head. 'That's what you think, of course. Yes, I have my pride. But you have more. That's how you do it, you know. Self-belief. The boldness to dream, to crawl down burrows of thought that others wouldn't dare enter.' Diancecht stepped closer. 'People think we are timid, us healers. But we are warriors. We see more blood than any battle-haunter; we labour long years after the warrior hangs up his spear. The healer encounters death in a soiled bed, beside a wailing widow, not in the red heat of the sword dance.'

'It is almost morning, and I wish to sleep soon,' said Miach. 'Perhaps you can continue the lecture tomorrow.'

Miach turned away from his father and walked away up the riverbank.

He halted when he heard the scraping of steel.

Miach turned to face his father. Diancecht's sword was in his hand, shining in the moonlight. 'Why do you draw your blade?' asked Miach.

'Pride,' said Diancecht, stepping closer to his son.

Miach backed away.

'I worked for centuries to be the greatest healer of the

sidhe,' said Diancecht. 'It is my name that should live on in songs.'

'Father,' said Miach, still backing away as Diancecht drew closer. 'You do not want this. This is not your way.'

'I shaped you. I made you. I have the right to unmake you.'

'Please,' said Miach as he found himself backed up against a hazel tree.

'What's the matter? You can always find yourself a silver heart.'

Diancecht lunged at Miach, driving his sword into Miach's chest. He was drunk enough to miss his son's heart. Miach fell to the ground, blood spurting from the wound. He closed his eyes and gasped an incantation.

Light shone from within the wound, Miach's blood glowing like molten gold. His wound healed.

Seeing this wonder, Diancecht roared in anger and jealousy. He struck Miach again. This time Miach rolled aside, but only enough so that the sword entered his shoulder.

Miach gasped. Again, he spoke evergreen words of healing. The wound on his shoulder closed.

It was too much. Diancecht held his sword up high and brought it down on Miach's head, cleaving his skull.

Miach would speak no more words of healing.

Miach was dead.

AIRMED SOUGHT out her brother soon after that. Sensing that the night's quarrel might worsen, she hoped to soothe her brother's temper. She found him lying dead beneath a hazel, his blood staining its roots, his once-glittering eyes now lifeless pools of pale moonlight.

She fell gasping to her knees. She searched his body for heat, she put her lips to his lips. But not even Miach could have healed a body so broken.

Airmed got to her feet. She searched for the murderer's trail, thinking Bres or one of his underlings had trailed Miach and taken revenge.

Airmed knew in her heart what had happened. But she was not yet ready to face it.

She returned to her brother's corpse. She lay down beside him, holding him tightly, soaking his cold cheeks with hot tears. When she had no more tears left to cry, she kissed his brow, closed his eyes, kissed his eyelids and returned to camp. The sun was rising and her father was sitting by their fire, drinking tea.

When he failed to meet her eyes, she faced the truth.

'Miach is dead,' she said.

'Yes.'

'You murdered him.'

'No.' Diancecht shook his head. 'This was not murder. When one sidhe insults the honour of another, he who delivered the insult lays his life on the line. Miach offered me insults uncounted. What happened on the riverbank was just.'

'You murdered your son!'

'Where are the herbs you gathered? Do not tell me you wasted this night. I have only one child now, and I shall expect all the more from you.'

Airmed ran from her father. She spent the day among the trees, bent double with grief.

In the afternoon she returned to camp, red-eyed and gaunt. She kicked awake her father, who slept by the fire.

'You deserve death for what you did,' she said. 'But I do not deserve the burden of delivering it. We need to bury Miach's body.'

'Of course we do. Return to the last farmhouse we passed and borrow shovels.'

Airmed did as her father ordered. She returned with two shovels and they set to digging a grave for Miach.

They buried Miach late that night. When that was done, Diancecht went off to gather herbs while Airmed remained by her brother's side.

Airmed stayed awake for another night. She sang to Miach, and told him tales he had loved as a child. She told him how proud she was of him; she reassured him that the sidhe would sing his name forever.

Exhaustion finally took Airmed. She succumbed to sleep.

At dawn, she awoke to a wonder that stole her breath.

Flowers grew on her brother's grave. They had sprung up overnight and now reached for the rising sun, fully grown. Dandelion and garlic, hawthorn and elderflower, nettle and mint all stood together, bright-leaved and wet with dew in the dawn light.

Airmed climbed to her feet, laughter mingling with sobs as she struggled to take in the sight before her. The flowers had grown in the shape of a sleeping person; the shape of her brother's body. It seemed that the root-and-leaf creatures which

Miach had loved now wrapped themselves around him, embracing his spirit, marking his passage with a festival of colour and beauty.

And there was more.

Some strange thought tugged at her mind. It was almost too much to accept; too beautiful and wondrous. It was agonising, for it made a blessing of her brother's death, and that was hard to bear.

And yet...

Mint grew where the stomach would be; nettles marked the passage of blood...

'It is true,' Airmed whispered.

Each plant grew upon the part of the body which it healed. Airmed understood this because she knew the uses of many plants. But there were others she only suspected the use of, or had no idea at all. Yet seeing this map laid out before her, she knew with utter certainty that her suspicion was correct. Medicine would never be the same again. All thanks to her brother. All thanks to his murder.

Airmed took off her dew-soaked cloak and laid it out on the ground. She began to pick the flowers and lay them out on her cloak, taking the utmost care to recreate their original arrangement. It took her all morning, so carefully did she work, but come midday she had finished. She needed to rest, but after she had done so, she would return and commit the arrangement to memory.

'Thank you, Miach,' she said. 'Twice you have changed the world.'

She returned to camp and awoke her father once more.

'What you did was evil, and has extinguished all my love for you. But you will be a better healer if you look upon what your actions have wrought.'

She led Diancecht to Miach's grave. He stood beside her in the afternoon sun as sparrows sang in the trees.

'Airmed,' said Diancecht eventually. 'Would you leave me for a while? I would spend some time alone here.'

She left without a word.

AIRMED RETURNED to her brother's grave that evening. The plants she had arranged on her cloak had been scattered all over the riverbank.

Airmed's memory of the arrangement was greatly flawed, so intricate had it been, and so worn was she by grief. Yet even her fragmented memories were enough to change medicine forever.

For the rest of her life Airmed worked tirelessly to pass on what she had learnt. She became the most beloved healer of the sidhe, while her father descended into infamy. Though Airmed's work brought medicine forward by great bounds, they could have known and passed on so much more, were it not for her father.

Airmed returned to camp that evening.

'This is the last you will see of me,' she said to Diancecht. 'I am tempted to slay you, but I choose not to let hatred poison my heart. Instead, I will forget you.

'From this moment I will travel alone. I will be the healer

you should have been. If by chance we ever cross paths, I shall turn and walk the other way. Though Miach sings in my heart, you are dead to me.'

Airmed left Diancecht and walked way into the night. She never did speak to her father or work with him again, save at the great battle that was to come.[1]

10

THE FLIGHT OF BRES

As Nuada grew reacquainted with ruling, Bres travelled north.

He went as furtively as a thief, keeping to bogs, moors and other untamed places. It was the tussling time between winter and spring, and many cold nights saw him shivering in his cloak, afraid to light a fire.

By raiding farmhouses and catching wild birds he fed himself. He covered ground as fast as he could, knowing that though danger was all around, warmth and sanctuary lay ahead.

Early one morning, Bres crested a hill and looked down upon a glen where smoke rose from a house nestled within birch woods.

His journey was over. He was safe.

Bres' mother opened her door to his shout. Eri stared at her son, hardly recognising him. His fine clothes were filthy, his hair knotted and his face haggard.

'The Tuatha have betrayed me,' said Bres.

SOON BRES SAT before a roaring fire, a mug of warm ale in hand.

'It was Diancecht,' he said as Eri brought him a plate of bread and cheese. 'And his brats, and that oaf Goibniu. They conspired against me. I told them they could not replace me, that it was against our laws, the laws of Danu herself. They did not care. The common people are to blame too, for not one of them fought for me. They chased me out like a dog.'

'What they did is indeed against our laws,' said Eri. 'You were their king – and still are,' she added as his nostrils flared. 'But while their actions cannot be excused, they can be understood. The sidhe have suffered terribly since the Fomorians began taking tribute.'

'What fault is that of mine? The Fomorians would have made war upon us otherwise.'

'And how did you know we could not have withstood them?'

Bres set down his cup. 'I did not know. But when the Fomorian envoy came, he told me something. Something that made me wonder where my true allegiance lay.'

Eri met her son's gaze.

'So,' she said. 'At last you know.'

'Yes,' he said. 'I know.'

'I see that look in your eyes,' she said. 'People have looked at me like that ever since I grew pregnant with you. I have not had a friend in the world since then, save my own son.

'Scorn. Distrust. They have long been my companions. Yet it hurts to see them in my boy's eyes.'

'What do you expect? You lay with an underworld creature! You made me an outcast. Everything I have suffered is because of what you did.'

'You exist because of what I did! Would you have worked your sword arm so hard if you were well-liked? Would you have learnt cunning if the other youths hadn't allied against you, the fatherless child? You may have lost your crown, but you might never have won it without such a life.'

Bres finished his ale. 'More,' he said.

Eri fetched him more ale.

'Tell me what happened,' he said as she knelt and stoked the fire.

Eri looked into the fire and smiled. It occurred to Bres that he had rarely ever seen his mother smile.

'When I was a young woman, I used to go out walking on the shore by my father's hall. I would walk all day if my duties permitted it, or steal out early to be by the water as the sun rose. I somehow felt more kinship with the sea than with my own family. I believed that it watched me, it knew me and would one day offer me a great gift.

'My favourite stretch of shore lay north of our home. I would walk for hours to get there, crossing headlands and rocky screes. To be there was to be the only person living in the world. Time seemed to stand still in that place. I would sit or swim or sing to the waves until the day darkened.'

Eri paused in her story and rose to fetch a cup of ale for herself. She seemed to struggle to find words for what happened next.

'One grey day, I was on that shore when I spied a ship. It was unlike any ship I had ever seen. It seemed to be made of starlight, casting a spell on sea and sky, so that all fell utterly silent and still.

'The ship drew into shore. I walked to the water's edge and saw a man standing at its helm. He held no rudder or oars; I was sure that he steered the ship purely with the power of his thoughts.

'The mariner beached his craft. He stepped out into the still water. He had dark hair and sky-blue eyes; his cloak shone like his ship.'

'If you are about to tell me how he spread his cloak on the sand and undressed you, please spare me,' said Bres.

'Very well,' said Eri, her voice cold. 'If you do not wish to know the little I can tell you of your father.'

'Did you see him after that day?'

'No.'

'So one meeting was all it took to make a mother of you.'

'Mock me all you like, my son. Have I not endured worse a hundred times? You cannot shame me. When the other girls saw my swollen belly and shunned me, I offered no excuses. I did not speak of his beauty, how he seemed to be ancient and child-like at once. How I felt I was in a dream, and knew with the certainty of dreams that lying with him was utterly right.'

'How noble of you.'

Eri sighed. 'Is there something you wish to know of him?'

'His name.'

'Whether he spoke truly or not, he gave it as Elathan of the Fomorians.'

Bres asked his mother no more questions. She brought him more bread and cheese, and he ate without speaking.

'I will stay here awhile to rest and regain my strength,' he said once he had finished eating. 'Then I will leave.'

Eri nodded. She did not have to ask where he would go.

A FEW DAYS LATER, Bres left Eri's hall, leading her best cow on a rope.

He took it into the hills west of the hall. As dusk fell he came to a high, stony glen. At its end lay a cave, which Eri claimed was a known gateway to the Fomorian realm. The skulls of men, beasts and otherworld creatures littered the floor.

Inside the cave, Bres cut the cow's throat. As it fell upon the cave floor he called out, 'Here stands Bres, rightful king of the sidhe and servant of Balor. I would speak with one of his servants.'

The cow's thrashing slowly diminished, her blood tracing patterns on the stone.

Bres waited.

Night fell. Darkness cloaked the cave. He shivered and stamped his feet. He had only guessed how to summon a Fomorian; perhaps he had guessed wrongly.

A shuffling sound came from the shadows.

Torchlight appeared in the depths of the cave, followed by a cloaked figure. It was the envoy who had first come to Tara, again wearing his monstrous shape.

'You are unwise to call on us. You lost your kingship. The Tuatha no longer pay tribute.'

'There is one among you whom I would speak with.'

'Who?'

'Elathan.'

The envoy grinned, revealing rows of sharp teeth. 'Come.'

Bres followed him into the rear of the cave, where a newly appeared tunnel led them into the bowels of the earth. The tunnel stretched on, guiding them down and forever down, until they emerged on the shore of a sea.

Sea and sky were dark. Tendrils of fire burned among black clouds, illuminating distant islands and the spine of great serpents which patrolled the bay. Thunder rumbled and wind howled.

The envoy led Bres to a waiting boat and they climbed in. At a word from the envoy the boat set off, taking them out to sea. Creatures rose from the water to gaze at Bres as they wove their way through a forest of islands. On some islands stood tents of skin, while others were home to castles of timber or stone. Everywhere, the sky burned.

At some point the boat turned towards an island, landing itself on her shore. Bres and his guide climbed out and took a path through gullies of sharp stone, finally arriving at a stone fort on a high hilltop.

The gates parted as they approached. Out strode a dark-haired, blue-eyed man.

He looked Bres up and down and curled his lip into a sneer. 'Why have you sought me?'

'The Tuatha Dé Danaan have deposed me.'

'This I know.'

'I do not wish to be a man of the Tuatha. Though I am Tuatha in form, I am a Fomorian in my heart. My place is here, Father.'

'What makes you think that we want you?'

'Nuada of the Silver Hand reigns at Tara,' said Bres. 'The sidhe are emboldened, and no longer pay tribute to Balor. Should we attack them, they will fight back fiercely.' He stepped closer. 'I can help you. I have fought among them in countless battles; I was chief among their champions. I know their every weapon, their every strategy; many are of my own making. If you fight with me on your side you will win, and be master of the Tuatha Dé Danaan forever after.'

'And what do you want in return?' asked Elathan.

Bres' eyes narrowed. 'I want to rule them,' he said. 'I want to sit once more on the throne at Tara, and ensure the Tuatha are so trampled in spirit that they never rise in rebellion again.'

Bres' father weighed his words. Eventually he said, 'Come with me.'

Elathan dismissed the envoy with a wave of his hand. He led Bres away, taking him down a steep set of stairs to a narrow harbour among the cliffs. There, Bres beheld his father's shining, silver craft.

'Get in.'

So Bres' voyage continued. They moved further into the forest of islands, the sky still burning above them. Bres noticed that the islands here were larger and more densely populated.

Eventually he spied a fort so mighty that fire-clouds swirled about its high turrets. A wave of dread hit him; an ancient, primeval fear he had never known. He wanted to turn back, but he was past that point.

They docked at what appeared to be a port. Bres followed his father through the docks and up into the lamplit streets of the Fomorian city.

Bres had had dealings with a dozen Fomorian envoys and tax collectors. That had not prepared him for what he saw. The streets were packed with the creatures – no, not creatures, his people – and they were so strange in shape! Many of them looked like Tuatha but taller, far more muscular, their bared skin covered in strange markings. They had a savage look to them, a predatory gleam in their eyes, as if they wore the bodies of men but had the spirits of hunting beasts. Others had scaled skin like reptiles, or were covered in fur and had the heads of cats, dogs, eagles, bears. Bres spotted a giant, easily five times his own height, lumbering down a nearby street. He passed an old woman who had one eye, one arm and one leg. She had an enormous fang which she used as a crutch to drag herself down the street.

The Fomorians made way for Elathan, who seemed to be well-known among them. Bres was jostled, shoved, given dark looks. Many Fomorians sniffed as he passed, then bared their teeth, as if they caught some foul scent off him.

'You may be half-Fomorian,' said his father without turning back, 'but you look like a sidhe and you smell like one too.'

The crowds grew thinner as they approached the fortress.

'Wait here,' said Elathan. He went forward to speak with the guards at the gates, each of which carried a sword in each of their four arms. They nodded as he finished speaking, and opened the gates.

Elathan gestured at Bres to come forward. They made their way into the fortress and down a dark hallway. Through stone corridors they walked together, passing more strange and brutish guardsmen, until they emerged into a vast hall.

Torches blazed on stone pillars, their light fading long before it could touch the ceiling. Bres' footsteps echoed as he followed his father forward to the front of the hall.

They halted before an enormous throne wrought from sinew and bone.

Its occupant was a giant. Tall as a tree, wide as a barn, dressed in the skin of some enormous serpent. To either side of the throne stood teams of five wretched-looking slaves, lank-haired and filthy, iron rings around their necks. Each of them held a chain, the other end of which was attached to an iron ring on the giant's right eyelid. If all the slaves gathered behind him and pulled on the chains, Bres guessed, it would cause his enormous, swollen right eye to open. At present, that eye was shut.

The other eye was fixed on Bres.

'My king,' said Elathan. 'I present to you my son, Bres.

'Bres, you stand before Balor, king of the Fomorians.'[1]

PART II

11

THE COMING OF LUGH

As Bres entered the Fomorian realm and Airmed wept over her brother's grave, the Tuatha went on feasting at Tara.

They came from every corner of the country. Tuatha arrived from the northern shores of Ulster, the rolling valleys of Clare, the shimmering hills of Killarney and the deepest Leinster forests. There were far too many to fit in the feasting hall, or even within the walls of Tara. Barrels of ale once hoarded by Bres were opened in the lesser halls and in hastily erected tents on the plain outside. Poets and musicians were everywhere, food was freely shared and everyone was overflowing with mirth, except perhaps the guards outside the great hall.

Nuada's hall was reserved for chiefs and master craftsmen. The choicest food and drink was served within those walls, yet as the days and nights passed, a shadow stretched across the feasting. The company rejoiced to be rid of Bres and to see

Nuada on the throne, his silver hand gleaming in the firelight. But a battle with Balor was surely coming, and Nuada had yet to speak on the subject.

It was midday on the twelfth day of the feast. The sun was bright in the blue sky; the hall shook with the sounds of revelry. Two guards named Gamal and Colum were on duty outside the hall, scratching their bellies and feeling thoroughly bored, when they noticed a young man striding towards them.

The man was strikingly handsome, with chestnut-red hair and soft, watchful eyes. Wolfhound-lean yet tightly muscled, he moved as lithely as a hunting cat. He carried slingshot and sword on his belt, wore a beautifully wrought spear on his back, and smiled broadly as he greeted them.

'The finest of spring days to you both,' he said, and made to enter the hall.

Gamal blocked his path.

'Who are you?' grunted the guard.

'Ah!' said the young man. 'My apologies. I am Lugh of the Long Hand, and I have come to join the feast. Now, if you wouldn't mind...' he tried to move around Gamal, but Colum stopped him.

'I hope you haven't come far,' said Colum, who was tired of listening to celebrations he couldn't join, 'because you're not going inside.'

'Really?' said Lugh. 'May I ask why not?'

'Because this feast is only for chiefs and masters of the arts.'

'I am not yet a chief,' said Lugh, 'but neither am I short of skills. Tell me: do you have a smith at the feast? For I am skilled in smithing.'

The guards looked at one another and laughed. 'Goibniu is in there,' said Colum. 'Are you a better smith than him?'

'Maybe and maybe not,' said Lugh. 'But do you have a great warrior in there? For I have mastered the fighting arts.'

'We have Oghma, who led our forces at Moytura,' said Colum. 'Try again, whelp.'

'I am a harper.'

'The Dagda is inside,' said Gamal.

'I am a healer.'

'Diancecht drinks in this hall,' said Colum.

'I am a poet.'

'Corpre's songs can make the rocks weep, and he weaves words inside,' said Colum.

'I am a fashioner of spells.'

'The Morrigan is the master of magic. She is here,' said Gamal.

'I am a cup-bearer—'

'They don't need a cup-bearer. They don't need someone to cut their meat, rub their feet or wipe their arses,' said Colum, who was losing patience. 'Off with you now.'

'Very well,' said Lugh. 'I will leave... so long as you answer a single question.'

'Fine,' said Colum, gritting his teeth. 'One question.'

'You have a master smith inside. You have the greatest of warriors, harpers, poets, sorcerers and healers. But is there a sidhe inside who is an ildánach, a master of all arts, as I am?'

Gamal and Colum looked at one another uneasily.

'Stay here,' said Gamal.

He went inside and picked his way through the heaving

crowd. Reaching the throne, he climbed the dais and knelt down by Nuada's side.

'Sire,' he said. 'There is a very unusual young man outside.'

'In what way is he unusual?'

'He claims to be an ildánach, a master of all arts. A great smith, fighter, harper, poet, sorcerer and healer.'

'Then he is not unusual, but extraordinary,' said Nuada. 'Assuming his boast is accurate. Take a gaming board outside and test him against our finest players. That is a good way to measure a mind.'

Gamal found two women hunched over a gaming board and explained the situation. Soon one sat on the grass outside the hall, lining up her pieces opposite Lugh's.

He beat her in a dozen moves.

She returned to the hall, shaking her head and proclaiming the might of the young man's mind. One of her peers went out to put Lugh in his place.

Lugh beat him in six moves.

One player after another faced Lugh and was defeated. Word spread through the hall that a handsome youth named Lugh of the Long Hand sat outside, trouncing all their foremost players.

'Bring him in,' said some. 'We would like to see this young man.'

Eventually Neit, who was acknowledged by all as master of the board, rose and went outside. He returned ten minutes later, snarling at the servants to refill his cup. The calls to bring Lugh in became a clamour.

Nuada cleared his throat.

Silence spread through the hall.

'Let Lugh of the Long Hand join the feast,' said Nuada.

The company cheered as Lugh entered. He walked through the hall, smiling at everyone who met his eye. Many noted that the spear he wore on his back was in fact the Spear of Victory, one of their four great treasures, which they had thought to be in the keeping of Manannán.

Lugh was halfway across the hall when Oghma, who was deep in his cups and had taken Lugh's boasts as a challenge, squared up to him.

'You... you think you're a big man, eh?'

'I know I am,' said Lugh. 'As are you, mighty champion.'

'Well then... let's... let's see you do this!'

Oghma bent down and dug his fingers in between the flagstones of the floor. Muscles straining, he picked up one of the great stones, spun around three times and hurled it through the wall. The drunken chiefs laughed and cheered, except for those whom the missile narrowly missed. The flagstone landed far out on the plain outside Tara.

Oghma turned to face Lugh again and raised his eyebrows.

Lugh smiled at Oghma. He left the hall through the newly made doorway. A few minutes later, the flagstone flew back through the wall and landed in the exact place it had been removed from.

The Tuatha's cheers were deafening.

'Young Master of Arts,' called the Dagda when Lugh re-entered the hall. 'Favour us with a song.' He rose from his stool and gestured to his harp.

Lugh took the Dagda's seat, plucked a few strings, cleared his throat and began.

He sang a bawdy song about a lusty farmer. The hall rang with laughter. A composition of his own followed, telling the tale of the Battle of Moytura. The chiefs cheered and wept.

Finally, Lugh sang of Connemara. His song was a summer wind sweeping through the western hills at dawn. The entire company fell asleep, awaking as the brisk, final notes filled the hall.

This time the chiefs did not cheer. Instead they watched as Nuada arose and beckoned Lugh to approach the throne.

'Lugh of the Long Hand,' said Nuada.

'King Nuada of the Silver Hand,' said Lugh with a bow.

'You are, as you claim, a master of all arts. My hall is enriched by your presence. But I think you came here to do more than entertain us.'

The chiefs gasped as Nuada stepped to his side and gestured towards the throne.

'I believe you have been sent here to lead us,' he said.

Not a man or woman breathed.

'We have enjoyed a well-deserved feast,' said Nuada. 'A respite from all our troubles. But those troubles cloud my mind, and the minds of every sidhe here. Bres may be gone, but Balor is with us.

'I know what you are all wondering. Will I order you to pay tribute to those monsters? Your hard-won grain, your beloved cattle, and even your children?

'The Morrigan has amassed knowledge of our enemy. They are a mighty race, their armies as vast as the western ocean.

Even had we five times our numbers, we would be hard-pressed to withstand them in battle.'

The silence that filled the hall was dagger sharp.

'I do not wish to pay tribute to Balor,' continued Nuada, 'yet I will not bring about the ruin of our entire race.'

'Let us leave this island then,' called someone. 'It was a mistake to come here.'

'No,' said Nuada. 'We will not leave. The Isle of Destiny herself spoke in our dreams. We were destined to come here and to rule for many centuries. And that we shall do, with the aid of this man.'

Nuada addressed Lugh again.

'I give you the throne,' he said. 'For thirteen days. Speak and we shall listen. Order and we shall act. Share with us your sea-deep shrewdness, your sun-bright mind. Lead us, Lugh of the Long Hand.'

Even the hounds beneath the tables held their breath as they waited for Lugh's response.

'For thirteen days,' said Lugh, 'I will lead the Children of Danu.'

Lugh climbed the dais, stood before the throne and sat down to rapturous applause.

'I have one last request, before your rule begins,' said Nuada as he took a seat at a nearby table.

'I will happily honour it,' said Lugh.

'This is a feast. You are a poet. So tell us a tale. Speak of your parents, and how you came to be born, and how you came to carry the Spear of Victory.'

'That is a good tale,' said Lugh, 'and I will tell it gladly.'[1]

12

THE BIRTH OF LUGH

It was in the first winter of Bres' reign that Fomorians came to Crow Island, intending to steal the Cow of Plenty.

Three envoys rose out of the ocean and stepped onto the stony shore. They took the path to Goibniu's forge and found him standing at its door. Grazing on the grass nearby was the Cow of Plenty. The Fomorians gawped at the cow and licked their lips as their leader addressed the smith.

'We have come to collect what is due to us,' said the leader. Like his comrades, he was humanoid in shape, with scaled skin and dense muscles. 'A third of your cattle, your grain and your children are ours.'

'Then this was a wasted trip,' said Goibniu, tapping the head of his hammer on his palm. 'I am father to no children, I grow no crops and I only have one cow.'

'Then you are fortunate,' said the leader. 'We will content ourselves with taking only the cow.'

'You won't feel content when I've pounded your brains to mince,' said Goibniu.

The Fomorian hissed at Goibniu. 'Balor himself covets this cow. Refusing us will earn you his enmity; that is a burden you do not wish to bear. Give us the heifer.'

'Here's another idea. You turn around and crawl back into whatever hole you came from. I'm done talking. If one of you takes a single step towards my cow, you'll feel the weight of my hammer.' Goibniu positioned himself between the Fomorians and the cow, his hammer held high and ready to strike.

The Fomorians looked to their leader.

'Have it your way, smith,' said the leader. 'This is not the last you shall see of us. Balor will take you and your cow, and you will wish you were mortal so that the pain might one day end.'

They turned and left.

GOIBNIU KNEW he could not remain alone on Crow Island. He would fight to the death to guard the Cow of Plenty, yet he had to work and he had to sleep. If the Fomorians were determined enough then they would get the cow eventually. He needed help.

The following day, a woman of the sidhe visited Crow Island to have a dagger made. Goibniu asked her to find his friends Cian and Samthainn and bid them come to Crow Island. They arrived a week later.

Goibniu greeted his friends and put mugs of sweet, dark ale in their hands. They listened gravely as he told his story.

'You are both powerful fighters,' said Goibniu. 'I plead your help in protecting the cow.'

'This is a dire situation indeed,' said Samthainn. 'I have heard tales of Balor from the Firbolgs of Connacht. They say that as monstrous as his race are, Balor is the most terrible of them all.

'As a child, it is said, he spied upon Fomorian druids who were brewing a deadly potion in a cauldron. The steam from the brew got into his eyes. One of his eyes grew grossly swollen and pregnant with power. Any person who that evil eye looks upon is instantly slain.'

'Is there a Tuatha whose situation is not dire?' said Cian. 'At least Goibniu has no children whom the Fomorians can take as tribute.'

'But the Cow of Plenty is no ordinary cow,' said Samthainn. 'She is sacred to all our people, kin to Danu herself. Balor must know that if he takes her from us, he is taking more than a source of milk. From her udders come the joy of the Tuatha, our hope and our good fortune.'

'Which is why I have sent for you both,' said Goibniu. 'If this quarrel was mine alone, I would have faced it alone. But if the Cow of Plenty is taken, all the Tuatha will suffer; I would not be surprised if the sun herself should go dark. Stay here with me, I ask you. Guard the cow; give your lives if you must.'

'You need not ask,' said Cian. 'To protect her is the sacred duty of the sidhe, and we shall do so gladly.'

CIAN AND SAMTHAINN remained on Crow Island with Goibniu. One of them would stay close to the cow, one of them would watch the path and the other would rest or go about his own business. Goibniu set to forging new blades for Cian and Samthainn, to thank them for their help and to aid them in protecting the Cow of Plenty. He intended that those blades be the finest he ever wrought.

It was not long before the Fomorians returned.

A team of seven warriors rose from the sea one morning. Samthainn spied them from the top of the hill. He blew his horn and Cian came running while Goibniu guarded the cow.

The scaled warriors climbed the path. They reached its top and spread out where the ground levelled out. The Fomorians drew their swords, swished their tails and snarled at Cian and Samthainn through sharp teeth.

'Balor wants the beast,' said the leader. 'Hand her over or lose your lives.'

'Tell Balor to come and get her himself,' said Cian. 'Unless he is scared, or too fat and lazy to fight.'

The Fomorian leader laughed. 'You are lucky that you will be dead soon, or you would live to regret those words.'

The Fomorians rushed at Cian and Samthainn, who stood firm. Cian lopped the arm off one warrior with his first strike. The Fomorian fighter fell, black blood spurting from his hewn arm. Cian turned just in time to meet his next opponent's strike. He glimpsed Samthainn holding off two Fomorians while the remaining three darted past them.

'They're coming!' he roared.

The Fomorians found Goibniu awaiting them, hammer in hand. He broke their skulls to bloodied splinters before running to join the fray. With Goibniu's help, Cian and Samthainn made short work of their opponents. Goibniu tossed their bodies from the clifftop, food for the fish.

'That was not so difficult,' said Samthainn, wiping blood and sweat from his brow.

'That was just the first of them,' said Goibniu.

GOIBNIU'S WORDS PROVED TRUE. The Fomorians returned again and again, increasingly often and in increasing numbers. It seemed to Cian and Samthainn that they only slept for a few snatched hours between bouts of fighting. Again and again their blades were blunted, and Goibniu worked every spare moment to forge for them weapons that would forever sing sharp.

'Our luck will not hold forever,' said Samthainn to Cian after a particularly bloody battle.

'Our swords will be ready soon,' said Cian.

'A sword is only as mighty as the man who wields it,' said Samthainn. 'And no man is mighty enough to withstand an army. I think Balor will send an army soon, if he does not come himself.'

But Balor did not send an army, nor did he come to Crow Island himself.

IT WAS MIDWINTER. Snow fell on Crow Island, to be quickly washed away by sheets of rain. Towering waves tore at the cliffs, spraying foam over the high ground where smoke rose steadily from Goibniu's forge.

Cian sat huddled in his cloak, shivering as he watched the path. No Fomorians had come for over a week, but that did not mean they would not come today. All the same, he wished he was inside with a mug of hot ale. The cow was in her winter byre, which at least meant that only one of them had to stand guard.

He looked up to see Samthainn approaching, a glittering new sword in his scabbard.

'The blades are ready?' asked Cian as his heart leapt.

Samthainn gave him a thin smile. 'This one is. I'm sorry, friend. Goibniu only forged one sword, and he gave it to me.'

Cian's hands curled into fists. 'He made a sword for you and not for me? After we have both lived here and fought alongside him?'

'The blame is not mine,' said Samthainn, showing his palms. 'If you have an issue with the smith, take it up with the smith.'

'I shall.'

Cian got to his feet and made for the forge, leaving Samthainn to keep watch on the cow. He threw open the door, entered the anteroom and found Goibniu sitting at the table with Samthainn.

'How dare you...' said Cian. 'How did you get in here, Samthainn? You were outside a moment ago—'

'Why aren't you guarding the cow?' interrupted Goibniu.

Too late, Cian realised he had been tricked.

He ran outside, followed by Goibniu and Samthainn.

The byre door was open.

The Cow of Plenty was gone.

Cian felt his legs quiver as Goibniu turned on him.

'I'm sorry,' he said. 'This was my fault. I swear I will bring the Cow of Plenty back to you, even if I have to fight Balor himself.'

CIAN DID NOT STAY another hour on Crow Island. He rowed to the mainland and set off inland, up into the toothy glens and windswept peaks of Beara. He sought the one person whom he believed could help him.

The following evening he spied smoke rising over the rocks ahead. Soon he stood before a tiny stone dwelling. Sweet-smelling smoke rose from the chimney; firelight filled the open doorway.

Cian entered to find Birog waiting for him.

Birog was known as the Wind Rider. She was on intimate terms with the spirits of the sky and lived as close as she could to their realm. Her white hair was sleek, her features sharp; she wore a cloak of eagle feathers.

'The wind brought word of your coming,' she said, 'and weeps for what is gone.'

Cian sat down on skins by the fire and faced Birog.

'Is it as bad as I fear?' he asked.

'It is worse,' said Birog, her raptor eyes boring into Cian. 'From the milk of the cow springs the strength of our warriors, the fertility of our fields. Without her, we will become wretched. Bards will sing songs of hatred, making neighbour quarrel with neighbour. Every oath ever sworn shall be broken; mothers will open the throats of infants. Our halls will burn and our armies will feed the crows.'

'It is my fault she was taken. I have sworn to retrieve her, but I need your help.'

Birog's eyes narrowed.

'That is why you call on the Wind Rider. You would have me take you over the sea and into the Fomorian realm, where the sky is fire and serpents scour the waves.'

'You have seen it?' said Cian.

'My gaze wanders far,' whispered Birog. 'Many nights has it flown to the home of our oppressors, roving unseen. But to go there in body is another thing entirely. It is yet another to take you along, and to bring the Cow of Plenty back. This is no small thing that you ask of me.'

'But you will do it,' said Cian.

Birog gave him a wide smile.

'What kind of sidhe would I be if turned down a little trouble?'

CIAN SLEPT by Birog's fire. Though images of the Fomorian realm troubled his rest, Birog's presence soothed his mind. He flitted in and out of sleep, awakening at times to see Birog hunched over the flames, eyes closed, singing spells in preparation for their voyage.

Morning came. Shivering, Cian arose and followed Birog outside.

Tendrils of mist wreathed the mountains. Birog led him up towards the high peaks. Cian fought to stay upright as the wind blew harder, buffeting him as if to test his strength. Birog muttered as she walked, talking to the wind as one might talk to an old friend.

They reached the mountain's peak. Sun-fire lit the eastern sky, illuminating the fang-sharp peaks all around them. Far beneath them, waves rolled and crashed on the restless sea.

'There are many ways to move between worlds,' said Birog. 'Caves and tunnels, pools of water, brews that give wing to the mind. We will ride the wind over the sea, and so slip through the veil.' She spread her cloak wide. 'The wind shall bear us; my spells shall enshroud us. Come.'

Cian stepped closer to Birog. She wrapped her cloak around him and began to sing. The wind responded instantly, its howl becoming a roar. Birog's wailing song gathered pace and soon she sang the final words of her spell. She spread her cloak wide and they shot into the sky.

~

OVER THE WAVES THEY WENT, leaving the Isle of Destiny behind. Birog sang all the while, her songs steering them as a rudder steers a ship. Eventually Cian looked up and saw a wall of grey clouds ahead. Lightning shot across it in sinuous webs; thunder shook the air.

Cian felt a jolt of fear. Was he mad? He was no druid; he was not made to wander between worlds. He opened his mouth to protest, to call for Birog to turn them back, but the wind stole his words.

A moment later, they struck the storm wall.

Cian lost all sense of direction as he spun this way and that, the air itself clawing and tearing at him. It knew he did not belong here; it would unmake him, scatter him across the sky...

They were through.

Cian breathed a sigh of relief, yet his relief was short-lived.

They had entered the Fomorian realm.

Birog's song changed. Cian somehow sensed that she wove spells of concealment. They would need them.

The Fomorian realm was a dark, storm-lashed sea, studded with rocky islands rising from the waves like broken teeth. Above them was a wall of black clouds suffused with flames, which spewed sporadic blasts of lightning. Cian made out immense shapes in the water that surfaced for a few moments before disappearing into the deep.

As they flew, Cian noticed pinpricks of firelight among the islands. He made out squat shapes that could only be Fomorian dwellings. At times he saw figures moving from house to house. He had fought against dozens of Fomorians by now, but he didn't know how he would fare against some of the hulking creatures he glimpsed below him.

Birog's course was straight and true; she had divined their destination. They shot over waves and jagged islands until there was nothing but dark water beneath them.

Then, in the distance, Cian spied another island.

It was shaped like the back of a whale, long and humped. Drawing closer, Cian saw a tiny cluster of lights at the peak of the hump. If the cow was kept here, might Balor be nearby? Cian shuddered at the thought.

No. Closer still, Cian saw that it was only a cluster of five low houses bordered by a high stone wall. The central house was large enough to accommodate a dozen occupants, while the four around it were much smaller. The Fomorian king would not live here. More likely the cow was guarded, and her guards slept here.

Over the dwellings they flew, gradually descending. Birog's song was a whisper now.

Cian saw one of the guards emerge from the central dwelling and move towards the wall...

They looked up.

Cian swore.

Birog flew to the far side of the island, out of sight of the camp. There were no guards in sight. Birog spread her cloak and Cian stepped out from under it.

'We were seen,' she said. 'I do not know why but for a moment, my spells of concealment failed. We must be quick.' She pointed in the direction of the shore.

Down at the water's edge was the Cow of Plenty.

Eithne stared into the sky.

'What is it?' said one of the guards at the gate, eyeing her suspiciously.

'Nothing. I...'

'You saw something?'

Eithne was about to reply, but hesitated. Balor had increased the number of guards on the island since bringing the sidhe cow here. He did not expect the sidhe to try to enter his realm. All the same, he had sent extra guards. All female.

'No. I saw nothing.'

The woman gave a brief bow. Eithne turned and walked away until she was out of sight, then looked up at the sky again. She had seen something. Just for a moment she had glimpsed a man in the sky, outlined by shadows that might have been wings, and whose face she knew.

It was the same face she had seen in her dreams. Last night, and every night for a year. It was the face she had seen in her waking hours too, for she did little now but lie in bed, eyes closed, summoning his image in all the detail she could muster. Caressing that sweet face with ghostly hands, imagining a thousand deep and gentle voices for him.

The guard came around the corner again, watching Eithne.

'You are sure you saw nothing?'

Could it have been him? Was he really real?

BIROG AND CIAN slowly approached the cow.

'Be careful,' said Birog. 'She might take fright.'

'No,' said Cian. 'She knows me and will trust us both.'

Indeed, she did not bolt, nor did she seem disturbed by their presence. Even here in this dark realm, the Cow of Plenty seemed as serene as ever. She raised her head, examining each of them with deep-seeing eyes. Then she returned to grazing on the thin grass which strained to grow among the rocks. She almost seemed to be smiling.

Birog drew closer. She placed her hand upon the cow's neck and whispered soothing words.

Meanwhile, Cian gazed up the hill, towards the Fomorian camp that was now out of sight.

'I will lay a spell of concealment on her,' said Birog. 'It will be difficult, given her power. To anyone sensitive to magic, she shines as brightly as a beacon fire. And if I succeed, Balor's druids will likely notice her absence.'

'How can I help?'

'Keep watch, and keep your sword-hand ready. I fear we will be discovered soon.'

Cian did as asked, watching the horizon as Birog worked her magic.

'We are ready,' she said after a time. 'Come under my cloak.'

But Cian kept back, his eyes on the horizon.

'What is it?' hissed Birog.

'I have to go up there.'

'What are you talking about?'

'There is someone I must speak with...' Cian ran away up the hill.

'Cian! Come back! You will be seen!'

But Cian ignored Birog. Cursing, she followed him as heavy rain began to fall.

EITHNE STOOD OUTSIDE HER TENT, the rain pouring down around her. Her gaze wandered over the huts where her guards dwelt, the stone wall that encircled their camp, and the women standing at guard posts atop the gates, gripping their spears. One of them turned back and glared at her for a moment before returning to scanning the horizon.

Then the woman fell to the ground.

Her companion did the same, as if suddenly overcome by sleep. Their spears clattered upon the rocks.

Eithne watched open-mouthed as the gates to the compound swung open. A young man and an old woman entered.

It was him. Truly, it was him.

She ran forward and wrapped her arms around him.

'Who...' said the man.

'It is you,' she said. 'I cannot believe it. After all this time, you finally came for me.'

'I... who are you?'

'I am Eithne,' she said. 'I am Balor's daughter.'

CIAN LISTENED, not knowing what to think as words tumbled from the beautiful woman in his arms. She spoke of how she had seen his face in her dreams, night after night. She had hoped that one day he would rescue her from this bleak place, and now he had come...

It made no sense. Yet to his heart, it was the only thing that had ever made sense. He had never lain eyes on her, not even in dreams. She was a Fomorian, Balor's daughter... yet in that moment when she had looked up at him, and their eyes had met, he somehow felt that he knew her too. And not only did he know her...

He loved her. He had never known such a love. It felt far greater than him, as if it were an ancient creature that had prowled the world since time began, and he was a vessel infinitely too small to contain it.

'We need to get out of sight,' said Birog as Cian and Eithne gazed at one another. For all the urgency of their plight, she recognised that this was no youthful fancy. Forces beyond her knowing were at work here.

Eithne turned to Birog and nodded. 'Come inside,' she said.

She led them into the central tent. A blazing fire lit the long central hearth; rich tapestries hung on the walls.

'My father keeps me in comfort,' she said, gesturing for them to sit down, 'but a prison is a prison.'

'Why does he keep you prisoner?' asked Cian.

'My mother, Caitlín, has the gift of prophecy. She told Balor that his death would come at the hands of his own grandson. I am Balor's only daughter.'

'So he keeps you here, away from men,' said Cian, gazing

into Eithne's eyes as he spoke. Fomorian she might be, but had ever a woman been so beautiful? Her lapis eyes were so bright, so entrancing...

'He tried to,' said Eithne. She knelt down beside Cian. 'But though he surrounded me by guards, they could not patrol my dreams, and in my dreams I saw you.' She put her hand to his face. 'I held you close. I ran my hands through your hair and pressed you to my body. I...'

Cian pressed his lips to hers as Birog went outside to watch the gates.

BIROG RETURNED to find the lovers dressing.

'We have been discovered,' she said. 'Balor's druids have sensed my presence. Come.'

They ran behind her, through the gates and down the hill as horns rang out across the sea. A distant roaring shook Cian's bones and reawakened him to the danger they faced.

Reaching the cow, Birog turned to face Cian and Eithne.

'I cannot carry both of you.'

Cian stared at Birog. 'But you must! She will—'

'Do not argue with me! There is no time. Look.'

Cian looked out to sea. Boats raced over the waves towards them. Between the boats swam enormous creatures, opening their maws to trumpet war cries to the sky.

'But I can't...' began Cian.

'Go,' said Eithne. 'You will return for me.'

'But your father will learn of this. When he learns we have lain together...'

'My father may be a monster, but he loves me. I will survive his wrath, as I have before. You will not. Go.'

'But you might be pregnant. I cannot—'

Birog ran out of patience. She had spied a druid at the head of one ship, waves of terrible power emanating from him as his song powered the ships forward. This was an enemy she could not withstand.

She wrapped her cloak around the cow, Cian and herself. They became shadows and took flight, shooting into the sky and away. Birog sensed the Fomorian druid's rage at her escape.

'Goodbye, brave daughter of Balor,' she whispered. 'May your faith in your father not prove misplaced.'

So goes the tale that Lugh told that evening.

When his tale was over, Lugh surveyed the silent hall. The entire company of Tuatha stared at him, enraptured. Night had fallen, the fires reduced to embers, every hound asleep with a full belly.

'My mother had the right of it. Balor could not kill his own daughter,' he said. 'He waited until I was born then threw me into the sea, for he could not kill me either. Kindness lives in even the darkest of hearts.

'Birog had been watching Balor. As soon as it was safe, she passed between the realms again, found me and took me to Manannán's hall beneath the waves. There I quickly grew to manhood, trained by the Lord Manannán himself, and attained mastery of all arts.'

Lugh rose from the throne.

'Now I stand before you at Tara, and I did not come here to feast. I came to say that our time beneath Balor's yoke is over. We will no longer bend to his will. No longer will we give him our crops, our cattle, our children. This fair isle which we won from the Firbolgs shall be ruled by Danu's children again!'

The sidhe cheered and hammered their cups on the tables, startling the hounds awake.

Lugh leaned forward, grinning widely, as the cheering subsided.

'This is how we're going to do it.'[1]

13

A GATHERING OF STRENGTH

'We cannot defeat the Fomorians,' said Lugh. 'Not as we are now. There is a hidden strength in each sidhe waiting to be awakened. For that to happen, it must awaken first in our leaders. Nuada, Oghma, Diancecht, Goibniu and the Dagda. Step forward.'

The named men stepped forward.

'In the morning we will leave this place. I will take you to a place I know, far from watching eyes. There you shall study until you are truly ready to lead.'

There were some who cast dark looks at Lugh, thinking that he insulted their leaders. But most accepted his words, for he had finally given them hope.

'Attend to whatever business you have. Gather at the gates at dawn,' concluded Lugh. The chiefs bowed to him.

The feast ended. The following morning, the lords of the sidhe left Tara with Lugh at their head.

THEY CROSSED THE COUNTRY, heading northwest. After a time, Lugh led them off the road and into the forest, down winding paths and then down no path at all until they reached Grellach Dollaid.

'Here we shall remain until our work is done,' said Lugh.

It was a marsh, the reeking air swarming with stinging insects, the ground spongy and dank.

'Why must we work in a place such as this?' asked Diancecht.

'Because here we shall work all the harder, knowing that when our work is done, we shall be free to leave this place.'

So they made their camp and commenced work. Night and day, under Lugh's direction, the company prepared themselves in body and mind to lead their people against Balor. Some days they trained at sword fighting under Oghma, or the use of the sling under Lugh. On other days Goibniu set them exercises to build their strength.

Other periods of work were more solitary. The chiefs would go off individually to some far reach of the marsh, fasting and praying for days as they sought new depths of insight into their own craft. At other times they would sit together for days, discussing battle tactics.

For a full year this went on. Finally Lugh said, 'We are done, and you are ready to lead.'

The leaders at last left the swamp. They were happy to return to more hospitable climes, yet grateful for all they had learned. Each of them now believed in their hearts that Balor could be beaten.

Back on the road, a cool breeze was blowing and the sun was shining.

'Return to Tara or wherever else you wish to go,' said Lugh. 'We shall meet again twelve days hence, on the Hill of Uisnech where all the provinces of the Isle of Destiny meet.'

'Where will you go?' asked Oghma.

'To Manannán's hall,' said Lugh with a grin. 'And I shall return with a mighty gift.'

Twelve days later, the chiefs gathered at the Hill of Uisnech. They summited the hill and looked around for a sign of Lugh.

The day passed and still Lugh did not come. But as the sun sank in the sky, the chiefs saw a cloud arising from the plain to the west, and heard a thundering that seemed to arise from beneath the earth.

From the dust-cloud emerged Lugh. He rode Enbarr, Manannán's shining white steed, at the head of a vast company of riders. They surged over the plain and up the hill, and moments later, surrounded the chiefs.

The chiefs were amazed at the sight of these riders, whose armour seemed to have trapped the light of the sun. Yet even the splendour of the riders did not compare to the splendour of Enbarr. Manannán's mount wore full battle-plate. Both Enbarr's armour and that of Lugh were inlaid with sparkling jewels, and with magical words engraved in ogham.

'I have been to the halls of Manannán, far beneath the ocean,' said Lugh. 'From there I rode Enbarr over the sea to the Land of Promise, where I gathered battle-trained riders to aid us in our cause. These riders I name the Riders of the Sidhe.' He wheeled Enbarr, who whinnied and stamped her hooves as if eager to go to battle that very moment. 'We have gathered our strength. We have gathered our allies. It is time to let Balor know that his dominion over our people is ending.'

'Then for the first time in my life,' said the Dagda, 'I am glad to see a Fomorian.'

They all turned to follow his gaze.

Climbing up the path to the hilltop was a band of Fomorians.

They drew close. The envoy who had first approached Bres made his way forward, approaching Lugh as the company reluctantly parted for him.

'I am told that you lead the Tuatha Dé Danaan now,' said the Fomorian to Lugh, his voice like the dripping of gore from a battlefield wound.

'I do, though Nuada remains our king,' said Lugh.

'Then I bring word to you from Balor.'

The envoy's voice changed and all present heard Balor speak.

'Greetings, grandson.' The envoy's many eyes roved the chiefs as he spoke. The chiefs all had the sense that Balor watched them through those eyes, and they shuddered. 'I am proud to see you take your rightful place in dominion over these underlings.

'Know that though you are Tuatha in form, you are Fomorian at heart. I see my own strength in you. Perhaps an even greater strength. Serve me and I will teach you to wield it. I will show you the path to true power—'

The envoy got no further. Lugh drew his sword and sliced the creature's head from his shoulders. In the same movement, he leapt from Enbarr's back, spinning and whirling so that all the other Fomorians lost their heads, save for one. The remaining Fomorian, a yellow-scaled, one-eyed and hairless creature, watched his companions' heads roll across the grass, and quivered.

'We are messengers,' he rasped. 'You cannot—'

'I can and I will kill every Fomorian who crosses my path,' said Lugh, sheathing his sword. 'Save for my mother and save for you, whom I send back to Balor with this message.' He leaned in. 'If you want our cattle, our grain and our children, come and take them. And if you want to know who I truly am, find me on the battlefield.'

The Fomorian turned and ran.

The Tuatha Dé Danaan and the Riders of the Sidhe cheered as the Fomorian stumbled down the Hill of Uisnech. But Lugh did not laugh.

In some deep place in his mind, he remembered the realm to which the envoy returned. He felt the chill of the crashing sea which he had drifted upon as a baby. He could faintly hear the chanting of the Fomorian druids, the battle cries of Balor's armies.

Balor could be beaten. Lugh knew that in his heart. But it was far from a certainty. One thing was certain; Balor would take swift revenge for Lugh's actions on the Hill of Uisnech.[1]

14

THE BATTLE OF EAS DARA

The walls of Balor's hall shook as he pounded his fists against them, leaving great gouges in the stone. His captains watched in silence, keeping a safe distance.

'I will destroy him! I will tear him limb from limb, and pound his bones to dust! I will...'

Balor's captains feared him, but they thought little of his words. They all knew that the red-haired upstart leading the sidhe rebellion was Balor's own grandson. Their king had cast the boy into the sea when he should have killed him. It was Balor's own fault that things had come to this, but no one was going to say so.

'They will suffer for this. Each and every sidhe. I will take every last child from them, break open their skulls and eat their maggot-ridden brains while their parents watch. I will—'

There was a commotion as someone pushed to the front of

the assembled chiefs and captains. The generals snarled as they saw who it was.

'My king,' said Bres with a bow.

Balor fell still as he heard Bres' voice. He stalked over to where Bres stood, his eye-chains clinking as his chain-slaves followed behind him.

'The Tuatha Dé Danaan traitor,' said Balor, his voice dangerously low. 'I can begin taking my revenge on the sidhe by pulling out your traitor's teeth.'

'You could make better use of me than that,' said Bres, trying to keep his voice steady. Balor terrified him; he knew how precarious his position was. Every person there would slit his throat or crush his skull without blinking, should Balor order it.

Bres had been observing Balor since coming to his keep. The Fomorian king, for all his great size and strength, was cunning. He sensed when to use fear and when to use force. He maintained his power by playing his captains against one another. But for all that, he had a temper, and took pleasure in inflicting pain.

Bres feared Balor, but his desire for power overcame his fear.

'And how should I make use of you?'

'You ready your armies to move on the Tuatha, but the muster is not yet complete,' said Bres. 'The longer you leave Lugh's crime unanswered, the bolder the Tuatha will grow.'

'So?'

'So give me a force to command,' said Bres, drawing growls

from the generals. 'I will strike the sidhe and strike swiftly, showing Lugh the price of his actions.'

'And why should I send you, a snivelling turncoat who was deposed by his own people?'

'Because I know them,' said Bres, a cruel joy in his voice. 'Your captains are yet to fight the Tuatha. They know nothing of their tactics. Me, I have fought as one of them. I have devised strategies with Nuada; I have sparred with Oghma; I have called the charge to battle. Allow me to deliver your message and it shall not be forgotten.'

Balor narrowed his eyes as he regarded the golden-haired warrior. Although Bres was a turncoat, he had traits that Balor recognised and valued, traits he possessed himself. Cunning. Cruelty. And he did indeed know their enemy well.

'Fine,' said Balor. 'Take a force. Let it be known,' he said, raising his voice as his captains muttered, 'that a Fomorian who disobeys you, disobeys me. Strike at the sidhe. Strike hard. Show no mercy.'

Bres laughed. 'You need not worry about that.'

LUGH SAW it in the flames of his fire.

He saw the northwestern sea. He saw a wall of glittering mist atop it: a way between the worlds. He felt in his bones a breaking of that wall, and saw a fleet of ships pass through it. Their sails were made of skin; corpses hung from their masts. The deck of each ship was rammed with men and monsters wielding swords, axes, maces and spears. At the prow of the lead ship stood a grinning, golden-haired warrior.

Lugh saw the fleet reach the Isle of Destiny and make its landing. Though he had never seen that shore, Lugh's vision told him it was Ulster he saw. Fomorian warriors leapt from the decks and dashed up the sand towards a tiny fishing village. Burning arrows struck thatched roofs, villagers ran screaming, and so the slaughter began.

There seemed to be few trained fighters in the village. Those who resisted were instantly cut down, the blood-drenched Fomorians wild with savage pleasure, drunk on slaughter. One group of villagers rallied and fought back, but it was like blowing in the face of a thunderstorm.

The golden-haired warrior was in the centre of it all. He directed the slaughter and took part in it too, his smile never leaving his face.

LUGH TORE himself from the vision. He ran from his chambers and made for Nuada's hall.

Striding through the doors, Lugh found Nuada sitting alone, apparently deep in contemplation.

'The Fomorians have struck! They attack Ulster now!'

Nuada listened as Lugh recounted his vision.

'So it begins,' said Nuada, 'and so Bres' betrayal deepens. He is the golden-haired warrior you saw.'

'We must march on Ulster! We need to gather every fighting sidhe!'

Nuada drummed his silver fingers on his throne.

'No,' he said.

'No?'

'You said it was a small force that Bres leads. Balor has chosen to send them ahead of his main fleet. Why?'

'Because he did not like my message.'

'Perhaps. And why send Bres?'

Lugh's jaw tightened.

'Bres knows how we fight. He has led our armies into battle. He knows that rules govern our warfare, and intends to outrage us with these atrocities.'

'You think Balor is luring us into a trap.'

'I know he is.'

'Fine. Our enemy has a plan. But you did not see the things I saw.'

'Which is precisely why I am better placed to judge our response than you are.'

Nuada held his breath as Lugh steadied himself.

The young man was a prodigy. Nuada had known it the moment Lugh stepped into the hall on that sunlit day. He had acted accordingly, even going so far as to lend Lugh his throne. It was an act of enormous trust, and one he did not regret. But he had been wrong before.

Watching Lugh fight for self-control, Nuada asked himself, had he made a mistake?

No. Lugh had lit a desperately-needed fire in the Tuatha. It pained Nuada that he had been unable to light that fire himself. His body was whole again, but had Bres' betrayal broken some deep part of his spirit? Many nights Nuada had lain awake, wondering whether to give Lugh the throne for good. Maybe that would avert the doom he saw coming.

Yet Nuada never acted. For despite his immense talents, Lugh was young, inexperienced and, Nuada now saw, he could be rash. Was that rashness simply something the young man would outgrow? Or was it something else; a battle-thirst borne of his Fomorian blood?

Lugh had taught the Tuatha chiefs about leadership. Yet Nuada knew that leadership could only be learnt one way; by making impossible decisions and living with the consequences.

'What is your plan of action, my king?' said Lugh.

'Bodb Dearg controls Ulster. It is his duty to repel this invasion. Balor will learn that I answer blade with blade, yet without blunting my sharpest weapon in the process.'

Lugh's eyes widened. 'Bodb Dearg's forces will not be enough.'

'Have some faith in your fellow Tuatha.'

'Yes, my king.'

'And remain here. Do not go to Ulster.'

'But—'

'One does not play one's best piece in the opening of the game.'

'This is not a game.'

'I know. It is war, which I have lived through and you have not.'

Lugh glared brazenly at Nuada.

'Do not forget who is king here, Lugh of the Long Hand,' said Nuada, lowering his voice.

'How could I?' said Lugh with a bitter laugh.

He turned and left the hall.

Nuada sat for a short while then rose and left the feasting hall. Looking out over the Plain of Breg, he saw a cloud of dust rising from the northwest road. Lugh rode for Ulster, leading the Riders of the Sidhe.

BODB DEARG STOOD atop a hill overlooking the village of Eas Dara.

Smoke rose from dozens of burning roofs. The screams of the inhabitants mingled with the roars and war-howls of the invaders, whose ships sat docked in the nearby bay.

'We are too late,' said one of his captains.

Bodb Dearg tore his gaze from the burning village. He stood at the head of a company of three hundred fighters. Word had reached him that morning that a Fomorian force was travelling east along the Ulster coast, attacking every settlement in its path. His company were hardened warriors who would die to defend these fishing and farming Tuatha.

Yet the Fomorians outnumbered them three to one. And they were waiting for them.

Eas Dara was a walled town. The gates looked inland and were wide open, looking towards the ridge where Bodb Dearg and his forces stood.

Bres watched Bodb Dearg from those gates.

He had tried to entice Bodb Dearg to attack, shouting insults and beckoning to the open gates. Yet it was all too clear what would happen if Bodb Dearg assaulted Eas Dara. Bres' force would surround them in the open ground through the gates, caging them like cattle in a pen. Then the butchery would begin.

Bodb Dearg could not delay the charge any longer. He was honour-bound to defend the Tuatha within those walls.

Yet he held back.

'Let us bring the fight to them! Why do we delay?' called Neit, one of his captains. There were noises of assent. Every moment Bodb Dearg held back, he was shaming himself, besmirching his own honour and that of his troops, as well as allowing the slaughter to continue. His fighters could not be restrained much longer.

There was movement at the gates. A group of sidhe women were dragged out into open ground by Fomorian warriors.

The Fomorians kicked the captives to their knees. Bres drew a knife and began to work his way along the line, opening the throats of each captive.

Bodb Dearg's vision turned red. He drew in a breath to call the charge.

Before he could speak, the earth beneath him shook.

A trap. A different trap. The Fomorians had surrounded them...

Yet it was not the Fomorians who came up behind Bodb Dearg.

With the swiftness of an arrow slicing the air, a company of riders drew up on either side of Bodb Dearg's force. Their leader rode up to Bodb Dearg, and he saw that it was Lugh upon Enbarr, her armour shining and her coat slick with sweat. Enbarr paced back and forth, snorting, eager for battle.

'I am pleased to see you, young ildánach,' said Bodb Dearg. 'Let us destroy these Fomorians and the traitor who leads them.'

'Gladly,' said Lugh, 'but you have not called the charge yet, and I would know why.'

'Bres hopes to lure us through those gates, no doubt to pen us in.'

Lugh surveyed the sight outside the gate, where more Tuatha had been lined up for slaughter. He could not make out Bres' expression from that distance, but he sensed his enemy's fear of him.

'And he wishes it all the more, now that the Riders of the Sidhe have arrived,' said Lugh. 'He has not met us in battle before; he did not account for us in his plans.'

'So what do you suggest, Lord Lugh?'

'Bres wants to goad us into a charge then pen us in. But my mounted charge will cut through his forces like a scythe through wheat. Do not give him time to reconsider his strategy. Sound the charge.'

Bodb Dearg did not hesitate. He drew his horn and blew the charge. His force roared as they descended the hill, yet their roaring was drowned out by the thundering of Lugh's force. The Riders raced ahead of the Ulster force, coming together to make a single unit, six horses abreast. Atop Enbarr, Lugh watched as Bres ran for cover, his forgotten captives fleeing.

The Riders of the Sidhe surged through the gateway, through the square and straight into the thickly packed Fomorian force awaiting them. The Fomorians fell beneath the horses' hooves, trampled and broken-bodied. Lugh sounded his own horn, the signal to disperse and re-engage. The Riders broke formation, each navigating a course through the village as they turned and came in for a second strike.

The Riders' second strike hit just as Bodb Dearg's fighters poured into the village. It was the Fomorians who found themselves penned in, pressed on every side. Many turned and fled, yet the Riders of the Sidhe had spread out so that there were few opportunities for escape. So instead the Fomorians fought, and many riders and horses were brought down. The square was soon red with blood, the air filled with screams of pain and bestial battle cries.

Among it all, Lugh moved like quicksilver. He was a red dart, a blinding flash as he revealed what he had learnt at Manannán's hall. He was master of spear and master of sword. He fought with blinding speed and a dancer's grace, sometimes with his sword in one hand and his spear in the other. He would slay a foe before they raised their weapon, fire a few stones from his slingshot then strike with sword and spear again.

He leapt upon the head of one gigantic warrior, felled a dozen enemies with stones then buried his sword in his mount's skull. He used his spear to vault into the air, taking out another giant with a kick to the throat. A circle of death widened around him until he spotted Bres.

Bres spotted Lugh, all alone among the corpses. Although the once-king had fled before the cavalry charge, he was not fleeing now. He knew that if he defeated Lugh, the crown would be his again.

The two fighters moved towards one another. They found a

clear space among the bodies and blood-slicked stones. They circled one another, eyes locked.

Bres struck first. It was his style to make an explosive opening, quickly exposing and exploiting his opponent's weaknesses before they could find a rhythm. He hit Lugh with a flurry of blows. Lugh answered each strike with no great show of effort. He had his own strategy, and quickly it began to tell.

Lugh was a warrior in his prime. Ever since he could hold a spear, he had trained every spare hour. Bres had been a master of the spear once, but had spent years growing soft as he sat the throne. Lugh knew this.

Bres continued his onslaught. Lugh met his strikes but offered none of his own.

Bres tried to press his advantage. But then he realised that his spear arm was tiring, ever so slightly.

Lugh shot forward as quickly as light from the sun. He struck a dozen blows in the time that another fighter would have struck two. Bres parried each blow but his strength was fading, fading...

Lugh's spear butt slammed into his skull, then across his shins.

Bres fell to his knees, white-hot pain exploding through his body.

He looked up at Lugh, his vision swimming.

The battle was over. The Tuatha survivors were helping fallen comrades to their feet, or putting an end to wounded Fomorians. Crows had gathered in a black cloud overhead, some already descending to feast. The sun was setting, the clouds as red as the blood-soaked ground, the evening shadows long and dark.

Bres turned back to Lugh. He saw Lugh's mind working. This young fool did not know when to finish an enemy.

'Mercy,' said Bres. 'I beg—'

A hand seized his scalp. A dagger touched his throat.

BODB DEARG STOOD OVER BRES, his dagger at the once-king's throat. Bres bled from a dozen wounds. One of his eyes was swollen; his cheek was cut open; blood dripped from his beard. The wild look in Bodb Dearg's eyes was not one Lugh liked; it was one Manannán had warned him of.

There comes a time immediately after a battle when all the laws which bind men seem to fall away, his foster father had said. *The very best comes out in some men, and the very worst in the rest.*

'Stay your blade,' said Lugh, the warning in his voice clear.

'This turncoat made us slaves,' said Bodb Dearg. 'It was by his law that monsters took my daughter into slavery.'

'And it is soon that you shall win her back,' said Lugh. 'And let it be the father she remembers who brings her home; not a monster like those who enslaved her.'

'What of the evil he will do if we let him live? Will you have it on your conscience? I will not have it on—'

'I can help you,' said Bres.

Lugh shot Bodb Dearg another warning look. 'What did you say?'

'I can help you.'

'How?' asked Lugh.

'Set me loose and I will return to Balor. I will persuade him to commit all his forces to an attack.'

'You have a strange idea of the help we want, traitor,' said Bodb Dearg.

'It is not what you want, fool,' said Bres. 'It is what Lugh wants, for he is wiser than you.'

Bodb Dearg looked at Lugh.

'He is right,' said Lugh.

'Why—'

'I want Balor to commit his entire army,' said Lugh. 'Because it is only by utterly destroying the Fomorians that we will be rid of them once and for all. He thinks we cannot defeat such a force. You may well think the same. But I know it can be done.'

Bodb Dearg reluctantly let go of Bres. It was clear from Bres' smirk that he believed he had made a fool of Lugh.

'I will deliver your message to Balor,' said Bres, 'and I will see you both on the battlefield.'

They watched him leave, stumbling through the mud with all the dignity his shaking legs would allow him.

'I hope you are right about this, lad,' said Bodb Dearg as a soft rain began to fall.

'I have to be,' said Lugh.[1]

15

THE MUSTER OF LUGH'S ARMY

Bres surveyed the grim-faced Fomorian captains.

Before him stood Octriallach, Balor's general. He was the height of a mounted man and wore no armour; it grew from his flesh in bony ridges lined with lethal spikes. Sword and axe would glance off him.

By Octriallach stood Indech, who was half-man and half-wolf. Goll and Ingoll, father and son, could have passed for Tuatha. In the shadows, apart from the others, stood the druid Lobais and his daughter Liath. Both wore headdresses which obscured their faces. Unlike the others, they seemed to have no interest in seeing Bres punished by Balor. His own father, Elathan, avoided his gaze, but Bres thought he could read shame and anger in his father's eyes, for Bres had failed in his mission to hurt the Tuatha.

What he had learned, though, was far more valuable.

Bres turned to face Balor.

'I know it might seem that I failed you,' he said. 'But in truth—'

He got no further. Balor's fist knocked Bres from his feet, sending him crashing into a pillar. He slumped to its foot, his vision spinning.

'Let me punish him, my lord,' he dimly heard someone say. 'I will hang him from my mast, and my fighters will make good sport of him.'

'No. I would have that sport myself. But he may still be useful. We will bring him with us and keep him alive.'

'When, my lord?' said another voice. 'When do we attack?'

'The muster is complete, my lord,' said Octriallach. 'Your armies are ready.'

'Lobais,' said Balor. 'Are you ready?'

'We have only one ceremony left to complete, my lord,' said Liath, Lobais' daughter. The arch druid rarely spoke himself. 'Tomorrow my father will open the gate and move your army between the realms.'

'You have my gratitude, master druid. To move my entire army between worlds is no small thing.' Even Balor spoke carefully to Lobais.

'I must be clear, my lord,' said Liath, her voice like the dark water of an underground well. 'As great as my father's power is, this feat will tax him to the utmost. His power will be deeply diminished once the deed is done. Both he and I will be of little use in the fight to come. You must win this battle with brute strength, not spellcraft.'

'It matters not,' said Octriallach. 'Had we not a single druid, we could still defeat the Tuatha by sheer strength of numbers.'

'Then sound the horns,' said Balor. 'We sail for war.'

LUGH SAW IT ALL.

He saw torches lit upon ten thousand ships. He felt the pounding of Fomorian drums even in the sunlit glade where he sat. They beat a rhythm of bloodshed, conquest and the coming of endless night.

The fleet set sail. Fomorian fighters of every size and shape packed the decks. Others rode enormous beasts through the water, or flew on the backs of demonic steeds. The fleet stretched to the horizon in every direction, beneath a sky of fire.

Lugh pulled himself from the vision and ran for Tara.

IT WAS EARLY EVENING. The hall was packed with Tuatha, both common folk and captains; other druids beside Lugh had felt the movement of the fleet. All conversation ceased as Lugh approached the throne.

Lugh and Nuada eyed one another. They had not spoken since Lugh returned from Ulster.

'Balor's fleet has set sail,' said Lugh. 'Their numbers are beyond count. How may I serve you in repelling them, King Nuada?'

Nuada took in the forest of eyes that watched him. It was in such times that a man showed his true colours. There was fear in those eyes; the fear of a tyrant. The fear that here and now, in their darkest hour, he would refuse to relinquish his power, clinging to it like a babe to its blanket.

'You may serve us by leading us, Lugh of the Long Hand. My armies are yours to command.'

The Tuatha cheered as for a second time, Nuada stood and offered his throne to Lugh. They fell quiet as Lugh climbed the dais and turned to face them, his face stern.

'There could be no greater honour than to lead the sidhe into battle.' He paused, his face grim. 'I have seen Balor's fleet, and divined his intent. The entire fleet will enter our realm at once, close to Tory Island in Ulster. It is a short sail from there to our shores. You must take up arms and leave Tara this hour, marching through the night.'

'What will you do?' asked Oghma.

'I shall ride the length and breadth of our country, calling our people out to fight.'

'Where will you meet us?'

'Make camp west of the Shannon. I will find you there.' Lugh paused for a moment. When he resumed speaking, everyone present felt his words were intended for them alone. 'You will feel great fear in these coming days. You will wonder if the sidhe can truly defeat such an enemy. You will wonder if you will live to see battle's end, and the breaking of a day free from sorrow.

'Let no lie be spoken. You may well die on the battlefield, food for the Morrigan's crows. But whether or not you feed the crows, victory is at hand. It is at hand here in this hall, in this very moment.

'The Fomorians would have us cower. They would have us

hear the pounding of their drums and give in before we even draw our blades. So choose now that you will not fear Balor's monsters.

'Choose not to falter before those who enslaved your children. Choose to face the Fomorians with the heart of a bear, the battle-grace of a wolf pack, with the cunning of the cat and with a song on your lips. Choose, and seal that choosing in your heart. Thus shall you stand strong in even the darkest hour of battle.

'Children of Danu, do you choose?'

The hall shook as the Tuatha answered.

'Then go now. Gather your weapons and don your armour. Meet upon the Plain of Breg and I shall guide you for the first miles.'

Lugh drew his sword and held it aloft. 'To battle!'

The Tuatha poured from the hall.

THE SIDHE MARCHED through the night and into the following day. They reached the Shannon and forded it while their scouts searched for a place to make camp.

Not far beyond the ford was a wide plain overlooked by a hill. There they camped as dusk fell, erecting tents and gathering firewood. Scouts set out to see if the Fomorian fleet had landed.

Late in the night, the first scout returned. He made for Nuada's pavilion, where the chiefs held counsel.

'My king, my lords,' he said, still catching his breath. 'I have news of the Fomorians.'

'Then give it,' said Nuada.

'I rode west as far as Carrowkeel,' said the scout, 'and summited the hill. From there I could see all the way to the ocean.'

'You saw the fleet?' said Oghma.

The scout nodded slowly. 'I saw it, my lords.

'If I had not known what colour the sea was, I would be none the wiser for that sight. There are more ships in the western waters than there are stars in the sky above us. As grass coats the ground beneath my feet, so sit Balor's ships upon the sea.'

'Thank you. You may go,' said Nuada after a moment.

The scout bowed and left.

'Can we really defeat such a force?' asked Diancecht.

'Have faith in Lugh,' said Nuada.

'Lugh is not here,' said Diancecht.

'He will return soon,' said Nuada. 'In the meantime, we must ensure the Fomorians do not attack us before we are ready.'

All eyes turned to the Dagda. If anyone other than Lugh could delay Balor's entire army, it was him.

The Good God smiled. 'I will see to that,' he said, plucking the harp that hung from his shoulder.

THE FOMORIANS PASSED through the portal.

The sky over Tory Island shimmered, then shattered. A great wave shot towards the land; the sea became a tempest. Many of the ships that first poured through the portal were destroyed, but it mattered little.

The sea calmed. Ships continued to pour through. They turned west and followed the Ulster coast, just as the Tuatha fleet had done all those years go. They landed in Connacht at Magh Scetne.

Camp construction began. Balor's whale-skin tent was erected by a team of slaves. His captains gathered there to listen to scout reports.

'The Tuatha have made camp west of the Shannon,' said the chief scout, a hound-like creature with dark, silken fur. 'They are not yet at their full strength, but new companies of fighters arrive every hour. I got close enough to listen to their talk, and learned that Lugh is not with his army.'

Balor grinned. 'He is out gathering recruits then. Fool. It is only when led by Lugh that the Tuatha stand a chance.'

'We should break camp now,' said Indech, baring his wolf-teeth, 'and crush them before Lugh can return.'

'That would not be wise,' said Octriallach.

'Why not?' asked Balor.

'The Tuatha infantry is no match for ours, but we must consider their magic-workers too. Lobais tells me the Morrigan is a force to be feared.'

'Lobais will recover from his exertions and defeat her,' said Indech.

'Lobais has only now finished transporting our entire fleet through the veil,' replied Octriallach. 'Such a thing has never been done before. I have been to visit his tent; he is dangerously depleted. Liath suspects it will be many days before he is ready to fight at all, let alone at his full strength. She will take his place until then, and she is not ready to face the Morrigan just yet.'

'We could send out raiders to the nearby villages,' said Goll. 'Catch those who were too cowardly to take up arms, and bring them back for blood-sacrifice. That would replenish the druid better than sleep.'

Octriallach nodded. He turned to the scout. 'Send word…'

He was interrupted by the sound of a harp being plucked.

THE DAGDA GLIDED through the Fomorian camp.

For all his great size and strength, his footsteps were as soft and delicate as his music. His huge fingers roved the strings as a quiet song took flight from his lips, putting all the camp to sleep.

The Good God looked about him as he walked freely among slumbering Fomorians. He took in the slumped figures around fires, the many-tusked monsters that had fallen and crushed their handlers. He saw warriors with one leg, one arm and one eye; he walked through an area of camp where only wolf-people slept. Yet for every grotesque creature he saw, there was a Fomorian who could have passed for a sidhe. Were they so different? Was there something that bound the two races together? Did a spark of the sidhe hide in each Fomorian heart?

The Dagda played and sang as night became day. He would

sit and strum by an untended fire before continuing his roving. Not for a moment did he cease playing; should he do so, the spell might break. For it was more than music that the Dagda called forth from his harp. His song was a spell, a calling forth of the peace which reigned in his heart.

No other sidhe could have done such a thing. No other being had such deep wells of peace and joy to call upon. He played and sang for a night, a day and another night, while Lugh crossed the country, calling the Tuatha out to fight.

The might of the Dagda's magic was immense. But he was not the only magic-worker in that camp.

THE DRUID LOBAIS sat upright by his hearth.

His daughter Liath lay slumped on a rug, as did their slaves.

Beneath his bone head-dress, Lobais' eyes were half-open.

He had been resting when the Dagda arrived at their camp. The ritual had been more taxing than even he had expected, for the three sisters of the Morrigan had laid protective spells across the veil, adding to his burden. Though he had succeeded eventually, the sum of his power had been spent. Thus the Dagda caught him off guard.

Lobais had entrusted Liath with watching the camp while he rested, but the Dagda's spell had overpowered his daughter. She slept with a joyful grin on her face, as did thousands and thousands of Fomorians.

But not Lobais.

Deep within the Dagda's web, he struggled like a captured

fly. There was a part of him that did not sleep and could not sleep. That spark of awareness wriggled and writhed, desperately seeking some weakness in the weaving.

He found it.

Though peace reigned in the Good God's heart, even he feared to sit alone amidst a legion of enemies. Doubt troubled his mind like the faintest flickering star, telling him that the Fomorians were too many; that they would conquer the Isle of Destiny and leave nothing of the Tuatha but bodies.

They were only the smallest of doubts, fading as swiftly as shooting stars.

But that was all Lobais needed.

His spirit slipped free of the Dagda's web.

The Dagda felt a shadow pass over his song. His fingers trembled and he fumbled his notes.

Lobais drew from his deepest well of strength and tore the Dagda's spell to shreds.

All around the Dagda, Fomorians opened their eyes. They stumbled to their feet, shaking their heads to dispel strangely peaceful dreams.

They saw the Dagda. They hissed, snarled, drew their weapons, bared their teeth.

The Dagda ran.

He shot through the camp. Fortunately he was near its eastward edge, and many of the Fomorians were slow to wake. The Dagda dodged left and right, swinging his skull-crushing club at those he could not avoid. He spied a tree line ahead and sprinted for it; in the forest he could lose his pursuit. But the entire camp was awake now, screeching for blood. He was prey surrounded by predators.

Entering the forest, he gasped the words of a spell which would hide him from sight. His strength was spent; the spell lasted moments then broke.

But it was enough. His pursuers halted, searching the shadows, while he sped away east.

THE FOMORIANS HUNTED the Dagda for hours, though with little chance of catching him. He was friend to the forest, which happily covered his trail while tripping and entangling his pursuers. In time they gave up and returned to camp.

The exhausted harper stumbled through the grey morning. Dawn was close when he reached the banks of the River Unshin, north of Lough Arrow. The singing waters soothed his shredded nerves, as did the sight of she who bathed in the waters.

The Morrigan.

The Battle Crow washed herself in the river. Her long, dark hair covered her naked white skin like a cloak. Ever so softly did she sing as she cleansed herself before the coming bloodshed. There was such peace in her song that the willows and rushes leaned in to listen.

Such capacity does she have for slaughter, the Dagda thought. *It is easy to forget that her war form is but one guise she wears.*

The Morrigan ceased singing and turned to him.

'You have wrought powerful magic,' she said.

'The spell was broken,' he replied.

'Every web is made and unmade. You gave us the time we needed, and now Lugh has returned. Our full strength is gathered. The battle is nigh and shall be fought on another plain of the pillars, this one by Lough Arrow.'

'So there shall be a second battle of Moytura,' said the Dagda. 'My spell was shredded by a druid of the enemy. He is a force to be feared.'

'Lobais,' said the Morrigan. 'Fear is his food; serve him none. I shall meet Lobais at Moytura, and I shall drink the blood of his heart.'

'I am glad to hear that.'

The Morrigan stepped closer to the Dagda, river-water dripping from her pale skin.

'Let gladness fill you, my friend. Feel the certainty of victory.' She smiled. 'Come, harper. Join me in the water. I will soothe your heart and we shall share our strength.'

So the Dagda disrobed and joined the Morrigan in the river. He remembered his colossal strength; she drank deep of the music of his heart. Thus the mightiest sidhe prepared for battle as crows flew overhead, impatient for blood.

THE DAGDA and the Morrigan entered the Tuatha Dé Danaan camp. They made their way to the high hill where Lugh awaited them.

A brilliant sunrise fired the sky, illuminating the camp. Reaching the hilltop, the Dagda was stunned by what he saw.

The sidhe had multiplied since reaching the Green Isle. Firbolg fighters swelled their ranks, for Sreng had come leading a mighty legion. They had even more cause to hate Balor than his own people did.

Lines of tents stretched across the entire plain, their ranks studded with the light of fires. Lovers shared last embraces; messengers hurried back and forth; parents showed their children how best to swing a blade. All knew that soon the battle horns would blow.

The lords of the sidhe had come together outside Nuada's tent. Lugh himself was there, along with Diancecht, Nuada, Oghma, Airmed, Goibniu, Bodb Dearg and many lesser chiefs. The Dagda and the Morrigan joined them as a westward wind arrived, buffeting the chiefs who awaited Lugh's orders.

'Our full strength is gathered,' said Lugh, his red hair lit by fiery dawn light. 'Today we meet the Fomorians in battle.

'Our numbers are great, yet Balor's numbers are greater. If we are to win, it will be because of you. You must surpass every sidhe who ever lived; you must all do impossible things. So I ask you, mighty chiefs of the sidhe: what will you do to win us this war?'

Mathgen the Magician stepped forward. 'We shall fight for this land, and the land shall fight for us. I will call on the twelve great mountains of the land to rise out of the earth. They shall take to the sky, and I shall hurl them at our enemies.'

Elathu the cup-bearer came forward.

'Twelve great mountains shall fight for us, and so shall the twelve great rivers and twelve great lochs. I will ensure that our foes grow fiercely thirsty, and leave the battlefield in search of water. But our lochs and rivers shall disappear from their sight, and thus they shall wander, lost, maddening with thirst.'

'From water to fire,' said Fingol the high druid. 'I shall call the sun herself to our aid, and she shall send showers of flame down upon our enemies.'

'All good, all good,' said Lugh. 'But more is needed! More! What else shall be done to defeat this savage scourge?'

'Let poetry play its part,' said Corpre. 'At dawn each day I shall stand upon a hilltop overlooking the battlefield, with my back to a thorn tree, a rock in one hand and a thorn in the other, the north wind behind me.

'I shall speak a satire with the coming of the sun, and her rays shall carry it far over the field. My satire will shatter the spirits of Balor's warriors, their weapons falling from trembling hands.'

Luchta the carpenter came forward. 'Fresh shields and spear-shafts for every fighter, every day and every hour of battle; I will supply them.'

'Rivets, hilts, shield rims and everything made of brass,' said Credne the brass worker. 'Though we are gathered in our legions, no sidhe shall want for them.'

It was Goibniu the smith's turn.

'No matter if we fight for seven years, I will be at my forge each day and night, labouring to replace every broken sword and spear.'

'Diancecht,' said Lugh, 'what words have you for us?'

Diancecht ignored the dark looks thrown his way. Rumours abounded of how Miach had met his end.

'I will be at the Well of Slaine at battle's edge,' he said. 'I will make every wounded warrior whole again, unless their head is cut off or their bone cut through.'

Lugh turned to the Morrigan.

'Well you know what I will do,' she said. 'My sisters and I will fly as dark birds, singing terror-songs to extinguish our enemies' courage.'

'And you, my friend, who has already done so much for us?' said Lugh to the Dagda.

The Dagda spread his hands wide.

'I will do all of these things,' he said.

The other chiefs laughed. 'That is why you are the Good God,' they said.

Lugh smiled to see his chiefs laughing together. The Dagda was the Good God indeed.

All eyes turned to Lugh now. It was his turn to speak, though not to his chiefs.

The lords followed Lugh to the brow of the hill. The rising sun shone upon him as he surveyed his army.

The battle-ready sidhe seemed to him a sea of gold, their spears a silver forest. At the sight of Lugh they roared, drawing their weapons and thrusting them into the air. Warriors, farmers, children and oldlings howled from the depths of their hearts for Lugh.

'Lugh! Lugh! Lugh! Lugh!'

The sight, the sound, the shock of their love was overwhelming. Some small part of Lugh wanted to shrink away, yet he stood tall and true before his people.

'Children of Danu,' cried Lugh, his druid-power carrying

his voice far through the dawn. 'I am honoured by your salute. But it is not me you howl for.

'It is yourselves. It is one another. It is every sidhe who answered my call to arms. Every sidhe who said, "No matter that I am aged and brittle-boned. I will fight." Every sidhe who said, "No matter that I am a beardless boy, a bent-backed farmer, a girl who has not yet given blood. I will fight!"'

Lugh waited for the echo of his words to fade before continuing.

'Now hear me, every one of you, from the battle-hardened to the battle-green.

'When Balor's forces charge, you will not flee. You will not! You will stand and fight, not for me, but for one another!'

The sidhe roared their assent.

'For our stolen children, you will fight!

'For our stolen cattle, you will fight!'

'For the Tuatha we have lost!

'For the Tuatha yet to be born!

'For the Isle of Destiny, the beating heart of the world, which we make today our own!

'For Danu!'

The sound the sidhe made in that moment still echoes through eternity.

Lugh blew his horn, and the Tuatha army took the road to Moytura.[1]

16

THE SECOND BATTLE OF MOYTURA

The sidhe army reached the field and faced the Fomorians.

The plain was long and wide, encircled by high hills. Grey clouds had drifted in from the west to cloak the sky. Poets took up position atop pillars of stone, their eyes peeled for great deeds to be immortalised in song and story.

Sidhe scouts had identified a hill overlooking the plain to serve as command centre. Lugh rode there at the head of his captains. His mind was busy with battle plans, yet he could hear his captains murmuring to one another, their tone fearful. He heard his name mentioned.

Arriving at the hilltop, servants set to erecting Lugh's command tent. He rode back and forth across the hill's brow, watching as his forces lined up across the plain. The Riders of the Sidhe took the centre. They would scythe through the

Fomorian front ranks then wheel around to make for safety. If they charged straight forward, they would be swallowed up.

Foot soldiers made up the rest of the army. Their ranks stretched the width of the plain and stood dozens of lines deep. Behind the rearmost ranks was a woodland, where a steady stream of smoke rose from among the branches. Goibniu's forge had been lit.

Somewhere near the forge was the Well of Slaine. Diancecht, Airmed and the other healers would be at work there, their herbcraft empowering the waters to heal wounded Tuatha.

Lugh looked across the field to the enemy army.

Their ranks stood deeper than even Lugh's eagle-keen eyes could see. For now, the Fomorian war drums were silent. They sang no battle songs. Studying the front ranks, Lugh saw that his own force had formed up quicker; the Fomorians were not ready to fight.

He should press his advantage.

Yet Lugh held back.

His gaze searched the Fomorian army.

Somewhere among them was Balor.

LUGH HAD NEVER SEEN his grandfather's face. He didn't remember the day Balor threw him into the raging sea. Yet sometimes in his dreams he would hear a woman crying, and feel a sudden shock of cold. In other dreams he saw an enormous eye, chains bolted to its closed lid, burning with an intense heat. The eye would become aware of him and begin to open...

'My lord Lugh?'

Lugh awoke from his daydream. A messenger stood at his side, awaiting an answer.

'Hmm? No. We will not attack yet. We have the advantage now, yet our advantage shall be still greater at noon, when Corpre speaks his satire. My power also rises with the sun; at noon I shall lead us into battle best.'

'No, young one,' said a voice from behind him. 'You shall not.'

Lugh knew that voice. He turned and saw Manannán, Enbarr at his side.

'What—'

'Come.'

Manannán led Lugh away from the clifftop. His chiefs had gathered outside the command tent. They eyed him as if he were a caged animal that could break loose and attack them at any moment.

'What is this?' said Lugh.

'We have agreed,' said Nuada, 'that you should not lead our army into battle.'

'What madness—'

'Listen, Lugh, please,' said Nuada. 'Think of all you have done for us since you came to Tara. You took a wretched people and made us warriors once more. The sidhe worship you.'

'So?'

'As great a warrior as you are, Lugh,' continued Nuada,

'there is a chance you may fall on the field. If you fall, the Tuatha shall lose heart, and flee, and all shall be lost.'

Lugh looked among his captains for support. He saw none. 'You cannot be serious.'

'I am deadly serious, Lugh. I am still your king, and I order you to remain at our rear. If you fall, the sidhe fall. I cannot risk that.'

'Madness,' said Lugh, shaking his head. 'Madness. Why do you think the Tuatha love me? It is not because I lurk behind the lines like a coward! It is because I lead! How can I lead—'

'The Tuatha have two kings, Lugh, strange as it may be. Would you have them clash at the very hour of battle?'

Lugh wanted to disobey Nuada. Whatever discord may come of it, it could not be as grievous as what might happen if he failed to fight. Lugh knew his own strength, and he knew the effect he would have on his people. He would awaken skill and cunning, grace and beauty in their battle-dance. All that a soldier of the sidhe could be, they would be it if they saw him amongst them. Such was the power, the poetry, the brilliant light of his prowess. He was worth more than a thousand fighters, more than ten thousand fighters; his worth could not be measured.

Clearly this was a hard choice for Nuada and the chiefs. There was pain in their eyes, as well as fear. The pain of the betrayer.

Well, Lugh could make hard choices too.

It would be hard to strike down Nuada and take the kingship for himself. It would be the hardest thing he ever did, the most infamous. Yet if he did, none of the chiefs – except perhaps the Morrigan – would be strong enough to stop him.

Lugh didn't want to usurp Nuada. But it might be the only way to win.

For a moment, he was dreaming again. A woman was wailing, sobbing, pleading. Immense hands held him; hands that could have crushed him. Instead they held him gently.

A terrible heat singed his flesh as a great eye, lidded and chained, began to open.

Lugh's vision cleared. He looked out over the field again.

Balor.

Balor whose blood ran in Lugh's veins.

Only he could defeat Balor.

Only he had Balor's own strength.

Perhaps if he were to defeat Balor, he would have to become Balor. If only for a moment.

Lugh made his decision.

He faced his chiefs and his silver-handed king, whom he was about to usurp.

Before he could speak, Manannán caught his eye.

Oghma, Nuada, even the Dagda, they all radiated fear of him. The Morrigan, of course, was inscrutable. Yet even in this moment, Manannán looked at him with love.

Lugh dreamed again.

He did not dream of icy water, shrieks and sobs. He dreamed himself back at Manannán's hall beneath the sea.

HE WAS A SMALL, *beardless boy, standing with a blunt practice spear in his hand. Manannán faced him beneath a roof of crystal, in a keep that lay deep beneath bright, blue waters. The hall was shaped from luminous coral and lined with weapons. Manannán was advancing on him, spear in hand.*

'Why won't the other boys practise the spear dance with me?' said Lugh.

'Because you always beat them, and hurt them.'

'I don't mean to. I try to give them a chance. But they're all so slow.'

'And yet you still can't lose every once in a while, even if you try?'

'No. I can't. When the spear dance begins...' *Lugh lunged forward; Manannán parried his blow.* 'It's like I become someone else. Something else. I can't stop myself from winning, or from striking too hard.'

Manannán swept in, feinting a jab before bringing round the butt of his spear to strike Lugh's thighs. The boy Lugh leapt high over the strike, somersaulting and landing atop Manannán's shoulders. The tip of his spear hovered over Manannán's head.

'So you do have a little self-control.'

'It's different with you. I don't know why.'

'There is ferocity in you, but just as much gentleness. Your father was a kind, gentle man.'

'My grandfather is not.' *Manannán had never kept Lugh's origins a secret from him.*

'No,' said Manannán.

'The boys say that's why I hurt them. Because I'm a wicked Fomorian.'

'Wherever your violence originates, you always have a choice,

Lugh of the Long Hand. Practise exercising it. Choose when to be fierce...' Manannán *suddenly flew at Lugh with a flurry of blows. Lugh moved swifter than Manannán could see, finishing with his spear tip at Manannán's throat. '...and when to be gentle. In time, you will learn to slip between the two faster than a sparrow beats its wings. Later, you will learn to be both things at once. When that happens, my young Lord Lugh, you shall change the fate of the world.'*

THE VISION DISAPPEARED. Lugh was back atop the cold, windy hill, surrounded by friends who feared him.

He knew his own strength. He knew his power to awaken strength in others.

Let them show that strength now.

In his blood he felt the movement of the sun. Beyond the clouds, she approached her zenith.

'Lead our army, lords of the sidhe,' said Lugh. 'I shall remain here.'

WINDS from the north whirled around Corpre. He stood atop a high hill on the far side of the plain from Lugh's command tent, a thorn in one hand and a stone in the other. A lone hawthorn tree clawed the air at his back.

He watched as the chiefs made their way from the command centre to the field, taking their positions along the line. Manannán sat atop Enbarr at the head of the Riders of the Sidhe. Nuada, Oghma and Bodb Dearg led the left, centre and right of the infantry respectively. The Morrigan, Badb and Macha had donned their crow forms and taken flight, disappearing among the dense clouds.

The Children of Danu were ready for battle.

So were the Fomorians.

Though they were creatures of chaos, their lines were in good order. Ranks of riders sat astride monstrous mounts. Corpre spied entire companies of giants; he spied creatures that might have been men or wolves; he spied fat, bloated beasts that could have been formed from the discarded parts of other creatures.

And prowling back and forth before the ranks was a being whom Corpre had never seen before, but whom he recognised all the same. His druid senses could not help but taste the tang of dark power emanating from that being.

It did not matter. For the sun was shining through a chink in the clouds, and Corpre wielded a weapon like no other.

The bard began his satire.

Do you truly call that an army, Balor?
Do you call this rabble of weaklings warriors?
I call it a stinking chamber pot
A puddle of vomit on a fine rug.

Courage is wanting in these wimps, Balor.
Piss runs down their scaly shins.
Looking upon Lugh's glittering ranks,

They slice their own stomachs
Take axes to their ankles
And beg to be excused from the fight.

Look at these war-weary wastrels!
These faint-hearted fools,
These crying cravens!
Should we fight them
Or wipe their weeping eyes?
Babes you have brought to the battlefield, Balor.
We shall slaughter them all the same.

Balor prowled before the front ranks of his army. His chain-slaves scurried behind him; his one open eye roved across his troops. He wore his necklace of fifty skulls and carried his twelve-foot, twin-headed axe on his back. Balor's great height allowed him to see over the giant-studded Fomorian ranks, yet even he could not make out where the forest of bristling spears ended.

The ranks parted as Octriallach made his way towards Balor. The Fomorian war-master rode an enormous, armoured hound, black-furred and twice the size as a bull. 'Our ranks are ready, my king,' he said as he drew up beside Balor, his mount snarling and baring its sword-sharp teeth. 'We await the order to attack.'

Balor nodded absently, his gaze now upon the glittering Tuatha ranks.

'Lobais said Lugh will strike with the midday sun,' pressed Octriallach. 'We should not delay. Lead us to victory.'

Balor glanced down the line towards where Caitlín, his queen, stood at the head of her company. All night he had argued with her.

'I will not lead the attack,' growled Balor.

'But...'

Balor silenced his general with a look. 'I will not lead. Not today. You will lead the fighting this day, and on every day until I am ready to enter the fray.'

'Why?'

'No matter how large our host,' said Balor, 'this battle will not go our way easily. Lobais read the bones before we left. Victory is uncertain. If it comes, it will come after many days fighting, and only by a hair's breadth.'

'All the more reason for you to lead us, King Balor. A king must be at the front and centre of his army, giving heart to his troops when the fighting turns hard.'

'No, fool,' hissed Balor, leading Octriallach away from the ranks. 'It is all the more reason to hold myself back. Let the sidhe await my coming to the field. Let them guess why I hang back, and fear what will happen when I finally enter the fray. When I strike at last, it will be against weary and wounded warriors.' He narrowed his gaze. 'And it will be against Lugh.

'Only I among the Fomorians can fight him. Lobais has seen it. Caitlín has seen it, and I know it in my bones. No other can match his strength, not even you. So I shall hold myself back while Lugh tires himself. When we face one another, I will be at my full strength, and my grandson will not withstand me.'

Octriallach listened to the words Balor spoke and the ones he did not. Those unspoken words were just as loud to him.

Balor feared Lugh.

Perhaps that knowledge would be useful in time. For now, it was time to fight.

'I will lead our army,' said Octriallach. 'I will bring death to the Tuatha—'

Balor was suddenly knocked to the ground as if hit by a wave. Octrillach's mount threw him and ran, its tail between its legs. All the Fomorian army fell to their knees, weeping and wailing. The noon sun was breaking through the clouds, and a voice that could have carried over oceans resounded over the Plain of Moytura.

Do you truly call that an army, Balor?
Do you call this rabble of weaklings warriors?

Corpre's satire struck.

The Tuatha horns sounded the charge.

MANANNÁN LEANED in to Enbarr's back as the Riders of the Sidhe raced across the plain. The mighty clatter of hundreds of hooves drove all else from his mind. Nothing had ever existed but this moment, this charge. He was no longer Manannán alone; he was every horse and every rider.

They arced to the right of the plain, surging past eager-eyed poets on pillars. The Fomorians ahead of them were still on their backs, knocked flat by the impact of Corpre's satire. Yet some were coming to their senses.

'Left turn!' called Manannán. The Riders of the Sidhe slightly changed their course. They would hit the Fomorian line at an angle, smashing through the enemy before circling around and retreating before they could lose momentum and be overpowered. They would repeat the move again and again, carving up Balor's line, breaking it into smaller segments to be dismantled by the Tuatha fighting on foot.

Closer to the enemy line. Closer, closer. Enbarr neighed and tossed her head, shining with sweat, eager to break Fomorian bones beneath her hooves.

Closer. Closer. A few stouter Fomorians were on their feet now. Closer, closer; the Riders of the Sidhe were bellowing for blood; the Fomorians on their feet were wide-eyed, turning and fleeing, seeing there was no withstanding this wave.

The Riders struck the Fomorian line. They tore through the ranks, flattening their foes, crushing bones beneath their horses' hooves. Further beyond the front line they went, their mounts wild now with the scent of blood, swords swinging left and right. They cut a broad gouge through the ranks, always wheeling as they went so as to ensure escape.

Manannán laughed as he stabbed at those Fomorians who dared strike at him. Their ranks were recovered now, on their feet and furious at the shame of the satire. Many threw themselves at the Riders, or even threw their smaller comrades, trying to topple Rider from horse. Manannán saw Riders go down. It was time to be gone.

'Tighten the wheel!' he called. The Riders responded at once, sharpening their turn to quicken their escape.

There; the front was ahead. A horse screamed and toppled on its side, its legs hacked off from beneath it. Almost there...

A giant bounded up before him, treading on her allies in her eagerness to reach him. She made straight for Manannán, landing with a crash before him. Manannán wheeled away, ducking down low as an enormous hand reached out.

Yet the giant was not reaching for him.

Manannán cried out as Enbarr was batted from under him by the giant's open palm. He and Enbarr both tumbled head over heel to the ground.

Manannán rose to the sound of Enbarr's desperate whinnies, unsheathing his spear. His only thought was to protect her, yet the giant had no interest in Manannán's horse.

She roared at Manannán and raised her spear arm. Her weapon came crashing down. Manannán rolled aside as the giant's spear buried itself in the spot where he had lain a moment earlier. He leapt at the giant, making a quick cut to the thigh before rolling away, and so their spear dance began.

In terms of strength, he was hopelessly outmatched. Yet his foe lacked guile, and Manannán was able to stay alive by ducking and dodging. He was tiring; he could only hope his opponent was tiring faster. When he had a moment to glance around, he saw many other Riders had fallen and were now fighting on foot. His stranded company were utterly surrounded; one by one they fell.

It was clear now to Manannán that he had underestimated the Fomorians. His company were not predators here; they were prey.

More Fomorians came at him, striking at his undefended

back. He took a dozen cuts within minutes; it was only a matter of time before he fell.

'FASTER! FASTER!' howled Oghma as his foot soldiers raced for the Fomorian line. Manannán's Riders had disappeared from view; he had seen the band of giants moving in to surround them. They would not escape that sea of foes unaided.

The Tuatha drew close to the Fomorian line. The Fomorians had recovered from the cavalry charge, and now ran to meet them.

Oghma had encountered Fomorians before. He had given their stinking tax-collectors his cattle, crops and children. Yet nothing prepared him for the sight of their army.

Creatures like giant toads, with the heads of old women and twelve arms, each hand brandishing an axe. Cat-headed men who hissed and yowled as they charged, swinging massive claws. He saw thickly muscled warriors riding bears; he spied armoured bats massed overhead, ready to tear open Tuatha faces with their fangs.

The two lines clashed together. A dozen Tuatha, whom Oghma loved dearly, died within moments. So the time outside time that is battle began. Oghma's well-trained mind emptied like an upturned cup; he knew this place. He had accomplished himself in this place. It was a matter of cruel, cold certainty; of knowing that he was the predator and every enemy he faced was his prey.

When he faced a Fomorian, he never took his eyes from

them. He studied them, he learned them, he solved them, he killed them. His mind did not wander; he did not indulge in fantasy or fear. He existed only to fight, to wound, to bring about death. He was death.

Yet he was a commander too. At the very first lull in the fighting, he forced himself free of his battle-trance and called to his men, 'To me! We aid the Riders!'

Those who could heed his call did so, rushing together and reforming into a spear-tip shape. Their numbers swelled as more Tuatha pushed forward. Very soon Oghma led dozens of fighters, their momentum building until they were mowing down their enemies.

MANANNÁN LEAPT aside from the giant's thrust. His opponent was tired and far slower than when the fight started. But so was Manannán, and the giant had no need to leap and roll. She took deep breaths as she swung and jabbed at Manannán, forcing the Son of the Sea to exhaust himself, knowing that sooner or later Manannán would give her an opening.

Another spear jab. Manannán dodged aside; the blade glanced off his chest plate. The giant swung her spear shaft around in the same movement. Manannán had seen the move coming, but the inevitable moment had arrived; he lacked the strength to evade it. The shaft smashed into his chest, lifting him into the air.

Manannán landed on his back with a crash. The world

spun above him. The giant loomed overhead, laughing to herself, death-lust in her eyes.

Before she could claim her kill, Oghma leapt over Manannán's prone form. He sprinted forward and used all his sidhe strength to make the salmon-leap, launching himself high into the air. He made a downward thrust with his spear as he did so, burying his blade in the giant's eye.

She gave a terrible howl as black liquid poured from her eye. Oghma let go of his spear and dropped to the ground, rolling away and drawing his sword as she groped for him. Sighting Oghma with her remaining eye, she brought her fist around in a wide hook, a blow which would have shattered him, but in that moment the Dagda leapt into the fray.

He ran, leapt and brought his club down with a two-handed blow on the giant's wrist, crushing it. The giant screamed, clutching her deadened hand, then roared at the Dagda, her pain and bestial fury terrible to behold.

Oghma had recovered now. He and the Dagda fought the giant together. Their adversary was steadily weakening as dark liquid rained from her ruined eye. She lost all battle-sense. Unsheathing an enormous sword, she began swinging wildly and without aim. Oghma moved in behind her. With a two-handed swing, he cut the tendons of her left heel. Down she went at last, and the Dagda's club made a cave in her skull.

The two friends had a moment of respite. Manannán got to his feet and whistled for Enbarr, a call that his steed would answer even were she in another world. She had been busy fighting too, smashing Fomorian skulls to splinters with her hooves, her finely wrought armour keeping her safe from spear thrusts. Now she turned and galloped towards Manannán; but so did another.

ATOP HIS GREAT HOUND, Octriallach sighted the island of Tuatha fighters adrift among a sea of enemies. He watched Manannán fall; he watched as Oghma and the Dagda defeated the giant. Octriallach had listened to Bres' descriptions; he knew who these three were. The Tuatha captains were dangerously depleted. Vulnerable.

It was time to move in. Slay these men and the battle would be won today. Won by Octriallach, not Balor.

He dug in his heels; his hound howled. His six finest riders raced through the ranks and soon were upon the beleaguered chiefs. Octriallach laughed as he witnessed sparks of fear awaken in their eyes.

OGHMA, Manannán and the Dagda backed away from the six enormous hounds prowling towards them.

They were the lords of the sidhe, the finest fighters of their race. They had reddened their spears on many a battlefield, and always lived to tell the tale. Yet they knew their luck had run out. Death had come for them.

The hounds smelt their fear. They lowered their heads, teeth bared, growling. Their riders let out low, mocking laughs as they tensed to leap.

But they did not leap. Instead they looked up, whined, and turned tail.

Octriallach looked up too, as a shadow fell over him.

ON A ROCKY HILL at the battle's edge, Mathgen wrought his magic.

His power burrowed into the hill. It reached out across the island, through soil and stone. It was a call for aid; a call to the mountains of the Isle of Destiny. Mathgen reached out to the chiefs of the mountains, the highest hills, the ancient fathers of the land.

It was a voice those beings of stone knew well. Ever since arriving on the Isle of Destiny, Mathgen the mountain-mage had wandered their slopes, made offerings of fine food in their caves, sang songs of devotion for days on end upon their storm-scoured peaks. He had given his body, his breath and his being to them.

When his moment of need came, they answered.

All the Isle of Destiny shook as the twelve chief mountains wrested their roots from the earth. They rose up into the sky and shot through the air, from Ulster and Connacht and Leinster and Munster, all in the direction of Moytura.

It was their shadows which caused Octriallach's hounds to shrink and cower.

Down came the mountains, perfectly aimed by Mathgen. Octriallach leapt from his steed's back just in time. A mountain crashed to the ground, breaking into a thousand vast rocks as it flattened legions of Fomorians. Oghma, Manannán and the Dagda avoided being flattened by a hair's breadth.

They picked themselves up and fled as the surviving Fomorians surged forward. Enbarr appeared, flanked by two other horses. The three chiefs leapt upon their backs and rode to safety.

WATCHING the Second Battle of Moytura unfold was the hardest thing Lugh ever did.

The fighting was relentless from dawn to dusk. Horns called out the retreat at regular intervals, summoning companies of Tuatha to rest while fresh units took their place.

Lugh left his hill. He descended to the plain and walked among those who limped and stumbled back from the battle, horror writ on their faces.

At least there was a way here for him to contribute. He slapped shoulders, listened attentively to battle tales, commended acts of bravery. But such words seemed small things to those warriors, even coming from their Lord Lugh. A woman with a shattered knee, a man who had lost his arm, they smiled at him while clearly wishing to continue on to the Well of Slaine.

Night came. The fighting did not abate. Lugh returned to his command centre. He watched from above as horns summoned weary warriors back to the front. Children cried as mothers and fathers lifted them to their feet, pressing weapons into their hands.

If only he were heading out there with them. To do what he did best; to dance the spear dance, dealing death so fast that no eye could follow him. But instead he hung about here.

He had to trust in his chiefs. Trust their wisdom.

The dark of night had fallen. The Fomorians came from a realm of darkness, and were stronger in the night hours; he could sense it in his own Fomorian aspect. The part of him that he kept buried deep within him. He could sense it growing stronger as the noise and battle smells filled the air.

The Tuatha had struggled all day to match their enemies. Now the Fomorians would fight even more fiercely. Would the Tuatha be defeated this night?

Yes, said his Fomorian aspect, rearing up like a serpent's head. *In the hours of darkness, the sidhe shall fall.*

As ever, Lugh turned his mind away from that voice, those thoughts. Manannán had taught him this long ago. Instead, he reached out to his chiefs.

Show me your strength, he said. *Show me that we can defeat this darkness.*

Lugh sensed the presence in his mind of Fingol, who was a leader among druids. He stood on a nearby hilltop, his allies all around him as they chanted a spell in unison. Lugh felt it reach its peak.

Do not fear, said Fingol. *Watch what we do.*

A streak of fire illuminated the sky. It struck the earth as fast as lightning, incinerating a whole company of Fomorians. A moment later another fell, then another, as Fingol fulfilled his promise to Lugh.

THE FIRST NIGHT PASSED. The Fomorians were stronger in the darkness, yet Fingol's fires decimated their ranks. The fighting never relented; it carried on through the second day and into the second night. Combat took place upon a carpet of corpses, for many thousands of both races had fallen. Yet there were far more Fomorian dead on the field than Tuatha. No mountains fought on the side of the invaders. There was only one among them who could craft spells on that scale, and Lobais was incapacitated.

Lugh's army was winning.

The second day passed, and the second night.

It was on the third day of battle that Liath, daughter of Lobais, entered the fray.

Her father had called her into his tent the previous night. She had not fought so far, instead tending to Lobais while attempting to recover her own strength.

'I shall not recover in time to win this battle for us,' he said to her. 'No druid is fit for the task other than you, daughter. I shall give what power I have to you.'

So Liath had knelt before her father. What magic was left in him, he gave to her. She was already a powerful druid, and this made her mighty.

Liath waited until the sun was sinking in the sky. At the liminal time when Lugh's power was fading, and with the power of the Fomorians rising, she worked her first spell of the battle.

As one, the Fomorians fighting in the front rank grew taller. Their hair and fur stood on end; fresh muscles formed beneath their skin as their eyes burned red. The ranks roared as ferocious, bestial strength exploded into their bodies.

The Tuatha they faced backed away in fear. The Fomorians pounced on them. Sidhe soldiers were torn limb from limb. Heads were pulled from shoulders, arms wrenched from sockets as the Fomorians grew ever more frenzied under Liath's spell. She stood upon a high pillar at the edge of battle, hands raised to the sky, her chant echoing out for miles.

The Tuatha front line collapsed. The fight became a rout, and as Tuatha in the rear lines saw their brothers and sisters flee, they turned and fled themselves.

Liath screamed with joy, finally feeling her father's power within her.

From the rear of the Fomorian forces, Balor looked upon Liath and laughed.

At the field's far end, Lugh watched in horror.

The battle was moments from being lost.

In that moment, the three sisters of the Morrigan came forth from the clouds.

They swooped down in their war forms, shooting towards the front line of battle. They shrieked their terror-song and even the hardiest Fomorians could not bear it. Giants fell down wailing and clutching their skulls.

The sisters circled the field, screeching ceaselessly, snatching up Fomorians and throwing them against the cliffs.

Liath had been expecting this.

She released her counter-spell.

Streaks of lightning shot down from the sky, too fast to avoid. Badb was struck. She tumbled from the sky, her burning black feathers carried away on the wind. She reverted to her sidhe form as she lay stunned on the ground.

Badb fell among the enemy, close to the front lines. Bodb Dearg saw it. He ran through the cowering Fomorians, who were still recovering from the crow-song. He put her over his shoulder and carried her away.

Macha and the Morrigan flapped their wings furiously as they fled the field. Both narrowly escaped Liath's lightning. Thus they were driven away, and could not harry the Fomorians with their screeching. Yet keeping them at bay occupied Liath, who could no longer lend strength to her army.

So the Tuatha Dé Danaan recovered, and the Second Battle of Moytura raged on.

BALOR SUMMONED Bres to his tent that evening.

'King Balor,' said Bres, hoping he looked suitably blood-soaked and battle-weary as Balor's massive eye turned towards him. Balor's crooked-toothed wife, Caitlín, sat by one of the fires that lined the enormous whale-skin tent. She seemed deep in thought. Other than Caitlín, and Balor's ever-present chain-slaves, they were alone.

'The sidhe should be defeated by now,' said Balor. 'Liath says that through some magic they fight even after they have fallen. She has not found the source of this spell. Prove that my faith in you is well-founded. Help me where my druid cannot.'

'I will help you in this, my king,' said Bres. 'Fallen Tuatha return to the field due to the powers of Diancecht.'

'Who is Diancecht?'

'The supreme healer of the sidhe. He and his underlings begin by locating a well. They awaken its healing powers, then enhance those powers through herb-spells. They did this at the First Battle of Moytura.'

'So we need only destroy the well.'

'That is not all, my king,' said Bres. 'The swords of the sidhe should be blunted by now, their spear shafts broken, their quivers empty. Yet they are not.'

Balor's grin twisted into a snarl. 'I know who is responsible for this. Goibniu the smith, who murdered my messengers when they came to collect the Cow of Plenty.'

'Goibniu is far beyond all other metalworkers,' said Bres. 'He supplies sharp-edged weapons to their entire army.'

'Then the path to victory is clear,' said Balor. 'We must kill Diancecht, destroy his well and deliver death to the smith.' Balor leaned down close to Bres, his eye-chains clinking. 'After that, I shall restrain myself no more. I will take to the field and slaughter sidhe by the legion.' He stood up straight. 'I am entrusting you with seeing these tasks completed. Tell me how many warriors you need, and you shall have my finest.'

'I will need only a small force to deal with Diancecht,' said Bres. 'Best to sneak around the Tuatha lines unnoticed.'

'Very well,' said Balor. 'And what of the smith?'

Bres hesitated. 'In truth, my king, Goibniu is among the very greatest of the Tuatha. If he sees our blow coming, it likely will not land. We should take him down with a knife to the back, not a sword to the front.'

'Then I know whom to send.' He called for a messenger. 'Bring me Ruadan,' he ordered. The messenger bowed and departed.

Balor turned back to Bres. 'Many times have my chiefs wanted you dead, yet I kept you alive. Serve me well and great rewards await you. The time shall soon come where the people who betrayed you will wear the chains of slaves.'

'Thank you, King Balor.' Balor turned away, dismissing Bres, but Bres did not leave. 'There is still another thing that might turn the battle.'

'What?'

'Lugh has not been seen on the field yet.' From the corner of his eye, Bres noticed Caitlín's eyes fix on him. 'It seems he is holding himself back just as you are.'

'You would have me send an assassin against Lugh?'

Bres shook his head. 'Lugh will be too well-guarded for that. But there is another leader whom the Tuatha love dearly, who fights on the field and whose death would drain the valour from their hearts.'

'Nuada,' said Balor.

'Yes. Nuada, the silver-handed simpleton. Send scouts out to find him on the battlefield. Have them follow him, so we know where he is at all times. Once Goibniu and Diancecht are dealt with, hunt down Nuada. Tear him to pieces and the sidhe shall scatter.'

'The smith, the healer, the king,' said Balor. 'Three blows in succession. You have a cunning mind. Perhaps the Tuatha Dé Danaan should have kept you as their king.'

'It matters not. They will have time to learn the error of their ways, in the world that is to come.'[1]

17

THREE BLOWS

Gamal yawned and scratched his chin.

He had been on duty outside Goibniu's forge since late evening. It was now early morning. At first, guard duty had come as a welcome respite from fighting. The screaming. The smells. The bolts of sky-fire blasting the earth. Mountains falling from above...

Soon he would go back out there.

Guard duty had turned out to be just as bad. His job was to stand by the door of Goibniu's forge, nodding through the little children who brought weapons for the smith to repair, or collect those with which he was finished. All the time, Gamal listened to the distant din of battle. He felt the earth beneath his feet tremble. He wondered which of his friends and kinsfolk still lived.

It felt wrong not to be out there. Surely Goibniu could protect himself? Yet Lugh had insisted that the forge be guarded. And if that was what Lugh wanted, that was what Gamal would do.

Strange that though the battle raged nearby, these woods felt peaceful. The fate of two races was being decided less than a mile away. Yet the grass just went on growing. The trees went on being trees.

Gamal heard a rustling in the treetops above. He glanced up. Nothing. A squirrel setting off to gather nuts.

He yawned again. He would have fallen asleep hours ago, were it not for the constant ringing of the smith's hammer.

That rustling again. Closer this time, louder.

That wasn't a squirrel.

Gamal took a few steps forward and peered into the branches overhanging the forge.

Something hit the ground behind him.

Something sharp pierced his back.

Everything went dark.

RUADAN DIDN'T BOTHER HIDING the guard's corpse. He would be gone before it was found. Besides, no one would care about one dead guard when his day's work was done.

He lifted the door-flap and slipped into the forge.

The heat was mind-melting. Swords, spears, maces and arrows lined the walls of the outer forge. Beyond, in the inner forge, Goibniu worked. Ruadan lifted the second door-flap and entered the inner forge.

Goibniu sat with his back to Ruadan, pounding on a sword

blade with his hammer. He was shirtless, the muscles on his sweat-slicked back bulging beneath his skin, his long hair loose and matted.

It was too easy.

Ruadan took a moment to watch the smith work. Such strength. Such skill. Such concentration. This man was a master artist, like Ruadan himself. A prize worthy of Ruadan's skill. His back awaited Ruadan's blade.

Yet Ruadan hesitated. Need it be over so soon? He would like to exchange words with this man. But he was an assassin, not a cat. He did not toy with his prey.

'Wait outside, boy,' said Goibniu. 'This one will be ready soon.'

Ruadan raised his blade. Hesitated. Lowered it. Why not have some fun? Why not let the smith live a few moments longer? An artist must take risks, after all.

'Are you doing magic?' asked the assassin, imitating a small boy's voice. It wasn't difficult; he owned four sidhe slaves. 'The other boys say you are not a smith but a druid.'

'The other boys are right and wrong,' answered Goibniu as he swung his hammer again, the sound making Ruadan's head ring. 'A man called Miach taught me that magic is not the sole preserve of druids. It can be applied to any craft, so long as a sidhe works with mind as well as body.'

'Can an assassin practise magic?'

Goibniu's hammer froze in mid-air.

'There is deep magic in death,' said Goibniu, 'but it is better meted out in battle's blaze than in dark rooms. The blade should break the skin of the chest, not the back.'

Ruadan lunged forward as Goibniu spun, bringing his hammer round in an arc. It smashed into the assassin's chest, making bone-dust of his ribs, even as Ruadan's knife pierced Goibniu's breast.

Goibniu dropped his hammer.

He looked down at the knife in his chest.

All went dark.

Goibniu awoke on the floor of his forge.

Blood flowed steadily from the wound in his chest. There was darkness at the edges of his vision; darkness that fought to devour everything it touched.

He tried to move, and screamed in pain. The darkness was poison. His assassin had struck with a poisoned blade.

He had little time.

Goibniu got to his feet, fighting the pain and creeping blackness. He stumbled from his forge. Which way to go? There. Through the trees he felt a pulse, a shimmering, a calling.

If only he could reach its source before the darkness took him.

Airmed opened her eyes.

She sat among a circle of healers. They surrounded the

Well of Slaine, but for the gap where the wounded entered the waters.

The healers' lips moved in unison as they sang forth the power of the waters. Each of them was devoted to some primal power, be it oak or rowan, wolf or bear, mountain or fire. Whatever the source of their strength, they poured its power into the well, which glistened like silver in the early-morning gloom.

There were over two dozen wounded Tuatha in the water, each assisted by two healers. Many of the injured warriors had to be held up by assistants, else they would have drowned. One was close to recovering, her broken arm almost healed. Airmed could sense the well-water filling the woman with strength. Soon she would climb out unaided, ready to take to the battlefield again, while another fallen fighter took her place.

There was no shortage of those. Nearby, a host of wounded and maimed Tuatha clung on to life as they waited to enter the well. Their groans and screams could be heard all too clearly.

Enough. *Focus,* Airmed told herself. Yet it was so long since she had slept... her eyes wandered the circle of healers again. Her father Diancecht sat at their centre, opposite the entrance to the well, leading the chanting. No doubt he sensed her lack of attention. Now that she looked for it, she sensed the current of his annoyance within the many strands of their song. He had to work even harder to compensate for her wandering mind.

Only that pompous fool could pass judgment on her after murdering his own son.

Airmed shook herself, seeing the water of the well turn cloudy. *Command yourself.* This was no time to think of Miach, nor to fan the flames of hatred. She had parted ways with her father after the murder; after this she intended never to see him again.

'Make way! Make room in the well!'

AIRMED TURNED to see four assistant healers crashing down the path, carrying Goibniu on a stretcher. His skin was deathly pale; blood dripped from a wound in his chest.

They helped him to the water's edge, set down the stretcher and strained to help him in. He tumbled into the water and disappeared beneath the surface.

The assistants jumped in after him, fighting to get his head above the water. Every other wounded Tuatha was forgotten. Without Goibniu, all was lost.

Airmed shook herself. This was no time to spectate. She forced her eyes closed, forced down her panic and sang again, throwing everything she had into the song. The other healers in the circle resumed singing, following Airmed's lead, and the song surged.

Goibniu was not merely wounded. Wrapping her senses around him, Airmed saw that some dark entity had entered the water with him. It fought back ferociously against their efforts.

Poison.

Do not give it ground, Airmed said to the others in her mind. *Fight!*

Airmed threw herself against the poison. She summoned strength from the earth beneath her, from the sun and moon and stars above her. She called on every tree she had ever prayed beneath, every hill in whose shadow she had dreamed. She opened herself to the soul of every plant which had grown upon her brother's grave.

Power surged in her. Within it, she sensed another spell-worker.

Miach.

Somewhere he was watching her, aiding her. His presence gave her a new burst of strength. Filled with that strength, she struck again at the poison.

The darkness receded. She opened her eyes a fraction; the well was glowing like a silver fire.

Goibniu was climbing out of the well.

He picked up his hammer and raised it, as if ready to fight. Yet there was no fighting to be done there.

Airmed opened her eyes wide.

'They are coming! Stand, arm yourself! They are coming now!' roared Goibniu.

Dark figures burst from the undergrowth.

AIRMED COULD NOT MOVE. She had been so deep in her spell and pulled from it so sharply that she could not make sense of what she saw. Monstrous warriors dashed towards the well. Was this a vision, some manifestation of the poison?

No. For at the head of the warriors was one she recognised; the sight of him snapped her awake. Bres the Betrayer.

The Fomorians were upon them. They swung at the healers, many of whom were beheaded where they sat. A hound-headed man dashed at Airmed, bringing his axe down in an overhead strike that would cleave her in two.

Airmed tumbled into the well, the hound-head's axe thudding into the earth. Sinking beneath the surface, she spoke a spell of concealment. Rising up, she saw her pursuer searching for her from the bank. He gave up and chose another target.

It was a massacre. Dead sidhe were being tossed into the well. Where was her father? She couldn't see him; either he fought out of sight or had fled. The weaponless healers were leaderless. This would be over in moments.

But for Goibniu. He tore through the Fomorians, swinging his hammer, roaring at the healers to fight back. Those who had survived the first rush were on their feet, evading their attackers; a few had found a weapon and were doing their best to retaliate. They would have broken and fled had the sight of Goibniu not given them courage.

But it wasn't enough. They needed more help.

Help arrived.

Nearby was a glade where wounded Tuatha awaited their turn in the well. Now those Tuatha came to fight. They came limping, bleeding, in some cases even crawling to aid those who would have aided them.

Goibniu was in sore need of them.

The master smith was a ferocious fighter, but he was only one man. Bres was no slouch with a spear, and he had encircled Goibniu along with a dozen dog-heads. They worked as a team, drawing his attention one way then thrusting at his unguarded back. Goibniu kept his hammer in constant motion, slaying foe after foe as he spun, but Bres' strategy was working. The smith bled from a dozen fresh wounds.

The wounded warriors joined the fight. They encircled the Fomorians who had surrounded Goibniu, giving him respite.

Airmed shook herself. Enough spectating.

She heaved herself out of the water and ran towards them, bending down to snatch a sword from a fallen Fomorian's hand. She brought it up to meet a dog-head's blade and so joined the fight.

Diancecht had insisted that she and Miach learn the sword dance. They had danced its steps at many a winter camp. Lacking her brother's strength, she had learnt to lean into her speed, her watchful eyes, her composure under pressure. Now she put her skills to use, slaying one, two, three Fomor before drawing back and surveying the battle.

The Tuatha were being slaughtered. These were untrained healers, or wounded warriors who had staggered from the battlefield; they were no fighting force.

But she was Diancecht's daughter, and he was gone. His territory was hers; it was her duty to keep her people alive.

She saw only one way to do that.

'Retreat! Abandon the well!'

Speaking those words tore her heart in two.

Another hound-head came at her. She blocked his thrust, backing away as pain shot up her arms, still calling the retreat. Those who could obey her did so.

Airmed dodged her opponent's next thrust and lunged forward, skewering him like a pig. She put her foot to his chest, pulled her sword free, turned and ran.

She was among the trees when she realised the Fomorians were not pursuing them.

Airmed turned and saw why.

Back at the Well of Slaine, the enemy had sheathed their weapons. They were hurling bodies and stones into the well.

Airmed ran, tears streaming from her eyes.

TWO MESSENGERS REACHED Lugh at the same time.

'Goibniu is missing from his forge, Lord Lugh,' said one. 'His guards are dead and blood stains the forge floor.'

'The Well of Slaine was attacked,' said the other. 'Many healers were slain. The well is now filled with stones.'

Lugh stared at them, barely able to take it in.

No more healing for their fallen warriors.

No more fresh steel for their blunted blades.

Lugh turned away from them.

He walked the few steps to his vantage point overlooking the battleground. Wind whipped his hair; smoke clawed at his eyes. For days and nights on end he had stood here, anxiously watching the battle unfold. It was difficult to even do that. Whether lit by the sun or the druid-fires that shattered the night, the field was a murky haze. Legions of crows swarmed though the sky; smoke rose from countless fires.

The Fomorians' numbers were beyond comprehension. They rode to battle upon creatures of nightmare. Yet Lugh had always believed the sidhe would triumph.

Until now.[1]

18

THE EYE OF BALOR

'I t is done, King Balor,' said Bres. 'The Well of Slaine is destroyed. The healers turned and ran; those who fought died.'

'And the smith?' Balor asked, his eyes eager.

'He must have survived Ruadan's attack, for he was at the well when we struck. For a while he fought us, but eventually he fled like the others.'

'It matters not,' said Balor. 'The sidhe have lost the Well of Slaine, and soon they will lose their king. It is time to end this battle and end this war.'

He looked to his chief scout who waited nearby.

'We have eyes on Nuada, King Balor.'

'Then finally it is time for me to fight. Take me to him.'

A TEAM of Balor's scouts ran ahead of him as he bounded down the hill towards the battle. Through the rear of his army he went, his warriors leaping out of the way as he passed, his chain-slaves running in unison behind him; they had trained for this purpose. Any Fomorian who was too slow to get out of Balor's way was trampled beneath his feet.

The noise of the battle grew louder with every stride. The press of the fighters grew closer, the ground ever slicker, becoming a soup of mud, blood, corpses and severed limbs as he reached the front line.

Balor drew his axe and swung it, howling his delight as it cut through three Tuatha. He brought it round in another swing, beheading another warrior, and so his bloody work began. The Tuatha fell back before him while the Fomorians took heart from his presence, pressing forward and cutting a wedge into the Tuatha line.

All the while, Balor kept track of his scouts, whose job was to stay alive while guiding him to his target.

NUADA GLANCED up at the sky as he caught his breath.

He had retreated from the front for a short while. Death awaited the warrior who succumbed to exhaustion beneath an enemy's blade. His fighters were under orders to take frequent rest breaks, and he had to lead by example.

He wasn't far behind the front, but it felt a world away. Children who looked barely old enough to walk scurried past him, laden with waterskins or bindings for wounds. He watched a man come stumbling from the front, holding in his own guts. The man fell to the ground at Nuada's feet, never to rise again.

The Second Battle of Moytura was a nightmare beyond imagining. Yet he could feel the heat of the sun streaming from somewhere beyond the clouds. Even such ugliness as this battle could not touch its light. Even if the Tuatha were defeated this day, slain and their names forgotten forever, still the sun would rise each morning. He took heart in that.

A new sound pierced the din of battle.

Someone was calling his name.

The ground was shaking beneath his feet.

Nuada turned and saw an enormous creature ploughing its way towards him.

Blue-black scales showed between plates of iron armour. The beast was three times as tall as a sidhe; only one of its eyes was open. Chains hung from the other eye, disappearing over the crown of the monster's head.

'Balor,' whispered Nuada.

In moments Balor crossed the distance between them. A wide circle opened up as Tuatha fled the oncoming duel. Nuada saw that the chains attached to Balor's eye were held by a team of slaves. Those slaves stared at him with dead eyes; Balor eyed him as a hound eyes a hare.

So this is how I die, said Nuada to himself. *By the burning gaze of Balor, or cloven by his axe. At least I shall fall to a king, even if that king is a monster.*

Yet Balor's death-eye remained closed.

'Nuada,' said Balor, his grin exposing rows of sharp teeth. 'The Once-King. Nuada Second-Best; Nuada Broken-Body. It was kind of Lugh to let you fight, as decrepit as you are. I suppose it saved him the bother of slaying you himself.'

'Spare me the stench of your breath, Balor,' said Nuada, drawing his sword.

Balor laughed. 'Gladly.'

With inhuman speed he raised his axe and brought it down on Nuada's helm, cleaving the sidhe king in two.

There was silence for a moment. Then Balor raised his bloody axe to the sky and roared his victory.

At that sight, the Tuatha lost heart.

'King Nuada is dead!' they cried.

The cry spread across the battlefield. The hearts of the Tuatha shattered.

The Fomorians poured forward, sensing battle's end. Their eyes gleamed, they foamed at their mouths; new strength filled their deadened limbs.

The Tuatha line broke. They turned and ran, falling with spears in their backs.

WATCHING FROM ABOVE, Lugh saw the line break.

Moments before that, he felt a breaking in his heart, and knew that Nuada was dead.

Lugh searched the faces of the Tuatha who stood at his side, their faces ashen as they watched their world end.

'You think the battle is over,' he said.

They looked at him without hope.

'You are right.'

Lugh leapt from the cliff.

LIKE A CAT he landed upon the plain. Without pausing he dashed forward, running towards the Fomorians as the other Tuatha ran from them. He reached the rear ranks of fleeing fighters and slipped like a shadow through the sweat and blood-slicked mass, speeding towards the grinding, deafening chaos of the front.

Lugh reached the foremost Fomorians. He unsheathed his weapons and went to work. Lugh leaped and twirled like the lights in the northern sky at winter, as swift and elegant as a falling star, his twin swords cutting through enemies as if they were made of silk. Somehow he used his twin swords and twin spears at once, throwing a spear then striking with a sword, leaving it in his enemy's chest before retrieving his spear and throwing it again. He moved so fast that no one, friend or foe, could keep track of him; many enemies stood and watched as he cut down their kin, then looked down to see his blade piercing their own heart.

Many Tuatha who saw him halted in their flight. They cheered and wept to see him fight, and their cries rallied their kinsmen. Though many continued to flee, others turned and faced the enemy again, for Lugh now fought beside them.

Yet Lugh was not merely fighting.

He was hunting.

Leaping atop a standing stone, he sighted his quarry.

Lugh jumped from the stone and dashed through the

melee. He became a blur, a streak of light, until he stood in the shadow of his prey.

His grandfather.

'Balor!' called Lugh.

The Fomorian king turned to face his grandson.

'The battle is over, Balor,' said Lugh. 'Call your forces back, leave this land to us, or I will utterly destroy your army.'

Balor laughed. 'I think your eyes are failing you, grandson. We have eaten our meal; now we chew on the bones.'

'Do not think that the fear in your words escapes me,' said Lugh. 'I know of the prophecy that haunts you. Your own wife foresaw that one day I would kill you. That day has come.'

Balor's mount twisted into a snarl.

'Enough words,' he said. 'It is time to cleave you as I did your king.'

Balor swung at Lugh as he spoke. Any other warrior would have fallen to Balor's blow. Lugh spun out of the way and landed two spear strikes of his own: one to Balor's thigh, the other to his hand. His blade sliced into Balor's knuckle bones.

Balor roared in pain. His hand fell to his side, leaving him to swing his mighty axe one-handed. He struck again, but far too slowly. Lugh salmon-leaped, whirling over Balor's head, cutting his grandfather's nose from his face as he passed.

Balor's cries were terrible as he spun round, blood fountaining from his face. Lugh came at him with a flurry of jabs that struck like a swarm of bees. Balor howled, his hand trembling upon his axe hilt.

Yet Balor didn't need his axe.

Lugh rushed him. Balor dropped his axe and with blinding

speed struck Lugh with his fist. Lugh hurtled through the air and slammed to the ground, half of his ribs broken.

Balor stalked forward, his shadow falling over Lugh.

'You gave a good accounting of yourself, child,' he said, blood dripping from his nose and into his mouth. He licked his lips, tasting its salty tang. 'Perhaps I should feel proud of you. But I feel more like killing you.'

Lugh groaned, the world spinning, every breath an agony.

'I will give you a good death, grandson' he growled. 'A death to be remembered.' Balor raised his voice. 'Pull on the chains!'

Balor's eye-slaves obeyed their master. They pulled on the rings in their hands as the watching Fomorians turned and ran in terror.

Lugh tried to get up. He made it to his knees, then collapsed.

'Run!' he called to the nearby Tuatha. 'Do not let the eye of Balor look upon you!'

Slowly, Balor's eye peeled back. An almighty heat blazed from it, as if they fought within a smith's furnace.

Higher climbed Balor's eyelid. It was as if a thousand dark suns burned behind that lid. Fires burst into life all around; men and monsters ran screaming as their hair and clothes caught alight.

Lugh did not move. He watched Balor, his skin reddening and cracking, his blood reaching an agonising heat within his veins.

All the while, he whispered words of healing.

Further back fell the lid. Further back. Those who had not run fell to the earth, becoming ashes and charred bones.

Lugh's broken ribs wove themselves together in his chest. His skin healed itself even as it burned.

Balor laughed as his burning eye looked upon the world. Looked upon his own grandson. Even Lugh could not withstand the might of that eye fully opened, at its fullest power.

But just as Balor's eye opened fully, its true power unleashed, Lugh leapt up and threw his spear.

It struck with such force that it carved a hole through Balor's brain, sending his eye out through the back of his skull, impaled by Lugh's spear. Manannán's spear, the Spear of Victory, which had come all the way from the far-off city of Finias, awaiting this moment.

Eye, brain and broken skull struck the red mud.

A moment later, Balor's body came crashing down.

The eye came loose from Lugh's spear-tip. It rolled through the Fomorian army, bringing instant death to all those it looked upon, until it finally came to a rest.

Its power faded and died.

Many Fomorians felt the death of their king in that moment. They fled the field, running west in the direction of their ships, and the rest of their army soon joined them.

Some Tuatha, overcome with rage and bloodlust, went after them. Other stood where they had fought, or fell to their knees. It was hard to comprehend that the battle was over, and with it the war. No more taxes on their cattle and grain. No more children enslaved.

Shafts of sunlight broke through the clouds. Warriors sheathed their swords and embraced, as the wounded wailed and the crows feasted.[1]

19

THE AFTERMATH

The next day the battlefield still churned and burned. Those among the surviving Tuatha who could stand now walked among the fallen, helping kinsfolk to their feet or providing the mercy of the spear. These spearmen were too few, though, and the wounded too many. The field seemed to be formed of endless writhing, jerking, blood-wet bodies, like a giant corpse riddled with maggots.

Some Tuatha found fallen friends and sat down beside them. Others, those new to war and some who were not, wandered with wide eyes, dumbstruck, insensible even to those screaming for death.

But a few had other matters on their minds.

Lugh sighted the Dagda crossing the plain towards him. Lugh had not rested since the slaying of Balor, instead traversing the field dispensing praise, condolence and death. All the while, he kept his eyes peeled for one man.

'We have him,' said the Dagda.

LUGH and the Dagda made their way west towards the beach where the Fomorian fleet had landed. The entire route was marked by Fomorian corpses. Many had succumbed to their wounds as they ran; others had been trampled by their kin in the rush to return to the ships. More than a few bore gaping wounds in their backs; it seemed the Tuatha had pursued their foe for many miles.

'Oghma did not stop fighting when the enemy fled,' said the Dagda as they walked. 'He rallied those around him to harry the fleeing Fomorians.'

Lugh nodded. It was ugly work, but so was the stealing of children.

They crested a rise close to the shore and met a sight which stopped Lugh in his tracks.

Ships crowded the water from the blood-soaked sands to the horizon. Barely a speck of blue could be seen. The skeletons on the ships' masts looked down on the last ragged Fomorian survivors, who tried to climb aboard the ships despite having lost limbs in battle. Many ships were on fire; companies of Oghma's archers were launching fire arrows from the beach. Soon there would be nothing left of those hulks but smoldering skeletons.

'May a storm come soon,' said Lugh, 'and wipe this wickedness away.'

'Down here,' said the Dagda.

The Dagda led Lugh to the water's edge as the sun sank in the sky.

Oghma awaited them in the shadow of the ships.

Kneeling before Oghma was Bres.

As Lugh and the Dagda approached, Bres grinned at them through the few teeth he had left. His eyes were swollen half-shut; he had been stripped of armour and clothing; his bruised and bloodied chest was a patchwork of gashes. Bres' captors had not been kind.

'The noble Lugh,' said Bres. 'Have you come to beat me like your friends did? You slew Balor, they are saying! Surely I am no prize to one such as you.' He spat out a mouthful of blood at Lugh's feet.

Lugh studied Bres, offering no answer.

'"Bres the turncoat, Bres the traitor," they keep saying,' Bres went on. 'I am not so sure. My father was a Fomorian. Did I not owe my loyalty to Balor as much as to the sidhe? Balor treated me better than the Tuatha ever did.

'I say this to you...' he broke off in a fit of coughing. 'I say this to you because you alone will understand. You are half-Fomorian like me, are you not? So are you not as much a traitor as I am?'

Oghma drew his knife and put it to Bres' throat. 'On your word,' he said to Lugh.

Lugh drew breath.

'Wait!' said Bres. 'Wait. Hear my offer first.'

'What offer is that?' asked Lugh.

'A third of your cattle were taken from you. They now roam,

fat-uddered, in Fomorian fields. Set me free and I will speak words which will return them to you, and ensure they never run dry.'

Lugh hesitated. He did not want to let Bres go; only trouble could come from letting him live. Yet he could not deny his people the return of their stolen cattle.

'My Lord Lugh.'

Lugh looked up. A crowd of bloodied and grim-faced Tuatha had gathered around them. One of them stepped forward.

'I am Maeltine,' she said. 'I am versed in the art of judgements, and I know something of spellcraft too,' she said. 'I would speak on this matter.'

Lugh nodded. 'Speak.'

'This one has the power to return to us our cattle and ensure the ripeness of their udders,' Maeltine said. 'But the Fomorians took more than our cattle from us; they took our children too.'

'Then I shall speak words so that when the Tuatha return home from battle, they shall find their once-enslaved children sleeping soundly in their beds,' said Bres.

Maeltine considered this.

'Few things could be of higher value than that,' she said eventually. 'But it was because of you that we lost our children. You speak of repayment, not reparation.'

Oghma pressed his blade to Bres' neck. 'Not good enough, turncoat,' he growled.

'Wait!' cried Bres. 'Wait. Spare me and I promise this: the

soil of this island will offer up a harvest not every year but every quarter. Four times as much food in the days to come. Endless feasting for even the poorest farmer. Surely that is enough to earn me my neck.'

'Not so,' said Maeltine. 'Danu decrees that crops shall be sown in spring, tended in summer, harvested in autumn and eaten in winter. To surpass her in this may seem like cleverness, but shall surely show itself to be folly.'

'No words from your lips ever did any good,' said Oghma. 'Time for me to open your neck.'

'To do so is justice,' said Maeltine.

'Wait,' said Lugh, stepping forward.

'He serves his own interests, yes,' said Lugh. 'And he can do so best by serving our interests. One more chance, Bres. Offer us something of true value.'

'Then hear this,' said Bres after a pause. 'And though it may seem like a little thing, its worth cannot be measured. The Tuatha would do well to plough only on a Tuesday, and to cast seed into the soil only on a Tuesday, and to reap only on a Tuesday.'

Everyone looked to Maeltine.

'He speaks truth,' she said.

They looked to Lugh.

'Let him go,' said Lugh.

Oghma reluctantly withdrew his dagger. Bres closed his eyes. He spoke strange words which had the feel of knotted muscle, jagged teeth and fire-smoke.

He opened his eyes and said to Lugh, 'Your cattle and children are returned.'

Bres got to his feet.

'Make way,' said Lugh, 'and do him no harm.'

The crowd reluctantly parted for Bres. He limped towards a nearby forest and soon disappeared from sight.

'What now?' asked Oghma.

'There is no shortage of work to be done at Moytura,' answered Lugh. 'Many suns shall rise and set before we see Tara again. Yet I would ask that you and the other chiefs take charge of it, for I have a journey to make.'

'You take the road to the Fomorian realm,' said the Dagda.

'Yes.'

'Then I will accompany you,' said the Dagda. 'I lost my harp when I left the Fomorian camp. It sings to me, yet so quietly that it cannot be in this world. I would find it and bring it home with me.'

'Very well,' said Lugh.

LUGH and the Dagda waded out into the water, disappearing into the gathering dark. Oghma watched them go then went the opposite way, east towards Moytura.

He reached the site of the battle where mounds of corpses burned, offering sickly-sweet incense to the unveiling stars. He walked beneath their light and, as he walked, his attention was drawn by a fallen Fomorian.

Oghma approached the man. This one was not just a warrior; he had been a king. He was half as tall again as the tallest sidhe; his armour had been forged from brilliant red gold; his skin was covered in dark fur, his teeth pointed. In his death-frozen eyes was an intelligence that Oghma recognised, for he had it himself: a battlefield-cunning, a dagger-slashed acquaintance with death from countless close meetings. This Fomorian king had met death and greeted him as an old friend.

'You see much, Oghma,' said a voice.

It came from the direction of the fallen king, yet the king's lips did not move.

'There is more you might see, more you might know, if you were to claim me for your own.'

The fallen king's sword was speaking.

Oghma picked up the sword, unsheathed it and inspected it. It was staggeringly detailed. Latticework encircled a jewelled pommel with the wild grace of hunting wolves.

'Take me in your hand.'

Oghma did as the sword bade. 'What are you, and who is this man?' he asked.

'Here lies Tethra, a king of the Fomorians and leader in war. I am Orna. I belonged to him, and to another before him, and another before him. Now, Oghma, I shall be yours.

'Sit, Oghma of the Tuatha Dé Danaan. Let me tell you of Tethra. I shall tell you of the duels he fought at Moytura. I shall tell you of things he saw in his life, the deeds he did and the people he loved.'

Full of wonder and forgetting all else, Oghma sat and folded his legs. He listened for days as the sword spoke in the high-leaping language of a bard.

Much of what has been written here is known because

Oghma heard it that night, sitting beneath the stars amid mounds of smoking flesh.

FAR FROM THERE, Lugh looked once more upon the Fomorian Sea.

Dim memories stirred in him as he gazed over the storm-tossed ocean, where rain fell in heavy sheets and thunder rolled overhead.

'This is where I was born,' he said to the Dagda.

They stood on the prow of a stolen Fomorian ship. The Dagda had used a druid-song to carry their ship across the ocean and through the veil between realms. 'When I was a baby, this sea was my crib. I floundered on the waves for many days until Birog bore me away. Somehow I feel a fondness for it.'

They continued on their way, the ship propelled by the Dagda's magic. Though the heavy rain obscured their view, they made out scarred ships in certain harbours, which must have returned from Moytura. Most of the harbours they spied lay empty, though. The Fomorian race had been decimated; few druids remained to guide them home to their realm.

'My harp is close,' said the Dagda suddenly. 'It lies that way.'

He took up his song again, and their ship turned towards a nearby island.

They moored in a sickle-shaped bay, jumped into the water and waded ashore. A path led them uphill through leafless trees. Soon they arrived at a feasting hall that perched on a cliff's edge.

Inside they went.

Fires burned in a pit which ran like a spine down the hall's length. Bedraggled Fomorians sat in silence on the benches. Lugh guessed that some of them had been left behind due to old age; others looked like they had been at the battle. These ones sat with horns of ale in hand, muttering and cursing, their weapons still strapped to their waists and their backs.

The Dagda did not spare the Fomorians a glance. Hanging on the far wall was his harp.

A shout broke the quiet; the uninvited guests had been noticed. The Fomorians leapt up, screeching and snarling as they drew their weapons, even some of the oldlings.

The Dagda called out to his harp.

It trembled for a moment then lifted into the air, sailing across the hall and into the Dagda's outstretched hands. He smiled his ocean-wide smile, cradling and stroking his harp like a long-lost lover.

The Fomorians ran at Lugh and the Dagda.

Lugh drew his sword.

The Dagda plucked his harp and began to sing.

He played a song of joy. Barely a note had quivered in the air before the Fomorians halted in their tracks, looking down at their weapons as if they couldn't quite remember what purpose they served.

An axe clanged upon the floor.

More axes, swords and spears followed suit as the Fomorians let their weapons fall. One three-headed warrior threw back her heads and laughed, and the others joined in. Another warrior clapped his hands and soon they were all clapping in time to the music, while the very oldest Fomorians nodded appreciatively upon the benches. Others danced, spinning one another around until the music slowed.

A new melody emerged upon the strings. It was a song of aching grief. The Fomorians found seats and sat staring at the floor or into their fires. It seemed to Lugh that there was as much beauty in the sadness of that song as there was in the joy of the first song. He wondered at that.

Finally, as softly and imperceptibly as light creeps into the sky before dawn, the song of sadness became a song of peace. The Fomorians lay down, closed their eyes and fell asleep with gentle smiles upon their faces.

The Dagda played a little longer, then finished his song.

'It is time to go,' he said to Lugh.

Lugh shook his head to rouse himself – he had sat down and nodded off too – and followed the Dagda out into the rain.

'I have my harp,' said the Dagda. 'I think there is something you must retrieve too.'

EITHNE PACED HER TENT, stopping again to listen for her father's returning fleet. Yet the night was quiet save for the endless thrumming of rain.

She went to the door and opened the flaps. Her guards stood there and at the gates of the camp. Why did her father still guard her? His fears had come true; she had made love to

Cian and birthed a boy. Balor had cast him into the ocean. Did he guard her in case it happened again? Did he think she would go on mating and spawning until one of her young survived, like the wild animals did?

Or did Balor fear that his grandson lived?

She had pleaded with the guards to tell her what they knew, without success. Clearly they had been ordered not to speak at all to her since it happened. So instead, she wondered. Had he survived somehow, her beautiful baby Lugh? Was he fighting Balor at that very moment? Or was he dead, drowned many years ago? Would some other man come for her, to use her like a brood mare to birth Balor's nemesis?

She gave up her pacing and lay down on her bed. Tears threatened to take her again. Let such a man come. She would open herself to him, no matter if her were ugly or hateful. She would lie beneath a thousand men to bring forth her father's slayer.

So her thoughts followed a familiar road until the sound of music struck her.

She was so surprised that she did not leap up to see who had come. Eithne lay still, listening. A moment later, all thoughts of who played the music were gone. What did it matter? The song was so merry, so at peace with all things; it was a balm for the deep cracks in her heart. Outside, she could hear the guards cheering and clapping their hands.

The song changed. It flew like a raven towards the land of grief.

Eithne knew a moment of panic. Too long had she haunted

grief's deep vaults. But swiftly it turned towards peace, and now she felt her heart mending again.

She sighed a deep sigh as sleep enfolded her.

Eithne awoke to find a young man cradling her in his arms.

She had never met anyone with such bright, blazing eyes. Save once.

'Lugh,' she whispered.

'Yes, Mother,' he said. He kissed her brow. 'Close your eyes. I'm bringing you home.'

EITHNE RETUNED HOME with Lugh and the Dagda. They beached their ship south of where the Fomorian fleet had landed, having taken their fill of such sights for a while. They burned the ship before taking the road to Tara.

At Tara they were met by a great host of Tuatha. The sidhe threw flowers at their feet as they passed through the gates. Not all the great Tuatha were there; many had gone to their homes, where their once-enslaved children awaited them.

Yet they left those homes upon hearing the news that Lugh would be crowned king.

So it was. Lugh was crowned king at Tara. The Dagda placed the crown on his head and the Stone of Destiny bellowed at his feet.

The celebrations went on for weeks. Many Tuatha observed that Eithne never ceased smiling as she watched her son laugh and dance with his subjects, rich and poor, young and old.

Goibniu had healed fully with Airmed's help. He arm-wrestled with Sreng, who had led a small party of Firbolgs to the celebration, and even managed to stop thinking about smithing at times.

The Dagda's fingers never left his harp-strings. Airmed found she could finally lay her grief over Miach aside. She laughed with great relief as she danced to the Dagda's music, ignoring her father, who drank alone.

The Tuatha did not forget those whom they had lost. Many a toast was drunk and tear was shed for their kindred who fell at Moytura. In bedchambers and in forest groves, the Tuatha ensured that a new generation would take the place of the fallen.

And what of Lugh?

How did he feel, he who had accomplished the great task of his life? Did he sit at ease upon the throne, at the very centre of the race who adored him?

No.

Lugh had the gift of prophecy. He did not need it to know that this peace, bought with so much blood, would not last forever. Just as the Tuatha had taken the Firbolgs' home, so a day would come when ships would carry a new race to their shores. A race hungry for new horizons, fertile fields and battle-fame.

Yet that was all the more reason to sing and dance now. So Lugh celebrated fiercely, his cup never empty.

As the Tuatha danced and sang at Tara, and those not in attendance toasted Lugh by their hearths, three great crows flew over the Isle of Destiny. Badb, Macha and the Morrigan flew from north to south and from east to west, carrying the news of victory. They cried the news to the great mountains and rivers and trees, who carried it to the hidden glens, nimble streams and rocky mounds, all the way to the deepest roots of the loneliest trees. Their screeching was both news and blessing.

'Peace upon this land,' they said in their night-speech. 'From the roof of the sky to the depths of the earth; peace and strength to all.'[1]

PART III

20

ENTER THE GAELS

L ugh ruled the Isle of Destiny for years uncounted. In time, he tired of kingship and passed his crown on until it came to a man named Cermait. The system of passing on kingship among the Tuatha had changed, and when Cermait died, he left the kingdom to his three sons.

It was in this time that the rule of the Tuatha ended.

The three sons of Cermait Honey-Mouth were Mac Cuill, Mac Cecht and Mac Greine. Following their father's death, they agreed to divide the kingdom equally among them. Yet each of them soon claimed that his share was too small, and sent out warriors to seize land, gold and cattle from his brothers.

Armies roved the land, reaving and burning. It seems that the nobility of spirit which Lugh awakened in the Tuatha faded during this time. Many took advantage of the chaos, mounting their own raids on vulnerable neighbours or settling old scores with knives in the night. Violence bred violence, harvests rotted and smoke filled the skies.

It was in this time that the Gaels came to the Isle of Destiny.

As the Tuatha had come in a great fleet from the north, so the Sons of Gaedhal, better known as the Gaels, came from the south.

It was not unknown for foreigners to visit the Isle of Destiny. They had always come in small numbers, usually as traders, sometimes as bards and wanderers. Towards the end of Cermait's reign, a Gael named Ith had landed with a small band of traders. A group of Tuatha slaughtered them and stole their wares. Only Ith's serving man escaped to carry the tale home.

Ith's family wept as they heard it.

Among them was a man named Amergin.

Amergin was a revered poet and druid, and a nephew of Ith. He was said to speak the languages of swallows and storm clouds; to sleep beneath the sea and have dealings with the dead. Kings and common folk sought his counsel and feared his judgement. He was not a man to be trifled with.

The fierce-faced druid listened to the tale of Ith's murder. Afterwards he went into the wild, seeking wisdom.

He returned with a purpose that would change the world.

Amergin went to the hall of his brother Heremon. He called a meeting, open to all, and let it be known that only a fool would miss it. Come the day of the meeting, curious people of

every station packed out the hall. The doors closed and
Amergin climbed the dais. The hall fell silent.

'My uncle Ith travelled to the Isle of Destiny,' said Amergin,
his words resounding like an eagle's salute to the sun. 'There,
he and his men were murdered.

'A tragedy, you might say. Yet nothing out of the ordinary.
Such things happen the world over.

'You would be right to say this. And yet.

'When I heard this tale, I itched for revenge, to lead a war-
band to those shores and spill the blood of my kinsman's
murderers. But a quiet voice in my breast said there was more
to this tale. I sensed a purpose, a design in Ith's death. So I went
into the woods and did my druid-work, seeking the counsel of
the gods.

'This is what they told me.

'The Isle of Destiny wishes to be ours. She is calling out to
us, not to avenge my kinsman but to claim her as our own.

'I know this will sound preposterous to many of you. You
have bonds to hearth and home, kin and king, and no desire to
break them. That is well. That is how it should be. But there are
always a few among a people who would leave all such things
behind.

'You know who you are. You who would risk everything to
take a chance upon a new life in a new land. It is the way you
were made. It is the way I was made.

'If my call rings true in your heart, whether you are woman
or man, young or old, I invite you to join me. Let us raise a fleet,
take the whale road west and wrestle the Isle of Destiny from
the Tuatha Dé Danaan.'

Cavernous silence filled the hall.

'We have heard tales of these sidhe,' said one woman. 'They are said to be fearsome fighters, skilled craftsmen and potent druids. How can we hope to take their home from them?'

'By trusting in me,' said Amergin, 'The Isle of Destiny herself spoke to me. If we fight for her, she will aid us in that fight. Who will fight alongside me?'

More silence. Then a hand was raised. Another, and another, and another. A voice cried out; another voice answered. Soon the hall shook with the cheering and stamping of Gaels thirsty for adventure.

Messengers set out across the Gaelic homelands. Most Gaels ignored the summons, yet many answered them.

MONTHS PASSED. Amergin's adventurers assembled and built a colossal fleet. They forged new weapons and trained their young in the ways of war.

Finally they were ready. They bade their kinsfolk goodbye and sailed west.

After many days at sea, they saw the green hills of Leinster upon the horizon.

Goatherds spied the fleet first. The goatherds ran down from the hills with the news. It raced across Leinster and soon reached the ears of some local druids, who gathered on the coast to establish the truth of the matter.

Their blood ran cold as they looked upon Amergin's fleet.

'Enough gawping,' said one of them eventually. 'Let us send these invaders back the way they came.'

The druids agreed on a suitable spell. They sent for reinforcements and soon every druid in Leinster was on their way to the beach, eager to lend their strength to the enchantment.

ON THE DECK of his ship, Amergin narrowed his eyes.

An hour before, the ship had rung with cheers at the sight of land. Yet that land was no longer there.

In its place was a boar the size of a mountain. Its red eyes were as big as houses; a well-aimed swing of its tusks could make driftwood of their fleet. It swung those tusks now, snorting and bellowing, warning them back.

The Gaels cried out in panic. Some called to turn the ships around, but others looked to Amergin.

'Do not fear this druidry!' he called out, his voice stern. 'Any kingdom worth taking is guarded with spells as well as swords. I would be concerned if I saw a smaller pig, for I would worry that this island was not worth the conquering.'

Some of the sailors nodded; others only stared at the boar. It raised its head and let out a bellowing that shook Amergin's bones.

'Stay strong, Sons of Gaedhal!' commanded Amergin. 'Feed not your fear; feed the fires of your courage.'

Still the sailors trembled.

Amergin closed his eyes and sent his spirit out towards the beast. He roamed its borders, probing, testing. This spell was the work of many druids, he discerned. He could have broken it with time and effort, yet there was a far easier solution to his problem.

'Turn south!' he called out. 'Let us leave these druids and their wind-pig behind!'

Oars creaked into action. Soon the fleet was sailing south. Amergin's ships were propelled by oar and wind; the druids could move no faster than their feet allowed them.

It wasn't long before the great boar was out of sight, replaced by the cliffs and coves of Munster.

THE GAELS finally landed at Inver Sceine, that is now called Kenmare Bay, in West Munster.

Amergin's boat landed first. He leapt from the prow into the water and strode up the soft sand.

'Greetings, Fair Green Isle,' he said. 'Thank you for calling my people here. May the time soon come when we call this land home. May we be good stewards to your fields, your forests, your mountains and rivers. May you call us in time your favourite children.'

Soon the beach was crowded with Gaels as ship after ship docked in the bay. Many made their own prayers. The air was charged with excitement and an undercurrent of fear. When would the Tuatha come? What would they throw at them next?

Amergin's chiefs, who were also his brothers, gathered about him. It was time to discuss their next move.

'That phantom boar was a sight to behold. If the sidhe are

as powerful warriors as they are druids, this island will not be easy to claim,' said Ir, scanning the horizon again for signs of an attack. He was a gentle man, a good leader in peacetime, yet Amergin feared he had no stomach for a fight.

'I would not be happy taking this land without a fight,' said Eber Finn, who was the most war-hungry of the chiefs. 'Yet we do not know who leads the sidhe or where their forces lie.'

'We could make camp here and send out scouts,' suggested Ir.

'No,' said Amergin. 'Now is not the time to sit idle. We should leave our ships behind and set off across country. The impetus of conquest is ours; best not to lose it.'

Though some would have preferred to rest after their long journey, everyone respected the wisdom of Amergin. He was warrior, druid and poet, the best of leaders in peace and in war. So the Gaels readied themselves for a long march.

Soon they were ready to travel. They left the bay behind and headed inland.

SEVERAL DAYS after leaving Inver Sceine, the Gaels made camp among the high hills now known as Slieve Mish.

During those days they had wondered at both the beauty of the land and its desolation. They had never seen such green hills, such verdant forests. Their druids spoke in awed tones of the power they sensed within the ancient oak, ash, hazel and birch. Yet every second habitation was deserted; every third field had been burned. Those who saw them coming fled, though that was to be expected. They were a mighty host, well-armed and armoured.

'This is a land in the grip of war,' said Eber Finn as the chiefs gathered around their fire one evening. They had made camp among a small copse of gnarled beech trees. The copse crowned a hill, commanding a good view over their surroundings. To their west lay the sea, and all about them was a hazy panorama of peaks. 'It is no ordinary war, for it is one fought without honour. Such savagery scars my heart.'

'If this war is fought without honour, then the Tuatha ruler is without honour,' said Amergin. 'As things are with the king, so things are with his kingdom.'

'Yet where is this...' Heremon ceased speaking as he stared past his brothers.

They turned and stared too.

A procession was climbing the hill, led by a woman who could only be a queen. She wore a crown of gold and a cloak of brilliant green; her beauty made the chiefs swoon. Behind her walked maidens in dazzling dresses, followed by men with the look of druids. Harpers and singers came last. They filled the air with music and song so that the procession seemed like something out of a dream.

Amergin and his chiefs walked out to meet their visitors.

'Greetings, newcomers to this land,' said the leader of the party with a warm smile. 'I am Banba, wife of Mac Cuill, Son of the Hazel. I am queen of all you see and far more.'

'Greetings, Queen Banba,' said Amergin. 'I am Amergin, Son of Miled. These are my brothers Donn, Heremon, Ir and Eber Finn. Our people are called the Gaels.'

'And what brings the Gaels to our shores?' asked Banba.

'I will speak plainly,' said Amergin. 'A kinsman of mine, a man named Ith, visited these shores and was murdered. His serving man escaped, made it home and told us what he had seen of your homeland. A land where the soil was rich and the woods full of game; a land that was neither too cold in winter not too hot in summer. I divined that we were destined to rule this land, and thus we have come to claim it.'

'I appreciate your candour, Amergin,' said Banba, 'and I shall return the favour.

'You have no doubt discerned that our country is at war. This war is fought between my husband and his two brothers, Mac Cecht and Mac Greine. Their father, Cermait Honey-Mouth, left the kingdom to the three brothers when he died. Their subsequent squabbles have bred chaos and bloodshed throughout the land.'

'I see,' said Amergin. 'No doubt Cermait Honey-mouth had his reasons for doing as he did. Even so, I gravely doubt the wisdom of his action.'

'He was a fool,' said Banba, 'and we have all paid the price of his foolishness.'

'I must ask, then, why you walk here without warriors to guard you? And is your husband nearby, that I may treat with him?'

'No sidhe is fool enough to cross me. If they did, the very land would turn against them. Roots would rise up around their feet to ensnare them; tree-branches would seize them and tear them in two. I am this land, and she shall brook no harm to me.'

Amergin nodded. 'I will not seek to cross you,' he said. 'But I would speak to your husband, and I would get to know you better if I may.'

'Turn your force towards Tara, which lies in the east. It is the seat of the High King, where the Dagda once ruled, and Lugh before him, and Nuada of the Silver Hand before him. The three sons of Cermait Honey-Mouth have agreed to meet there in an effort to end the war.'

'Then to Tara we shall go,' said Amergin.

'That is well.'

'Forgive me,' said Ir. 'But I must ask. We come as conquerors to your land, yet you welcome us. Why is it so?'

'The Tuatha Dé Danaan are immortal. Swords can kill us but the turning of time cannot. Yet time still flows by, and with it the world turns. One age ends and another arises. The time of the Tuatha will end, and if that moment has come, there is no sense in fighting it. Yet I do have an offer to make you.'

'What is that?' asked Amergin.

'You will face fearsome warriors in your fight for this land. We defeated the Firbolgs, a race of savage strength and iron will. The Fomorians came to our shores, as numerous as the stars in the sky, and we slaughtered them. Your fight with the Tuatha will go better if you have my blessing.'

'You would give that?' asked Heremon.

'I would,' said Banba, 'provided that should you win this war, you name this island after me.'

'It shall be done,' said Amergin.

Banba smiled warmly at him. She gave Amergin her

blessing that night, and their followers feasted and celebrated together until dawn.

As the sun rose, the Gaels set off for Tara.

THEY MOVED northeast across the country. Their path led them down from the mountains and across plains scattered with smoking farmsteads and abandoned villages. Their scouts reported war bands moving nearby, and they gave these a wide berth.

After several days of walking, they spied high hills ahead and climbed one in order to view the surrounding lands. They crested Slieve Felim and looked out over the hills, forests and green fields of Tipperary. Standing atop the hill, Amergin and his brothers spied another procession headed their way.

This one was also led by a woman who could only be a queen. She wore a golden crown and green dress like Banba, and she too had a retinue of maidens, druids and bards.

'Greetings, travellers,' she said. 'I am Queen Fodhla. My husband is Mac Cecht, Son of the Plough.'

Amergin stepped forward and introduced himself, his brothers and his people.

'You are not the first queen we have met on our journey,' he said. 'We crossed paths with Queen Banba, wife of Mac Cuill, on our way here. She told us how things stand in the lands.'

'This I know,' said Fodhla. 'I sense that her blessing is with you.'

'I wonder, then, if we might ask for your blessing too?' asked Amergin.

'You are bold,' said Fodhla. 'Boldness is sometimes punished. At other times, it is rewarded. I will offer you my blessing on one condition: that you name this island after me should your conquest succeed.'

'It shall be done,' said Amergin without a pause, earning him sideways glances from his brothers.

'Then my blessing you shall have,' said Fodhla.

She led Amergin to the hilltop's eastern edge. 'That way lies Tara,' she said. 'To get there, take the road northeast along the eastern shore of Lough Dearg. Follow the road until you come to the Hill of Uisnech, where the provinces of Ireland meet. The road leading east from Uisnech will take you to Tara.'

Amergin bowed to Fodhla and thanked her for her assistance. She invited the Gaels to make their camp alongside hers, which they did. Gael and Tuatha ate and drank together that night. Come morning, the Gaels resumed their journey to Tara.

THE NEXT LEG of the journey was much the same as the last. It took three days for them to reach the Hill of Uisnech while avoiding raiders. They arrived late in the morning as a powerful wind blew in from the west.

Upon nearing the hill, Amergin said to his brothers, 'Climbing hills has brought us good fortune thus far. I think we should see what lies atop this one.'

The chiefs agreed. The army climbed the hill as rainclouds blew in from the west. They soon reached the hill's peak, for it was not of great height.

Awaiting them at the top was a queen.

She was dressed like her kinswomen. She greeted them and said, 'I am Eriu, wife of Mac Greine, Son of the Sun.'

Amergin was about to reply when a strange thing happened.

As the clouds raced by overhead, Eriu's appearance shifted. She went from being a woman to a huge, grey-eyed crow. Amergin blinked and she was a woman again. Looking around, it was clear his brothers had seen what he had seen.

'You are close to Tara,' Eriu said. 'There you shall find my husband and his brothers quarrelling like children. Should it come to battle between you and they, I could aid you by giving you my blessing. I only ask that, should you be victorious, you name this island Eriu.'

'It shall be done,' said Amergin.

'Then go from here with my blessing,' said Eriu. 'Keep walking and you shall reach Tara tomorrow evening.'

The Gaels did as Eriu bade. They retreated down the hill and carried on east towards Tara. On the road, Heremon said to Amergin, 'I wonder at the wisdom of your actions, brother. You have obtained for us three powerful blessings, yet you promised to each queen that you will name the island after them.'

'And to that promise I shall hold. For cannot we call this island Banba at times, and Fodhla at other times, and Eriu when the mood takes us?'

Heremon saw the truth of that and smiled.

'What do you think it means that so fair a queen is also a crow? Is this an ill omen?'

'Gold is silver and silver is gold,' said Amergin. 'Summer wears a gown of winter. A queen is a crow, a swan a falling star; the best man is the worst. Do not be fearful, brother. We will claim this kingdom soon enough.'

THE GAELS REACHED the western edge of the Plain of Breg.

Tara lay before them.

Amergin halted, savouring the sight of the fort which would soon be the seat of a Gaelic king. Then he led his people to the gates of Tara, which were open and unguarded.

Amergin selected a band of his chiefs and finest warriors and bade them follow him. Entering Tara, they saw that many of its buildings were in disrepair. Broken doors lay among overgrown grass or hung on their hinges, creaking in the wind. An enormous rat ran across their path and disappeared into a storehouse.

'The high seat of the sidhe has been abandoned,' said Amergin.

The Gaels climbed the hill. At its peak, they finally found life other than rats. Three bands of warriors sat idly on a stretch of ground leading to the hall. Each group eyed the other groups warily, as well as the approaching strangers.

A man from the closest group stood and drew his sword.

'Who are you?' he called out.

'I am Amergin of the Gaels. These are my chiefs and finest

warriors. We have come to treat with the three sons of Cermait Honey-Mouth, for we wish to make a claim to this kingdom.'

The warriors stared at the Gaels and whispered to one another. Amergin and his brothers tensed.

'Let them try,' said a warrior from one of the other bands. 'They can't do a worse job than the fools we call our kings.'

Amergin waited for someone to contest this, but no one did. He was relieved, but also saddened to see a great people fallen so far. He bowed to the warriors, and the Gaels entered the hall.

THREE MEN in golden crowns and crimson robes stood beneath a dais at the hall's far end. A collection of wooden chests stood between them, each brimming over with golden necklaces, silver cups, jewelled daggers and other treasures.

'I am merely expressing my surprise,' said one of the men, 'that you would give up the chance to cease our feuding over a few chests of treasure.' He wore a hazel brooch; this must be Mac Cuill, Son of the Hazel.

'It is you who is spoiling our chances of making peace,' said another, whose brooch was in the shape of a plough; this must be Mac Cecht. 'If you did not demand for yourself what should be divided between all of us, we would have no quarrel.'

'Our father said we should divide the kingdom equally between us. Equally!' said the third son, Mac Greine, Son of the Sun.

'And the lands Father left me are not equal to the lands he left to you. How am I supposed to tax farmers whose fields are stone and bog? The division of land I have proposed compensates for this.'

'Compensates the two of you, at my expense,' said Mac Greine. 'It has always been the same. Just because I am the youngest, you think—'

'Silence!'

Amergin's voice crashed through the hall like a thunderclap.

The three kings turned and stared as Amergin strode into the hall, followed by his chiefs. Before Cermait's sons could respond, he spoke again.

'Broken men stand before me. Or are you men at all? Better I call you infants, squabbling as filth run downs your rears.

'To think there are people who call you their kings! I once heard of a warrior who sent his sick father to take his place on a battlefield. There was less shame in his deed than in what I see before me.

'My party and I are from far over the sea. We came here because our kinsman, Ith, was slain upon your shores. His serving-man escaped, returned home and told us of your bountiful island. Her fish-rich seas, her verdant meadows, her forests where the deer outnumber the trees.'

Amergin went on speaking as the warriors who had been sitting outside entered the hall. They did not draw their weapons; they only listened.

'There were some among our people who doubted the truth of the tale. But when we arrived here, what did we see? We saw that Ith's man had not been generous enough with his words! My most battle-hardened men wept for joy while walking your roads. Such a prize you have in this isle, such a jewel!

'On our way here we met your wives, the Queens Banba, Fodhla and Eriu. They were each as graceful and cunning-tongued as a queen of this land should be. Yet they had no fine words to speak of you three. Far from it; they offered to help us! How could such a thing be? Was it all a trick, I wondered at times?

'I almost wish it was.' Amergin shook his head. 'I truly do. For the sight of you three is a knife-slash on my soul, and the sight of this island ravaged by your war is even worse.'

'Who are you?' demanded Mac Cuill, finally finding his tongue. His brothers seemed stunned into silence by Amergin's scolding.

'It is well you ask,' said Amergin with a sly grin. He raised his voice, addressing everyone present in the hall and clustered at the doorway. 'I am Amergin, Son of Miled, and my people are the Gaels. I led a mighty army here, and it is camped outside your gates. We are here to take this island from you, just as you took it from whoever came here before you.'

'Then see us put aside our arguing,' said Mac Cecht. 'We will unite to repel you as we did the Firbolgs and the Fomorians—'

'Good!' said Amergin. 'Then our bards might find some good to speak of you, in the winters to come when they sing of your defeat.'

'A moment, please, Amergin of the Gaels,' said Mac Greine before Mac Cecht could reply. He gestured to his brothers, who huddled around him and whispered furiously to one another.

They ceased their conference.

'There is one issue with all this,' said Mac Cuill. 'We do not fear to fight you. But our armies are scattered, and it would take time to gather them. Surely you would not wish to face us at less than our full strength.'

'So what do you propose?'

'We propose a different kind of duel,' said Mac Cuill, failing to keep a wicked grin from his face. 'We propose a battle of magics. Our finest druids against your most esteemed spell-weavers.'

Now it was Amergin who fought to suppress a smile. He was the most esteemed spell-worker the Gaels had known in generations.

'Very well,' he said. 'In that case, may I suggest the manner of our engagement?'

Mac Cuill nodded.

'We Gaels will retreat to our ships. We will then row our ships away from your coast, over the length of nine waves. At that point, we shall reverse course and try to land again, opposed by your druids.

'If they succeed in stopping us, I swear we shall turn our ships around and sail away forever. But if we cross those nine waves, this island shall be ours.'

Mac Cuill glanced at his brothers. None of them doubted that the druids of the sidhe were the finest in the world.

'It is done,' said Mac Cuill. 'Retreat to your ships.'[1]

21

THE SONG OF AMERGIN

The Gaels retraced their route across Ireland. Mac Cuill, Mac Cecht and Mac Greine followed at a distance, making separate camps each night.

Before leaving Tara, each of the three kings had sent out riders to gather his finest druids and send them to Inver Sceine. So it was that when the three armies finally reached the coast, they found a formidable band of druids awaiting them.

The Gaels were camped at the edge of the sands. Seeing that Cermait's sons and their armies had arrived, Amergin ordered his people to break camp and return to their ships.

The sea was still, the sky grey. The Gaels crossed the sands and waded out to their ships. A few among them filled their hands with sand, a souvenir should they lose the coming battle of magics. But most of them had faith in Amergin, and they laughed and joked as they boarded the ships.

The Gaels took up oars. Amergin mounted the prow of his ship and surveyed the scene.

Three armies lined the bay, any enmities forgotten as they awaited the coming spectacle. The druids of the sidhe had chosen a hill overlooking the bay on which to make their stand. Women and men, old and young; the most potent spell-casters in the land stood united. Their kings watched them from close by.

Mac Cecht put a horn to his lips and blew, its sound ringing out over the waves.

It was time.

'Turn about and row,' called Amergin, 'over the length of nine waves.'

The order was obeyed. The Gaels crossed the length of nine waves.

'Halt!'

Amergin's command rang out again, and they halted.

'Turn about and face the Isle of Destiny,' commanded Amergin.

The fleet turned in unison. Soon the water was still again.

The Gaels were ready.

'DRUIDS!' shouted Mac Cecht, eager to give the order before his brothers. 'Summon a wind and scatter those ships to the four corners of the world.'

At once the druids began chanting. Those sensitive to magic among the Gaels immediately felt the spell's potency.

Moments later, the waters stirred.

The sky turned black. Winds whipped at the three kings, moaning then howling then shrieking. Mac Cecht fought the urge to run for cover as he kept his eyes on the Gaels.

Waves reared up to pound their ships. Soon the waves were towering over the masts. Swirling storm clouds, wreathed in lightning, shot towards the fleet as if fired from a great catapult.

The storm broke over the bay. Nobody on the shore or the ships could see more than a few feet in front of them. Every Gael dropped their oar and clung to whatever they could. One after another the storm tore them loose and tossed them overboard. The fleet was scattered as the storm swept them out to sea.

'We are doomed!' cried some. 'The sea will swallow us!'

Others cried out, 'Have faith in Amergin!'

AMERGIN WAS OCCUPIED.

The storm assailed his ship too. No words of power could he speak to combat the storm, for his lungs were choked with seawater. He clung to the prow of his ship and spluttered, incapable of answering magic with magic, just as the Tuatha druids had intended.

Upon the bay, the three kings and their armies ran to take shelter wherever they could find it, cowering behind rocks and among sand dunes. Only the druids stood their ground. They continued to chant, their hands held high, veins of light twisting about them as they channelled the vast powers of the storm.

The druids did not escape unscathed. Many of them were overwhelmed by the spell. They fell writhing to the ground as the storm pulled them apart from the inside, snapping necks and wrenching limbs from sockets. Druid after druid was lost this way, but the strongest stood firm and the storm raged on.

As THE LESSER DRUIDS FELL, so did many of the Gaels.

One ship crashed into a skerry and was smashed into splinters.

Two ships clashed together and capsized.

Other ships were blown out to sea, never to be seen again.

A druid fell to the ground as his neck snapped. Another.

Out on the waves, Amergin sensed the storm weaken.

'Hold on!' he called. 'The storm's full strength has passed! Stay true and we shall win this battle!'

Another wave crashed over the ship. Two of his people were tossed into the water.

'We can't go on any longer! Our strength is spent!' screamed one woman. A moment later, she lost her grip and was blown over the side of the ship.

Snarling, Amergin closed his eyes.

The storm was no doubt weakening, yet its power was still vast. His own druids were too scattered, too preoccupied to rally.

He would have to answer the Tuatha Dé Danaan spell alone.

He needed more time. Given time, the spell would weaken enough for him to break it.

But there was no more time.

Pain split his chest as if a spear had pierced his ribs. Amergin saw with his inner eye that Ir's ship had been lost.

With that, Amergin found the fury he needed.

He roared out to sea and sky. No more waiting; he would fight the Tuatha now.

Clinging on tightly to the prow, Amergin turned his body until he faced the sidhe druids. Though he could not see them, their spell was like a beacon fire to him.

Drawing on the deepest reaches of his power, Amergin unleashed his own incantation.

The Tuatha druids had channelled the fury of the storm. Amergin went further than that.

He spoke these words.

I am the wind on the sea;
I am the wave of the sea;
I am the bull of seven battles;
I am the eagle on the rock;
I am a flash from the sun;
I am the most beautiful of plants;
I am a strong wild boar;
I am a salmon in the water;
I am a lake in the plain;
I am the word of knowledge;

I am the head of the spear in battle;
I am the god that puts fire in the head.
Who spreads light in the gathering on the hills?
Who can tell the ages of the moon?
Who can tell where the sun rests?
It is I.

As he spoke of water and wind, salmon and spear, so he reached out to them and became one with them. The power of eagle and moon, bull and boar, spear and setting sun filled Amergin. He reached out across all creation, channelling the brilliance of those beings into words.

With those words, he silenced the storm.

The sea obeyed Amergin as a hound obeys a huntsman. Within moments it was as smooth as marble.

An oystercatcher called out, its cry echoing across the bay.

The surviving Gaels wiped their eyes and surveyed the carnage. Wreckage from dozens of shattered ships floated serenely among corpses too numerous to count. Only a handful of ships remained upright. Their fleet had been all but destroyed.

'Do not weep yet,' said Amergin to his crew. 'Many ships were blown out to sea; some surely survived. We will look for our surviving kinsfolk, but first let us claim our prize.'

The Gaels took up oars and rowed into the bay. They jumped from their ships and waded ashore.

The Isle of Destiny now belonged to them.

～

AMERGIN and his surviving brothers stood upon the sand before Mac Cuill, Mac Greine and Mac Cecht.

'We have won this island, which we shall call Eriu,' said Amergin. 'Do you deny it?'

'No,' said Mac Cecht sullenly.

'I would hear it from each of you.'

Mac Greine and Mac Coull assented.

'Congratulations, then, on a battle well-fought. I wonder, where will you go now?'

Mac Greine's answer surprised Amergin.

'I ask you,' he said. 'I beseech you. Send us not from these shores.' Amergin's brow furrowed. 'Instead,' he quickly continued, 'Let us retreat not over the sea, but under the ground. We will build halls beneath the earth, and cloak ourselves in such mystery and magic that later generations of Gaels will doubt we exist at all.'

'It is your right to take this land from us, as we took it from the Firbolgs,' said Mac Cecht. 'Yet we love this island so dearly. Surely you understand; you have only just arrived here and already you love her. Please, give us leave to remain, and we will become but a tale to amuse your children.'

Amergin pondered these words.

Eventually he said, 'So shall it be.'

And so it was.

The Tuatha retreated underground, building splendid halls where they danced and delighted and lived out their lives. Some chose not to go underground and went instead over the sea. They made homes on Tír na nÓg, Land of the Ever Young, and other isles far out to the west. The Gaels, meanwhile, established themselves on the land that they sometimes called Banba, and sometimes called Fodhla, but mostly called Eriu.

The Tuatha did not remain totally unseen, of course. Many Gaels encountered and even coupled with Tuatha over the years, giving rise to legends to which we now turn. Thankfully, the Gaels never went to war against the Tuatha, though it was not long before they went to war with one another. Amergin refused the kingship, so his brothers immediately set to contesting it, just as Cermait's sons had done.

There is not much to say of that. Heremon became the first Gaelic king of Eriu following a bloody feud with Eber Finn. Their children continued the feud, and so it went as it always does. Brother against brother, kinswoman against kinswoman, iron against iron as the centuries rolled by.

But there are other tales I wish to tell you.[1]

22

THE BIRTH OF ANGUS

While the Gaels established themselves as overlords of Eriu, the Tuatha Dé Danaan lived out their lives on lonely shores and in underground halls. Some had dealings with the Gaels, though this lessened as time went by. The Gaels began to wonder if the sidhe existed at all.

There came a time when the Dagda was chosen as king of the Tuatha Dé Danaan. They loved him dearly and were sure he would be a great king. For was it not the Dagda, they said, who led their forces at the Great Battle of Moytura? Did he not accompany Lugh into the Fomorian realm? And was it not the Dagda who warned Nuada against backing Bres as king?

The Dagda was flattered by his people's adulation, and at their pressing he accepted the kingship. Yet he doubted whether he deserved it. He knew that even if he ruled the Tuatha, too often his appetites ruled him. Rarely could he refuse a plate of meat, a cup of ale or a turn on the dance floor. Nor could he resist a beautiful woman, even if she were another man's wife.

THE DAGDA WAS FEASTING at Brú na Bóinne. The hall lay in the east of the country, close to Tara, concealed beneath a mound on the banks of the River Boyne. Elcmar, a chief of the Tuatha, ruled there with his wife Boann. The Dagda did not like Elcmar, who was proud and mean-spirited, but as king he had no choice but to keep his chiefs close. He himself ruled from the new seat of the kings of the Sidhe, beneath the Hill of Uisnech.

The feast went on for five days. During those days, the Dagda found himself admiring Boann more and more. She was one with the river which we call Boyne after her, and bore all the power and beauty of those waters. The curve of the river was the curve of her hips; her words were as sharp and clear as its waters.

And she was Elcmar's wife.

She is not available, the Dagda told himself. *Stop looking at her.*

Yet as mug after mug wet his lips, it grew harder to stop stealing glances. It grew even harder when, on the third day of the feast, he noticed Boann looking back at him. There was no mistaking the intent in her eyes. Red-nosed, lank-haired Elcmar did not notice; he only paid attention to his cup and his plate, and roared at his servants whenever either grew empty.

It matters not where she looks, the Dagda told himself. *She is Elcmar's wife. You are king now; you must be better than this.*

But another part of him said, *If she turns away from Elcmar, that is Elcmar's fault. Such a woman should be kept satisfied. Why deny her what she craves? If Elcmar cannot satisfy her, he does not deserve her.*

No! the Dagda told himself, knowing the insidious voice of his own appetites. *Treachery is treachery. If my strength is only in my arm then I am no king at all.*

The best thing would be to leave, but the king could not do so without giving grievous offence. So the Dagda turned away from Boann and did his best to ignore her. It worked for a while. But willpower waxes and wanes like the moon.

On the fifth day of the feast, the Dagda approached Elcmar and asked for a quiet word.

Elcmar leaned in to listen, wiping ale from his chin as the Dagda spoke in a low voice.

'Something is on my mind, friend. You know that Bres rules now at Mag Ninis?'

'I do,' said Elcmar with a sneer. 'That traitor should never have been offered pardon, let alone a lordship.'

'I do not disagree. Nevertheless. Word has reached my ears that Bres is plotting a rebellion, and we must take action.'

'You would make war on Bres?'

'No,' said the Dagda. 'Not yet. What I wish is for you to visit Bres' hall. Go there as my envoy. Stay a while, saying I sent you to ensure all is well in the region.

'Make it clear that you are not checking up on Bres. You are merely basing yourself at his hall, as befits my emissary, while you conduct your business. If he is indeed plotting rebellion, he will know that I know of it. Yet no trouble will be stirred between us.'

'Very well,' said Elcmar with a belch. 'How long would you have me remain with him?'

'Oh, I don't know... let's say a year.'

Elcmar paled. 'Very well. If I must. But I do not like to go a night without enjoying my wife. You'll allow me to bring her with me?'

'Best not, in case Bres is up to his old tricks. You would not want her endangered. I will bring her to the Hill of Uisnech. She will be well-guarded and always entertained.'

Elcmar bristled, but knew he had no choice. 'Very well, my king. I will go to Mag Ninis, and I only ask one thing in return: that I may visit Uisnech each evening to lie with my wife. She's a pretty thing, and needs to be kept satisfied,' he said with a wink.

The Dagda thought for a moment.

'Very well,' he said.

The following day, the feast ended. Elcmar left Brú na Bóinne for Mag Ninis, and Boann departed for Uisnech with the Dagda.

AT THE HILL OF UISNECH, the Dagda wasted no time in visiting Boann's chambers. They fell on one another with the hunger of bears in spring.

'You must leave me,' said Boann as the evening shadows

lengthened. 'I am glad we did this, for I have long desired you. But my husband will return to me tonight and every night.'

'No,' said the Dagda, 'he will not.'

'Why not?'

'I put a spell on Elcmar before he left Brú na Bóinne. When night comes, he will perceive it as day. Darkness shall be unknown to him. He will remain at Mag Ninis for a whole year, yet will perceive that only a single day has passed.'

Boann gave the Dagda a sad smile. She did not care for trickery, and would have thought the Dagda above such things. He had his faults, she saw now. Yet who did not?

Boann closed her eyes and kissed the Dagda. They did not leave the chamber for a week.

WEEKS PASSED. Boann grew great with child just as spring's first flowers blossomed. Nine months later, as Elcmar lingered in Bres' hall and wondered impatiently when night would come, Boann gave birth to the most extraordinary child.

The child was a boy, with golden hair and lazuli eyes. Boann gave birth to him in a glade on the riverbank, as the Dagda played music to soothe her pains and bless the child. The moment their son was born, sunlight burst out from behind the clouds and birdsong filled the air. Four bright-winged birds flew down and circled his head, singing sweet songs as if in praise of him.

'We should call him Angus,' said Boann.

'Angus Mac Óg,' said the Dagda, which means *The Young*

Son. 'For he was conceived and born in a single day, as some would perceive it.'

Soon after that, Elcmar's year with Bres came to an end. He returned to Brú na Bóinne, feeling greatly confused about the passage of time yet overjoyed at the thought of seeing Boann again. He sent word to Uisnech that it was time for her to come home.

'I would rather stay here with my son and with you,' said Boann to the Dagda. 'In my heart, you are my husband.'

'But not in the eyes of our people,' said the Dagda. 'I must pretend to be a king, even though in truth I am no king at all.'

'Do not berate yourself again,' said Boann. 'There is nothing so true as desire. You of all people should know that.'

'I do,' said the Dagda with a sad smile. 'I do.'

Boann returned to Brú na Bóinne and lived as Elcmar's wife again. She spoke not a word of the boy called Angus Óg.

ANGUS DID NOT REMAIN at Uisnech. It was the custom at that time for children to be raised by foster parents, so the Dagda arranged for Angus to be fostered by his friend Midir. The Dagda confided the circumstances of Angus's birth to Midir, and asked that Midir pretend to be Angus' father.

Midir was happy to oblige. His hall was at Bri Leith, not far from Uisnech, and he and his wife Fuamnach had scores of foster children. Over the long years of their marriage, the love Midir felt for Fuamnach had waned, though she still cared as deeply for him as she ever did. As their marriage grew ever more strained, Midir poured more of his love and attention into his foster children, seeing that they had the best of everything and training them in the many arts he knew.

Angus arrived at Bri Leith and settled into his life there. Of all the children in Midir's care, he soon loved Angus best of all. The boy proved to be as warm-hearted as his father, quick to laugh and quick to forgive, a natural leader among the children. He settled disputes among the hot-headed boys. He took care of the quieter children, sensing when to encourage them to join the games and when to leave them in peace. Wherever he went, his birds flew around his head, causing the smaller children to gaze at him in wonder.

Everyone at Bri Leith adored Angus.

Everyone except for Triath.

Triath had been the leader of Bri Leith's children before Angus came along. He was older, taller and stronger than Angus, and did not tolerate rivals. Triath did his best to mock and belittle Angus, but while his former subjects feared him, they loved Angus. It became clear to Triath that he had lost his place to Angus, and would not win it back anytime soon.

Triath complained to his father, a warrior in Midir's court. His father would not hear it.

'If one of your companions is stronger than you are, make yourself his friend and things will go well for you,' said Triath's father. 'Make him your enemy and you will only suffer. That is the way among men young and old.'

'But he is not stronger than me. I am the better fighter.'

'I have watched this boy, son. I have taken his measure. You are a born warrior, but he is a born king, whoever his true parents might be. Learn your place and you will know peace.'

'What do you mean, whoever his true parents might be? He is Midir and Fuamnach's son.'

Triath's father halted, his mouth hanging open. Midir had put it about that Angus was his own son, but the men of the court had known that to be false, and guessed that Angus was an orphan. He glared at his son.

'I should not have said that. Keep it to yourself.'

'Angus... Angus Óg is an orphan?'

'Say that again and I will beat you black and blue, boy.'

Triath bowed to his father and ran outside, suppressing a grin. This would be worth a hundred beatings.

IT WAS A CRISP AUTUMN MORNING. Wet brown leaves blew across the meadows beneath a grey sky. The children of Bri Leith had come outside and were choosing their game for the day.

'I think we should play at battle,' said Triath.

'Or we could go into the forest,' said Angus. 'The fallen leaves will be good for making dens.'

'Yes!' said many of the children. 'Let's go into the forest!'

Triath had been waiting like a coiled viper ever since his father's slip. In that moment, he struck.

'Why should we do what you say, Angus? You're only an orphan.'

Some of the children laughed, thinking it a joke. Others stared in shock at Angus. Was it true?

They looked to Angus for guidance, but Angus was speechless. He stared at Triath, pieces falling into place in his mind. He had grown up knowing Midir as his father, yet he did not remotely resemble Midir. And more than that... hearing Triath's words, he somehow knew they were true.

Midir was not his father. Fuamnach was not his mother. He was an orphan.

A tear ran down Angus' cheek.

A young boy laughed.

Another joined him, then another, then another. Many of them felt sorry for Angus, but children are herd animals. Soon they were all laughing at him, and Triath laughed loudest of all.

'Out of here, orphan!' he cried. 'Out of here, orphan!'

The other children laughed harder as they took up the chant. The balance of power had shifted; Triath was their leader again and they knew they must obey him.

'Out of here, orphan! Out of here, orphan! Out of here, orphan!'

Angus fled in tears.

MIDIR WAS at breakfast when Angus came crashing into the hall and ran to his side.

'Tell them it's not true!' said Angus, rubbing his red eyes. His birds flew about him in slow circles, singing sadly.

'Tell what to whom?' said Midir.

'Tell the children I'm not an orphan, and you are my father.'

Midir sighed and put down his cup.

'Sit down, lad. It's time we had a talk.'

So Midir at last told Angus the truth of his birth. Angus learnt that he was the son of the Dagda, High King of Eriu, and Boann of Brú na Bóinne. He learnt that his father had loved a woman who was not his own wife, and thus kept Angus' existence secret. 'But I love you no less for it,' finished Midir.

'I... I would like to meet my mother and father.'

'I think that you should,' said Midir. 'I will take you to see your father first.'

MIDIR AND ANGUS left Bri Leith that day. They travelled south and came to the Dagda's hall beneath the Hill of Uisnech that evening.

As usual, a feast was underway. Midir and Angus were shown in and brought before the Dagda's throne.

The Dagda looked down upon Midir and the boy with his blue eyes, his golden hair and four birds flying about his head.

He got to his feet. The hall hushed.

'Some truths must linger in darkness,' he said, 'until it is time to let them see light. Thus I declare that this young man is Angus Óg, my son.'

There was a moment of stunned silence; then rapturous applause. Angus ran to his father and embraced him, burying his head in the Dagda's beard.

Midir stayed and partook of the feast for a few days. It pained him to lose Angus, but seeing father and son reunited gave him great joy. Yet there was still the matter of Elcmar.

'You must have given thought,' he said to the Dagda one evening, 'as to how Elcmar will react to this news, and to what lands the boy will call his own.'

'I have,' said the Dagda, waving Angus over.

'Son,' he said, 'I know you are keen to meet your mother, and are aware of the complications that will arise when you do. I have considered this and determined our best course of action. Listen carefully.'

SAMHAIN CAME A FEW WEEKS LATER. It was the custom among the Tuatha to never bear arms or go to war at Samhain, and instead to celebrate the night with feasting.

Elcmar let it be known that he would hold a Samhain feast at Brú na Bóinne. The day came and guests streamed in through the unguarded gates.

By the light of the moon, when the hall was already full and the feast well underway, Angus Óg passed through the gates of Brú na Bóinne.

He made his way down torchlit tunnels to a vast feasting hall far beneath the ground. Looking around, he saw everything was as it should be. People ate and drank, danced and played games, fed scraps to hounds that ruled beneath the tables. At the high table, sitting beside her husband, Angus saw Boann.

His mother.

Angus crossed the hall and approached Elcmar and Boann.

'What do you want?' said Elcmar. Boann, meanwhile,

looked at Angus and froze. She would have known her son anywhere, even without his escort of songbirds.

A wolf makes its kill then defends its kill, the Dagda had said to Angus. *If a lord of the sidhe is fool enough to be tricked, he deserves to be tricked. Especially an oaf like Elcmar.*

With blinding speed, Angus drew the sword hidden beneath his cloak and held it at Elcmar's throat.

Screams rent the air. The hall fell silent.

'Shame on you,' said Elcmar, his voice hoarse. 'It is not our custom to come armed to a Samhain feast.'

'That is true,' said Angus. 'It is also true that red blood will spill upon your red cloak, unless you meet my one simple request.'

'What is that?'

'That you lend me your hall and its lordship for a day and a night.'

Elcmar eyed the golden-haired, blue-eyed youth. He saw both gentleness and ferocity in those eyes, like fire which gives warmth and light yet can also burn and destroy. The boy would make good on his threat.

'Very well,' hissed Elcmar. 'From tomorrow morning, for a day and a night, you shall be lord of Brú na Bóinne.'

Angus nodded. He withdrew his sword, sheathed it and left the hall.

He returned the next morning. Elcmar waited on the riverbank.

'Take care of my hall, young one,' he said to Angus. 'Though you won it dishonourably, I hope you have enough honour to do at least that.'

Angus watched him go, then joined the feast.

He took Elcmar's seat beside Boann, who hugged him fiercely. Some gave him dark looks, thinking that his trick had been dishonourable, yet others admired his boldness. As for Boann, she could pretend no longer.

'My boy,' she said to him, loud enough for all at their table to hear. 'My beautiful Angus.'

'Yes, mother,' he said. 'It is me, Angus Óg, your son by the Dagda.'

She wept, then laughed, then embraced him, as the feasters looked on and wondered and whispered. It did not take long for the news to spread, and soon everyone wondered what would happen upon Elcmar's return.

ELCMAR CAME at dawn the following day. He entered the hall and found Angus sitting in his seat, Boann at his side. She gazed at Angus, enraptured like everyone else, while he and his birds sang in harmony.

It seemed to Elcmar that Angus had claimed his wife as well as his hall.

The song finished. The feasters applauded, then hushed as they noticed Elcmar.

He crossed the hall.

'A day and a night have passed,' said Elcmar in an iron voice. 'It is time for you to leave, young usurper.'

'A day and a night have indeed passed, Lord Elcmar,' said Angus. 'But it is not time for me to give up Brú na Bóinne.'

'You said—'

'I said I would take Brú na Bóinne for a day and a night. And is the passage of time not made up of days and nights?'

Elcmar stared at Angus, slack-jawed. In the Irish language, to say 'a day and a night' can also mean 'day and night'.

'That does not mean... you know perfectly well what I understood...'

Laughter broke out as the company realised that Angus had tricked Elcmar, making himself lord of Brú na Bóinne in perpetuity. It was a cruel trick, but a fine trick all the same.

'Hush,' said Angus, getting to his feet. 'There is no call to mock this man. We all at times fall prey to one with wits more agile than our own.'

'More agile...' Elcmar drew his sword.

Angus drew his own sword with a practiced grace. It was clear to everyone who would win a duel between these two, including Elcmar.

'You are despicable,' said Elcmar. 'You have stolen my hall and my lordship from me, and by the looks of it, the love of my wife as well.'

Gales of laughter met that, which Angus silenced with a glare.

'I love this woman,' he said, 'but not as you do. She is my mother, and the Dagda is my father.'

Elcmar gasped. He fell to his knees. There was no laughter

now; Elcmar's pain and rage were so great that everyone feared what might come of them.

'Then I shall go to your father,' he said. 'For as low a creature as he is, the Dagda is our High King. He must settle this.'

ELCMAR AND ANGUS both set out for Uisnech that day, travelling separately. In the last hours of day they stood before the Dagda, who listened from his throne as Elcmar made his petition.

'The Mac Óg is indeed my son,' said the Dagda. 'And you are right that he and I both tricked you. Yet a man must carry his wits even when he carries no sword. I shall uphold Angus' claim to the lordship of Brú na Bóinne.

'That said, you have suffered greatly since we crossed paths, and this shames me. I would not see you without a home. I thus grant you the lordship of Cleitech, its hall and all the lands about it. You shall rule there in perpetuity, but not with Boann at your side; she shall remain at Brú na Bóinne with her son.'

Elcmar's face went purple; his sword-hand trembled. Yet after a few moments he gave a long sigh and bowed to the Dagda. He left the hall, not meeting Angus' eyes.

'My dealings with that man are no credit to my name,' said the Dagda to Angus. 'He is a fool and deserves to be fooled, or so many of our people would say. I am not so sure, yet I fooled him anyway. Alas, I think I sat better on the harper's chair than on the throne.'

'I am grateful for the lordship of Brú na Bóinne,' said Angus. 'I will try to rule it well, and to be a good man.'

'You shall be a great man,' said the Dagda, meeting Angus' eyes and smiling. 'Far better than your father. I see that you will be a hero to our people and even to the Gaels. You shall protect those in need of protection, and surpass me in bringing song and laughter and love to the world.'

So the Dagda spoke words of blessings to his son; words which proved true in the years to come.

Angus returned to Brú na Bóinne, where he has ruled from that day to this one. If you go to Eriu and visit the tomb of Newgrange, listen carefully for the sound of feasting in Angus' hall far beneath your feet.[1]

23

MIDIR & ÉTAÍN: PART I

A ngus Óg was Lord of Brú na Bóinne. He was famous both for the splendour of his hall and the cunning turn by which he had won it. Angus held the finest feasts in Eriu, and among those who regularly attended his feasts was Midir.

Midir took immense pride in seeing Angus flourish, yet he missed the lad keenly. So he comforted himself by visiting Brú na Bóinne, staying for a few days, a few weeks, a few months; it mattered little to a sidhe.

It was on one such journey that Midir met Étaín.

MIDIR WAS TRAVELLING on foot from Bri Leith to Brú na Bóinne. As he walked, he took note of the changes wrought on the country by the Gaels. Land cleared for cultivation, expanding settlements, red cattle covering the hills.

It was early in spring. The sky was blue, the air full of birdsong. Midir was passing through a woodland carpeted with bluebells when he heard voices ahead of him.

Midir turned a bend in the road and saw a sight that would change the course of his life.

A group of women sat on a carpet of bluebells between the road and riverbank. They were laughing at some jest, and then fell silent as one of their number broke into song.

The birds ceased singing. The breeze ceased to blow; even the rushing river was silent. Midir forgot to breathe as he listened. He had never heard such a voice; it was apples and honey, starlight and wine, dark ale and the crashing of thunder over mountains.

Midir fell in love as he listened; a love that would last until the end of days. Back in Bri Leith, his wife Fuamnach let out a cry of pain, though she knew not why.

The song ended and Midir approached the party.

'I hope I do not intrude,' he said to the singer, a golden-haired and blue-eyed young woman, 'but your song delighted me, and I would know your name.'

'My name is Étaín,' she said with a wide smile.

'And mine is Midir, Lord of Bri Leith. I am on my way to Brú na Bóinne, home of my once-foster son, Angus Óg. Angus delights in music, and I would do ill if I failed to invite you all to join me.'

'I have long dreamed of feasting at Angus Óg's hall,' said Étaín, her eyes full of youthful excitement. She looked hopefully at her companions, who nodded at her. 'We will gladly join you,' she said.

So Midir, Étaín and her companions travelled onward together. As they walked, Midir and Étaín conversed. They went on conversing as they approached Brú na Bóinne, and continued at Angus' table. Fine food went unattended on their plates; when they danced, they danced together.

The march of time is barely a whisper in the halls of Danu's children. A full year passed in which Midir and Étaín stayed together at Brú na Bóinne, only leaving to walk in the woods and on the hills together. They fell in love on those first days and lay together soon afterwards. As the year went by, their love only deepened.

Yet Midir knew that eventually he must return home.

'I would gladly stay here with you forever,' he said to Étaín as they walked beneath the sun of a new spring. 'But I have my own hall, my own lands and my own people to care for. I must return to Bri Leith.'

'And to your wife,' said Étaín, shame writ on her face. Every day she knew the guilt of lying with another woman's husband, yet still she stayed with Midir. She was young and had never known love before. To deny herself his touch seemed utterly impossible to her.

'Yes.'

'Then we must part,' said Étaín.

'No.'

Étaín looked at Midir, perplexed.

'Though I must return home, I will not be parted from you. Come to Bri Leith and live there as my guest.'

'Live with you and your wife, as your "guest"? Fuamnach—'

'Fuamnach will see that I have brought a talented singer to our hall. My wife and I are not poor farmers huddled in a hut. Our hall is home to hundreds. You will be one among many and Fuamnach will scarcely notice you.'

'And you? Will you remember me as you sit with your wife at table and kiss her at night?'

'No matter where I am or what hour it is, the only face I will ever see is yours.'

'And you think you wife will not notice this.'

'Would you prefer that we part?'

Étaín was silent.

'No,' she said eventually. 'I will come to Bri Leith.'

A SERVANT RUSHED into Fuamnach's chamber with the news.

'Lord Midir is on his way here,' he said.

Fuamnach's heart lurched like a drunkard at sea in a storm. It had been over a year since Midir left. She knew how deeply he loved Angus, so she took no issue with his long visits to Brú na Bóinne. Yet this one had been so long. She had keenly missed her husband's touch, and her dreams had been dark on so many nights. Often she had awoken to evil whispers in her mind, telling her exactly how Midir passed his time.

No, she would convince herself come the day. *My husband is a good man. It is a different kind of love that keeps him away; he would never betray me.*

Yet in the darkness, those whispers became a web of night-shade, a choking prison with no corner to hide in.

And now he had returned.

'Sweep the floors,' she said. 'Stoke the fires and bring in fresh flowers from the meadows. Let these halls look no less sweet than the home of Angus.'

Her orders were obeyed. Soon Midir approached the gates where she stood awaiting him.

A beautiful young woman walked beside him.

'My dear Fuamnach,' said Midir, stepping forward and embracing his wife. 'I am so pleased to see you after my long absence.'

'And I you,' said Fuamnach. She looked pointedly at the woman who fidgeted at his side.

'Ah!' said Midir, as if he had forgotten the woman was there. 'This is Étaín. She arrived at Angus' hall while I was there, and swiftly won fame with her singing. Indeed, Angus' guests would hear no other singer while she was present. I thought that she might stay with us a while and brighten our evenings with her songs.'

'I see,' said Fuamnach.

Silence fell. Fuamnach watched as Midir and Étaín looked everywhere but at one another, their faces reddening.

'Well, you must be tired from your journey, Étaín,' she said eventually. 'We have many fine rooms available. Allow me to show you to one.'

'Thank you,' said Étaín. With a hurried glance at Midir, she followed Fuamnach through the gates, down winding corridors and into a guest room.

'I hope this will do?' said Fuamnach.

'Oh yes,' said Étaín, 'this is lovely. You are very kind.'

'And will you rut with my husband here or in my bed?'

Étaín's mouth fell open. 'I...'

'Midir always had a fine tongue. He thinks he can convince anyone of anything. I think he genuinely believed I would accept this charade! But a woman sees much, and a wife most of all. You should have known better than he, Étaín. Was it lust or love that clouded your mind?'

'Please... I didn't mean...'

Étaín fell silent. She backed away as Fuamnach reached into her cloak and pulled out a wand of red rowan.

'You are young and weak-willed,' said Fuamnach. 'It is Midir I should punish, not you. But I am love's fool too.'

Fuamnach lunged forward and struck Étaín with her wand. She spoke a spell and Étaín screamed as water dripped from her nose, her hair, her hands and chin. Her screaming grew louder as the dripping became a pouring; her whole body was becoming water. Étaín's fingers dripped to nothing, then her hands, her arms. Her screaming stopped as her tongue, lips and teeth turned to liquid and poured onto the floor. She splashed to the ground, reduced to bare bones in a few moments, and even her bones melted like icicles in spring.

All that remained of Étaín was a heap of clothes lying in a puddle of water. Fuamnach lit a fire in the hearth, burned Étaín's clothes and departed.

THE DAY PASSED QUIETLY at Bri Leith. Fuamnach walked with her husband, catching him up on all he had missed. Midir desperately wanted to check on Étaín, but he made a point of spending time with his wife.

Meanwhile, in a guest room, before a flickering fire, ripples appeared in a puddle of water.

The water bubbled, steamed and became fire. That fire became a fly, with glittering red jewels for eyes and wings bedecked with intricate patterns of colour.

The fly flew into the air and around the room. As it flew, sweet music and fragrances emanated from it as seeds fly from a dandelion in a summer breeze.

Étaín flew about the room for a while, accustoming herself to her new form. When evening came, she flew beneath the door, down the corridor and through the hallways of Bri Leith, following the sounds and scents of feasting.

MIDIR WAS SITTING at table with Fuamnach. The feasting hall was packed to the rafters to celebrate Midir's return.

As Midir sipped his mead and watched the dancers, a fly began buzzing about him.

He was about to bat it away when he noticed a peculiar scent, like a garden of fresh flowers after spring rain. He heard a wondrous music and realised that it emanated from the fly. It flew down and landed on his finger, and he noticed its jewelled eyes and enamelled wings.

Midir cried out, loud enough that the musicians stopped

playing. The dancers stopped dancing, the feasters stopped feasting and all turned to face him.

The Lord of Bri Leith held his finger close before his face, inhaling deeply of the fly's fragrance. It was a fragrance he knew.

'Étaín,' he whispered.

He turned to face his wife.

'You did this.'

Fuamnach leapt to her feet, sending her chair clattering to the floor behind her.

'Yes, husband. I did this. I took your harlot and changed her shape. Yet I see that she has taken another shape, and even as a filthy fly she ensnares you.' Fuamnach's voice quivered as she went on. Though her voice was angry, there was pleading in her eyes as she said, 'Show me that you are my husband, Midir. Squash her.'

Midir shook his head. 'I am no husband of yours.'

Fuamnach stared at Midir, open-jawed, seemingly waiting for him to change his mind. But he did not; he only stared at the fly which had come to rest on his hand. So Fuamnach ran to her chambers, packed a bag and left Bri Leith.

MIDIR REMAINED at Br Leith with Étaín. She kept close to him in her fly form, and he gave orders that no fly was to be harmed, lest she be hurt by accident. There was little need; no one could mistake Étaín for an ordinary fly. Besides, she never left Midir's side. She went everywhere with him, buzzing about him, trailing beautiful scents and music in her wake. Though the people of Bri Leith felt sorry for Fuamnach, they could not help but be charmed by Étaín the fly.

As for Midir, it hurt him deeply to see Étaín that way. Yet he was relieved that he need no longer hide his love. He found that despite her new form, his love for Étaín was undiminished. Though they could not talk or dance or lie together at night, her music and scent brought joy and peace to the deepest reaches of his heart. He found satisfaction in protecting Étaín from a world that was so dangerous to one so small.

Midir succeeded in keeping Étaín safe. But only for a while.

FUAMNACH WENT to stay with her father, a druid named Bresal. It was Bresal who first taught her magic.

'I do not wish to speak of Midir,' she said to her father when she arrived at his deep-forest hall. 'I ask you not to seek knowledge of him.'

Bresal agreed. His dealings were with the unseen world; the doings of Tuatha mattered little to him. So he asked no questions, and seasons passed as Fuamnach remained at her father's hall, her heart slowly healing. Yet the boundaries of Bresal's dreams were porous, and knowledge would sometimes come to him uninvited. So he saw one night that Midir flaunted his love for a fly, shaming Fuamnach, and he was angered.

At breakfast the next morning, as the snow fell outside, he told his daughter what he had seen.

'You weaken yourself by letting Midir away with this,' he said. 'For the sake of your honour, you must act.'

'I would rather remain here in peace,' said Fuamnach.

'Then my door is closed to you,' said Bresal. 'I do not shelter cravens. You have been hurt, daughter, but you are strong. You have the will for vengeance and the tools to enact it. Go forth and put right what is wrong.'

Fuamnach looked into her father's eyes; there was no uncertainty there. Perhaps she could have that peace for herself.

'Very well,' she said. 'I leave today for Bri Leith.'

FUAMNACH TRUDGED through snow as she walked the wintry roads to Bri Leith. She spoke words of power to warm her body and wished they would warm her heart.

At length, she saw the hills of home before her. Her husband's servants watched the roads and, sure enough, she soon spied a figure on the road ahead of her.

The figure drew closer. It was Midir.

As Fuamnach neared him, she smelt a sweet smell and heard subtle music. She choked back a sob. So he would not even show her the courtesy of leaving his fly behind.

He would regret that.

They stopped a few paces from one another, snow falling softly about them.

'What brings you to Bri Leith?' said Midir.

'I learned that you still keep that creature at your side. You dishonour me in doing so, Midir, and I will not stand for it.'

'It is no business of yours who keeps me company.'

'I am your wife.'

'Not since you worked evil magic on one I care for.'

'On your "guest", you mean? The whore whom you bedded for a year then paraded before me?'

'Love commands and the heart obeys. Why fight love? Look what love drove you to do, Fuamnach. Are you so innocent?'

'You seem happy enough.'

'I am happier now than I ever was with you.'

Fuamnach took a step back. With those words, every memory of her former happiness was shattered. Midir saw it.

'I am sorry. I went too far. I did not mean—'

'Yes, you did,' said Fuamnach. 'You meant to hurt me, husband, and you succeeded. Now it is my turn.'

Before Midir could say another word, she drew her wand from her cloak. Drawing on her power and that of her father, Fuamnach summoned a storm.

The sky howled. Trees bent double and crashed to the ground. Midir backed away from Fuamnach as Étaín buzzed furiously, searching for a pocket among his clothing to shelter in. Yet she was not quick enough. Fuelled by Fuamnach's pain and fury, the summoned storm was immense. Lightning split the sky and thunder shook the earth.

Midir was thrown to the ground. Étaín shot into the sky. Spinning around and around, she soon forgot everything but the howling of the wind and the crashing of lightning as Fuamnach's storm carried her across Eriu, away from Midir.

FUAMNACH'S STORM roved Eriu like a wild creature released from a century in chains. Tuatha and Gaels watched for its coming and dashed indoors when it darkened the horizon. After it passed, their peace resumed. Yet Étaín knew no peace. All she knew was sorrow, and the battering of the storm.

There came a day when the storm entered Leinster and passed over Brú na Bóinne. Angus felt the storm's coming as a charge upon his skin. While all others fled indoors, he strode outdoors and onto the hill to experience its power. He did not know that Fuamnach was the source of the storm, nor that Étaín had become a fly and was trapped within it.

The storm reached Brú na Bóinne. Angus met it with his arms outstretched, his cloak and golden hair flapping about him. His birds had remained indoors. The booming and crashing and screaming of the storm was a magnificent music to him... yet he heard another music within it. A melody, faint, yet wild and frenzied.

Angus strained his ears. He shielded his eyes from the lashing rain and searched the sky.

There was a tiny creature riding the storm.

Angus spoke words of magic that pulled the creature down to earth. He reached out and snatched it from the air.

Angus cupped the creature in his hands. It was a fly, with red jewels for eyes and enamelled wings. The music he had heard was emanating from the fly, and as he held it, the frenzied music took on a new, calmer tone. A sweet fragrance filled Angus' nostrils.

'What manner of magical being are you?' he asked.

Instantly, images filled his mind. Angus saw the whole

story; he learnt that this was Étaín, the lover of Midir, and knew all her troubles.

Carefully closing his hands over Étaín, he carried her into Brú na Bóinne.

ÉTAÍN'S PLIGHT moved Angus deeply. He carried her to his own chambers, stoked his fire and sat with her, singing or speaking soft words, promising that her troubles were over. Étaín responded in the only ways she could, with sweet scents and sounds. Soon her music and Angus' singing were entwined like the necks of swans in spring.

Angus let it be known that the jewelled fly was Étaín, that she was his guest and that all who crossed his threshold should see to her safety. No fly was to be harmed within a league of Brú na Bóinne. Yet he worried that even this might not be enough to protect her. Moreover, Angus was concerned not only for her safety but her happiness. So Angus ordered the building of a little room of glass and crystal on the uppermost floor of his underground hall. Open to the world outside, it was bright with sunlight and fragrant with freshly gathered flowers. Once it was completed, he brought Étaín there and proclaimed it her home.

Étaín remained within the chamber. Time passed and it seemed to Angus that Étaín was happy there, her heart healing day by day.

But what of Midir?

Angus guessed that Étaín must miss Midir terribly. Yet if Midir came to Brú na Bóinne and reunited with Étaín, Fuamnach would surely hear of it. Midir was sure to visit Brú na Bóinne at some point though, and when he did so he would learn of Étaín's presence. He probably thought her dead, and suffered greatly for it.

Angus decided that the wisest course of action was to bring Midir and Fuamnach together and attempt a reconciliation. Otherwise, Étaín would never truly be safe, and none of them would truly be happy. For better or worse, Angus tended to see the best in people, and he believed that even after all that had happened, he could bring about peace between Midir, Fuamnach and Étaín.

So Angus sent out invitations for Midir and Fuamnach to join him at Brú na Bóinne. He let them both know that he had found Étaín, and that she now lived under his protection.

His messengers returned; the invitations had been accepted. On the appointed day, Midir and Fuamnach arrived and sat down at opposite ends of a long table, with Angus between them. Étaín remained out of sight in her glass bower.

Angus looked from husband to wife. Each regarded the other with unconcealed contempt.

'I see that you both hold your grievances close,' said Angus. 'Yet you have shown faith in me by coming here, so I hold out hope. You have also shown that you desire the same thing as me; that we find a way forward. No heart is the better for harbouring hatred, especially where love lived before.'

'Hatred can be a poison,' said Fuamnach, 'that leeches away life. Yet it can also sustain life when there is nothing else to live for. So it has supported me since my husband betrayed me.'

'If you wish to live as a creature of hate, you are free to do so,' said Midir. 'Yet you have made your own misery mine, and Étaín's too.'

'What did you expect, husband? That I would welcome her with open arms? Did you think me stupid enough not to see through your pretence? Or was I supposed to play along, feigning sleep while you crept from our bed each night?'

'I loved you,' said Midir, 'and I loved Étaín too. I love her still. I could not deny what I felt for her, and why should I? Why must a heart's endless depths of love flow only in one direction? Yes, you can dam a river for a while. But whether it takes a day or a thousand days, every dam will burst in time. So it is with love.'

'And so it is with hatred,' said Fuamnach, 'and vengeance. I took my vengeance upon you and I will not regret it, not until the end of days.'

'Perhaps we should halt for a little while,' said Angus.

Fuamnach took a deep breath. 'Yes,' she said. 'I think I will go outside and get some air.'

Angus nodded and Fuamnach left.

As soon as she was out of sight, Fuamnach began to search Brú na Bóinne. She moved quietly. She kept out of sight and out of earshot. Eventually, she came to a glass room open to the sunlight, and heard sweet music coming from within it.

'It is good to see you again, Angus,' said Midir. 'Even under such circumstances.'

'And you,' said Angus. 'It pained me greatly to learn what

you have suffered; though I must say that having Étaín here has given me joy.'

'I have been a fool,' said Midir. 'I lied to myself; I told myself everything would be as I wished it. In doing so, I caused great pain to the two women I loved most.'

'Who does not act a fool when in love? It brings forth our deepest passions and darkest shadows. Yet you are here, Fuamnach is here, and we will find a way forward.'

'I am not so sure,' said Midir. 'It seems there is no room for forgiveness in Fuamnach's heart.'

'There must be. Otherwise why did she come here?'

Silence fell as they realised Fuamnach should have returned by then.

They leapt from their chairs just as thunder shook the hall. Cups crashed to the floor; sleeping hounds leapt up and set to barking.

Angus ran from the hall. Midir followed.

They arrived at the sun bower.

Fuamnach stood there, surrounded by shattered glass, bleeding from a dozen places where flying glass and crystal had struck her. Storm winds howled and Étaín was nowhere to be seen.

Fuamnach laughed as she saw them; but not for long. Angus drew his sword and cut off her head.

MIDIR REMAINED WITH ANGUS, crushed by grief, while Étaín rode the storm winds again. Though Fuamnach was dead, her storm did not dissipate. For hundreds of years it wandered Eriu. Being an immortal child of Danu, Étaín lived for hundreds of years within it.

Life among the deep-dwelling Tuatha remained the same. For the Gaels, generations lived and died in the storm, which was a part of the tapestry of their world. Yet in time, it finally lost its power, and Étaín found herself drifting down towards the ground.

So long had Étaín lived within the storm that it is hard to say how she felt to be free, or if she still had the capacity for thought or feeling at all. But it is known that, whether seeking sustenance or drawn by warmth and merriment, she entered the hall of a Gaelic man named Etar, who was holding a feast.

Étaín flew unnoticed into the hall. As she flew over the head of Etar's wife, her strength gave out, her wings ceased to shiver and she dropped like a tiny stone into the woman's cup.

Etar's wife, who was named Clodagh, lifted her cup to her lips and took a drink.

She set her cup down and a moment later, an ancient knowing unfurled in her mind. She turned to her husband.

'Etar?'

'Yes?'

'I am with child.'

24

MIDIR & ÉTAÍN: PART II

Clodagh's utterance proved true. Nine months after the feast, she gave birth to a baby girl.

She named the child Étaín.

Étaín grew up as befitted a lord and lady's daughter. Her mother and father doted on her; servants saw to her every need. She had a kind and gentle nature which her lavish upbringing could not spoil, and some said she made them think of the sidhe.

There were few Gaels in Eriu at that time who could claim knowledge of the Tuatha Dé Danaan. More than a thousand years had passed since the Gaels drove the Tuatha into their underground halls. Though there had been mingling and even marriage between the races over the years, the Tuatha had grown steadily more distant as time passed. Most Gaels knew them only through stories; many claimed they did not exist at all. Eriu belonged to mortals.

ERIU WAS RULED at that time by the High King Eochaid Airem. He had come to the throne at a young age and had enjoyed every day of his reign. Everyone he met fawned over him and flattered him. He hunted every day, feasted every evening and a different woman warmed his bed every night.

Eochaid's allies tolerated his indulgences. He had a likeable way about him and was quick to put down any threat to his reign, charging to the battlefield as eagerly as to the feast. He was clever enough to let his advisors take care of tasks that ill-suited him, so the country was peaceful under his rule.

There came a time, though, when the other kings of Eriu began to say that Eochaid had feasted, flirted and fornicated long enough. It was time he took a wife and produced an heir.

Eochaid listened to the lesser kings and promised to consider their words. In truth, he gave them not a moment's thought. He had lived as he did for so long that he could not imagine another life, and convinced himself that things could go on as they were.

When the kings saw that Eochaid was playing them for fools, they started meeting in secret and muttering against him. A king with no heir was vulnerable; a vulnerable kingdom would sooner or later be attacked. Was it not then their duty to make Eochaid see reason, by force if necessary?

A day came when Eochaid invited the lesser kings to a feast. Each of them refused his invitation.

'What is this? Why did the kings of Banba shun me?' Eochaid asked his chief advisor.

'It is as I have said before,' said his advisor, 'many times. Eriu is insecure when the High King has no wife or heir. The lesser kings well know it. Even if no outsider attacks us, I fear that in time they will move against you. This refusal is but the first breath of rebellion.'

'So I, High King of Eriu, must obey the wishes of men beneath me?'

'You are a ruler and a servant, sire. The highest and lowest of men.'

Eochaid rolled his eyes. He drummed his fingers on the arm of his throne. 'Very well,' he said after a time. 'I will marry.'

His advisor looked set to cry with relief.

'I will marry the most beautiful maiden in Eriu, whoever she is. Find her for me. Scour the country from Munster to Ulster. Bring her here and I promise you this: heirs shall be in no short supply.'

EOCHAID'S ADVISOR deemed it best to accept his demand. He sent out riders to every corner of the kingdom, from the Aran Isles to Ratho, from Connemara to the Mountains of Mourne. These riders were tasked with visiting every single dwelling-place of the Gaels, from grand halls to fishing huts and mountain bothies. Every young woman they met, they judged her beauty. Each rider was well familiar with Eochaid's tastes.

This survey went on for three seasons before a rider named Hogan took the road to Etar's hall. Beneath a bright spring sun he approached its door, dismounted and knew at once that his journey had ended.

A golden fountain stood on the grass outside the hall. Four golden birds perched on its rim, and standing beside it was the most beautiful woman Hogan had ever seen. Her hair was spun gold, her eyes gleamed like sapphires and more than that, she had an air about her which the messenger had never encountered. He felt a peace in his heart as he looked at her, as if he had stood all his days beside a deep, clear pool but only now entered its waters. A sweet fragrance filled his nostrils; he almost fancied he heard faint music. If he had encountered this maiden in some deep forest glade, he would have sworn she was a woman of the sidhe.

'Greetings,' he said. 'My name is Hogan, and I come on behalf of the High King Eochaid Airem. He wishes to marry the most beautiful woman in Fodhla, and I believe I have found her. Will you tell me your name, and will you consent to marry the High King?'

The young woman studied him before replying.

'My name is Étaín, and I will marry the High King if my mother and father deem it wise.'

So Hogan waited as she went into the hall. She was not gone long.

'It is done,' she said. 'My parents and I will accompany you to Tara, and I shall marry the High King Eochaid Airem.'

HOGAN SENT word ahead of him to Tara. By the time they arrived, preparations for a royal wedding were complete. Eochaid's chief druid bound his hand to that of Étaín, and Étaín was named High Queen.

Life at Tara was quieter after that. To the surprise and relief of those close to him, Eochaid did not tire of his wife, nor did he find excuses to leave her at home while he lusted after excitement and adventure. On the contrary; Eochaid was enamoured of Étaín, to the extent that some whispered she must be a sorceress and he under her spells. As soon as the hunt, the council meeting or any other duty or pleasure was done with, Eochaid went straight to Étaín.

As for Étaín, she found Eochaid to her liking, but Tara less so. It was too busy for her tastes. She left daily to walk in the woods and wild places, or to shelter in quiet shoreside caves. Peace and tranquility were ever a balm to her heart. She did not remember the life she had lived before, either as a woman of the sidhe or a fly trapped in a storm. Yet she knew she was different from those around her, and always she yearned for quiet and stillness.

Eochaid embraced his wife's ways. He joined her sometimes on her wanderings, but also allowed her ample time alone. With Étaín as queen, Eriu grew more peaceful. The Gaels attended to the music of rainfall and lapwings, lowing cattle and corncrakes. It is said that a delicate fragrance rode the winds to Eriu's every corner, faint yet sublime in its sweetness.

So passed the first years of Eochaid and Étaín's rule, until Eriu's serenity was broken.

EOCHAID HAD A BROTHER NAMED AILIL. He first met Étaín at her wedding, and from the moment she first smiled at him he was lost. It seemed to Ailil that Étaín was his destiny; that the world had been made so he and Étaín could enjoy it together.

But his brother was in the way.

Ailil swore that if he had met Étaín first, they would have married, sharing a love the bards would sing of until the end of days. That love was in every drop of his blood. What warrior had the strength to defy such a foe?

Yet defy it he did. Eochaid was his older brother and closest friend. As boys they had been near inseparable. Eochaid had taught Ailil how to swing a sword, aim an arrow and talk to a woman. So years passed in which Ailil suffered in silence, telling himself he need only be patient. He had seen Eochaid cast aside so many women; surely his brother would tire of Étaín in time. Then Ailil could make his move.

But Eochaid never tired of Étaín, and Ailil tired of waiting.

EOCHAID WAS due to tour the country. On the day of his departure he strode among his travelling party, finding fault wherever he could. Everyone knew the cause of his anger: Étaín refused to go on such tours, and Eochaid loathed to be parted from her.

Eventually all was ready. It was time for Eochaid to depart, and he had not seen Ailil all morning.

'Where is my brother?' he asked. 'Why has he not come to see me off?'

'He did not wish to trouble you, King Eochaid,' said his chief advisor. 'Lord Ailil is sick. He said that if you asked, I was to tell you not to worry about him.'

'If he is sick enough not to see me off, then he is sick enough for me to worry,' said Eochaid, dismounting. He pushed through the crowd and made for his brother's chambers.

Eochaid found Ailil in bed. The hearth fire blazed yet Ailil shivered.

'I am sorry to darken your day,' said Ailil. 'Please, put me out of mind. I am...' he broke off into a fit of coughing. 'I am not so poorly as... as I may look.'

'I will not put my own brother out of mind,' said Eochaid, 'nor will I leave him without knowing he has the best care. Ailil, I will ask the High Queen herself to care for you until I return.'

'Thank... thank you, beloved brother.'

Eochaid kissed his brother's brow. Back at the gates, he agreed with Étaín that she would care for Ailil. He embraced her one last time and the royal retinue departed.

Étaín went to Ailil's chambers soon afterwards.

'Thank you for coming, Étaín,' said Ailil as she closed the door behind her.

'How could I not, when the brother of my beloved is sick?'

'I am not sick.'

Étaín frowned. She looked more closely at Ailil. Indeed, there was no change in his colouring nor in the tone of his voice. No sickness-stench pervaded the room. 'What is afoot here?' she asked.

'I lied to my brother. The only sickness afflicting me is love, and the love I bear is for you. I have lived with this love, which is both my dearest treasure and most terrible affliction, since the moment I saw you. I thought I would live this way until I died, for I would never betray my brother. But there has been a change in me, and now I see that if I do not have you, I will die.'

'That is not true.'

'It is true. I have seen it in my dreams. If you do not lie with me, I will die. Eochaid, your husband and your king, will lose his brother.'

'He would not have me do this.'

'Only once, Étaín. If you lie with me but once, I will be cured. So I saw in my vision. I swear it.'

Étaín studied Ailil. Was he telling the truth? She could not tell. The thought of lying with him disgusted her. But could she risk his death for the sake of her own discomfort? She had known Ailil for many years. He was a good man, or so she had always thought. He would not stoop so low as to lie about this, would he?

Whether he was false or not, it seemed to Étaín that her answer must be the same.

A tear ran down Étaín's cheek. 'Once I shall lie with you. Only once.'

'It is enough, Étaín. It is more than enough.' He pulled back the furs.

'No,' she said. 'Not here at Tara, where anyone could walk in and see us. Meet me at top of the An Cnoc Breac at dawn tomorrow.'

'Very well,' said Ailil. 'Tomorrow.'

Étaín left, closing the door behind her. Ailil grinned. His ruse had worked.

ÉTAÍN HARDLY SLEPT THAT NIGHT. Many times she told herself that she would not go; she would deny Ailil, whose story rung false. But what if Ailil spoke truly? And what would happen when Eochaid returned? How could she tell him what she had done? How could she not tell him?

So her thoughts went until the world turned towards morning.

Étaín rose from her bed and dressed. She left her chamber and stole out of a side gate in Tara's wall, heading east in the grey half-light.

Étaín reached the hilltop. Ailil had not arrived yet. She stood alone, the wind tossing her hair as the gates of dawn slowly opened.

Étaín looked towards Tara and waited.

She spied a man approaching from that direction.

He wore a dark grey cloak. A deep hood obscured his face. Ailil had come, his face in shadow, to take what had been promised.

And yet...

As the man made his way up the hill, Étaín noticed that he did not move the way Ailil moved. He seemed taller than Ailil and slimmer of build. It was hard to judge at that distance, amid the wraiths of morning mist. But there was something about this man which filled her with a deep knowing, as if he had stepped from a dream long forgotten and suddenly recalled.

This man was not Ailil.

He frightened her. It was as if he himself was a man of peace, yet he came as a messenger from a world of turmoil and torment. Étaín looked at him and felt a presence: that of a nightmare which had hovered for years at the edge of her awareness, just out of sight, as if she were a mouse and the nightmare a circling hawk.

Étaín turned and ran. She ran all the way to Tara, slipped in through the same side gate and returned to her bed.

Later that day she went to see Ailil.

'I was waiting for you atop the hill,' she said. 'But I saw a man in a grey cloak coming towards me. I grew afraid, for I knew he was not you.'

'It was me,' said Ailil from his bed, his expression dark. 'You have broken your promise to me.'

'Then I shall go to the hill again tomorrow,' said Étaín.

ÉTAÍN RETURNED to the hilltop the following morning.

She stood alone again. The wind was fierce and she shivered as she awaited Ailil's arrival.

Eventually she spied that same grey-cloaked and grey-hooded figure.

'It is Ailil,' she told herself. 'I will not run. I will do what must be done.'

Yet as the man climbed closer she felt the same certainty as on the previous day. This man was not Ailil. He was not even a man of the Gaels. He was something else, something she had not encountered before, something which terrified her.

She ran.

Ailil did not hide his anger when she visited his chamber.

'You break your promises to me and betray your husband. Would you let the High King lose his brother in order to spare yourself my embrace?'

'No! But I swear to you, the man I saw approaching me this morning was not you.'

'It was me! I told you as much yesterday, and you do not even bother to invent a new excuse. You are a dishonest woman as well as a heartless one.'

Étaín's fists tightened. 'I will see you tomorrow. In the name of Danu, I will not run.'

Ailil dismissed her with a wave.

A THIRD TIME, Étaín waited atop the hill.

The figure in grey broke the mists.

Étaín steeled herself. She waited as the figure climbed the slope. Though a thousand voices screamed at her to flee, Étaín stood rooted.

The figure in grey drew close.

He stood before her and pulled back his hood.

This man was not Ailil. He scarcely seemed a man at all, but rather a dream of a man visiting her from another world. It was the world she sought in her solitude and wanderings; a world glimpsed in the music of the harp, the words of poets, the play of sunlight on a silvery stream. A world she longed for and a world she feared.

This was no glimpse. As she gazed into his silver eyes, his stern face and his black and silver hair, she saw that he lived in that world; it was his body and breath.

The hawk was circling closer; she could hear its cry…

'Étaín,' he said. 'My name is Midir. I am a lord of the Tuatha Dé Danaan. Sit down with me, please. I have a story to tell you.'

They sat down together.

'Oh, Étaín. I have so much to tell you. Where do I begin? Since we last saw one another, a thousand years have passed. I lived for countless years before that. I have fought in battles that live on in legend; I have seen one age of the world make way for another. Yet when I look back on my life, the face that I see is yours. The face of a girl I met one spring day, among the bluebells on the road to Brú na Bóinne.'

So Midir began his tale. Sunlight crept into the sky as he told her of their days together in Angus' halls, their ill-fated journey home and Fuamnach's wrath.

Étaín listened in silence, entranced. The tale was the kind the bards wove, not the kind that anyone lived through. Yet for all its strangeness it spoke to her, lighting torches in the deep caverns of her mind and illuminating images scrawled on the stone there. Memories. Nightmares. Love.

'I lived without you for so long,' Midir was saying. 'I

watched the Gaels make our world their own and I cared not, for still I thought only of you. Acorns grew into oaks while I lingered in my hall, caring only to recall the music of your wings, the scent of your perfume, the touch of your hand in mine as we danced.

'And then, after so long, my fire spoke to me. I saw a vision in the flames; I saw that Fuamnach's storm had dissipated and that you walked on two feet once more. I learnt that you were birthed by Clodagh, had grown up and married the High King. So I came to Tara. I watched all that went on from the shadows. After your husband left for his tour, I wove spells upon Ailil's mind which would lead you here.'

He reached out and took her hand.

'And so here we are, at the turning of night and day. At the turning of one season of life to another, should you wish it.' Midir's and Étaín's eyes met. 'I know that you have been happy with Eochaid, Étaín. I do not wish to rob you of your happiness. But I can offer you so much more.

'More than safety and comfort. More than contentment. I can offer the world your heart longs for. You know that you do not belong among the Gaels; I can see it in your eyes. You will ever be the outsider here, for you are of the Tuatha Dé Danaan. If you come with me you will live among them once more. The peace, the joy, the world that your heart longs for; they shall be yours.

'And last of all, I offer you love. Not the kind you have with Eochaid, but the kind that lives in bard-song and on the blades of knives. A love that is beyond the heart of a Gael to hold.

'Be with me again, Étaín. Be where you belong. Dance as you once did. Love me as before and our love shall never die.'

Étaín looked away, out towards the sea and the rising sun. She did not speak for a long time.

'Now that I see you and hear your words,' she said eventually, 'I do remember my life among the Tuatha. I do remember your love.' She turned to face him. 'And I remember your foolishness. I remember you took me into your home and exposed me to your wife's vengeance. I remember that for every day I lived with you as a woman, I lived for another as your pet fly. And for every day I lived as your pet, I lived for ten years in torment, thrown back and forth on Fuamnach's storm.

'You think it was hard for you to spend an age of the world missing me? It was harder for me, up there in the freezing sky. I assure you of that.'

Étaín stood.

'No,' she said as Midir made to follow. 'I am leaving now. I am going to Tara, for I am a Gael. I am High Queen of the Gaels. I will await my husband there and never be false to him.'

'That life is a lie. You are a Tuatha—'

'I am a daughter of the Gaels! Whatever sorcery brought about my birth, I was born to a mother and father, I am married to my husband, and I am a mortal woman. Your tale is but a tale to me; your promises a fancy for cold winter nights. Leave me, Midir. Leave me to my life.'

Midir slowly stood. He bowed to her and pulled his hood over his head. 'Very well, Étaín of the Gaels. I wish you happiness.'

He turned, walked away and vanished into the mists.

Weeping, Étaín ran for home.

25

MIDIR & ÉTAÍN: PART III

It was Beltane, the first day of summer. Hundreds of Gaels had flocked to the plain beneath Tara to celebrate the coming of the sun. Gaily dressed couples danced to pipes and drums. In the oak groves, druids spoke binding words as young lovers twined their hands together.

Étaín walked alone through it all.

She had left Eochaid's side, feigning a headache. She wasn't sure if he had believed her. She didn't much care.

Things were different between them now. Ever since meeting Midir, Étaín had found it harder to be with her husband. She couldn't help but find fault with his every word and deed; his ways that had once charmed her now irritated her.

He had noticed the change in her and asked after its cause, but what to tell him? How could she say that she was over a thousand years old, that she had lived most of those years as a fly, and before that as one of the sidhe? He would think it madness. Perhaps it was. How could she trust a stranger who claimed to be Midir from the stories, Midir who had fought at Moytura and raised Angus Óg?

And yet so much of it made sense. Her hatred of strong winds. Her love of caves and beech groves, her discomfort among her fellow Gaels. And when she heard those tales of the Children of Danu, the world of the tales felt like home to her. It was as if that world was the waking world, this one the dream.

That world felt closer now. It exacted a price. The hovering hawk, which she now knew was not a hawk but a storm, had drawn closer. It was harder than ever before to be queen; to flatter guests at feasts and dance with rank-breathed drunkards. It was hard to sit by her husband's side and hear the rasp of his voice. When they went to bed she feigned sleep, wishing desperately that his hands would not reach for her.

Happiness had fled like a fox at dawn. All thanks to Midir.

Étaín stopped to watch a band of musicians play. Their fingers moved as swiftly as snakes; sweat soaked their brows as they poured their passion into the music, delighting the dancers. It was clear that the players loved to play; all was right in their world so long as they played and the dancers danced.

A grey-clad man came to stand beside her as she listened. He was tall and sharp-nosed, with black and silver hair.

'You once knew such happiness as theirs,' said Midir.

'Until you took it from me.' Somehow Étaín was unsurprised to see him there and then, on the day when two worlds met.

'I do not speak of your happiness among the Gaels.'

'I know. You cannot bear to think that I might have known happiness other than as your pet.'

'It was not me who made you a fly.'

'I was your pet before I was a fly. You were a fool to bring me home to your wife. You were a fool when you took me to meet your wife on the road, and again when she left the table at Brú na Bóinne.'

'I—'

'No! No, Midir. Do not apologise to me. Just leave me. Let me attempt to claw back some of the happiness you have stolen from me, yet again.'

Midir's jaw tightened.

'I offer no apologies, then,' he said. 'But I do offer to bring you home. Whatever I have done, you know you do not belong here. Come home to the world which calls to you, every moment of every day. Fuamnach is no more. Her storm is no more. Everything you desire, you will find among the Tuatha Dé Danaan.'

'With you.'

'Yes.'

'I refuse you, Midir. I refuse you utterly. Leave me. Now.'

'Very well. Yet let me ask one question first. If your husband gives you to me, will you come with me?'

Étaín laughed bitterly. 'If that will make you leave. Yes, Midir. I will go with you if my husband gives me to you.'

Midir bowed and left.

Eochaid stood on the ramparts of Tara, looking across the Plain of Breg.

He often began his day with a walk along the ramparts, surveying what could be seen of his domain. It gave him a sense of order and control to see the sun rising again in the east, to know that no horde of enemies prepared an attack from the west.

His walks also helped him to feel better about Étaín. Ever since he had returned from his last tour, she had been different. Colder. Her love for him had never blazed like a bonfire; that was not her way. It had been gentle yet ever-present, like a stream that continued to flow beneath a mantle of winter ice. Now she found excuses to leave his side, and made a battlefield of their bed.

Enough of such thoughts, he told himself. The sun was rising, making a golden temple of the sky. *Settle your mind there.*

He stood still upon the rampart, watching the dawn unfold, until a grey-clad man silently drew up beside him.

Eochaid turned to face the stranger, his hand on his sword. His grip quickly loosened. For some reason, looking into this man's eyes, Eochaid found the peace he had been searching for. This man felt like an old friend. He was tall with silver-streaked hair, and wore a cloak of brilliant purple bound by a gold brooch. He carried a gold-mounted spear, the blade of which caught the rising light.

'Greetings, Eochaid, High King of the Gaels of Ireland,' said the man.

'Greetings,' said Eochaid. 'May I know your name?'

'You may know my name and my title. I am Midir, a lesser king of the Tuatha Dé Danaan.'

Eochaid laughed and immediately regretted it. There was something about this man which made his outlandish claim ring true. He truly was a king of the sidhe.

'It is an honour,' said Eochaid.

'I am honoured too. I wonder, Eochaid. Have you ever observed that while stablehands talk to stablehands, and smiths drink with smiths, a king has no one to pass the time with? No one, that is, whom he can truly relate to?'

Eochaid thought of Étaín with a bitter pang.

'I have often felt that way.'

'Well, then. Perhaps you and I, two kings, could enjoy a game together?'

'I would like that.'

'Then sit with me.'

Midir sat down on the rampart. Eochaid followed and saw that a gaming board sat between them, its pieces in position.

'You play?' asked Midir.

'Of course.'

'And you are not afraid of a small wager?'

'I am not.'

'Then shall we say one game? A wager of fifty horses?'

'Fifty horses it is.'

Midir nodded and made his first move.

The game gathered pace. Eochaid was pleasantly surprised by his own performance. It was daunting to game with a lord of the sidhe, yet Midir was no great player. He thought no more than two moves ahead and fell into simple traps.

'And the game is mine,' Eochaid soon said.

Midir smiled, his eyes on the board. 'It seems I am a little rusty. You would not have beaten me in the days when I played regularly.'

Eochaid's eyes sparkled. His old love of gaming and wagers, which he had suppressed since meeting Étaín, uncoiled like an adder in the sun.

'Those are easy words to say. Harder to prove,' he said.

'True,' said Midir. 'In that case, when I deliver your horses at dawn tomorrow, we could game again.'

'For what stakes?'

'Fifty boars,' said Midir.

'Done.'

'I shall see you here tomorrow.'

Midir and Eochaid met again the next morning. Eochaid did not tell Étaín of the meeting. It was only a small wager or two, yet she would take it as an excuse to remove herself further from him. And even if he was returning to his old ways, what of it? It was her fault for denying him the companionship he needed.

The game began. Midir played better than on the previous day but still fell into Eochaid's clutches. After playing they talked a while, laughing and joking.

'Same time and place tomorrow? For fifty cattle?' asked Midir.

Eochaid won Midir's cattle. He won fifty sheep the

following day. By that point his thirst for a wager had opened its jaws wide and sunk its teeth into him.

'I will bring the sheep tomorrow,' said Midir as he rose to leave.

'I wonder if I might set the stakes for our next game,' said Eochaid.

'Oh yes? And what stakes have you in mind?'

Eochaid's face flushed. He had been lying awake at night, remembering stories of the Tuatha Dé Danaan and their magical powers. Powers which might be turned to his advantage.

'These stakes. The land around Tara which is stony; to clear the stones and use them to make a causeway over the Bog of Tethbae.

'The land around Tara, which is choked with rushes, to make soft and fertile.

'The hills around Tara which are bare, to clothe them with trees.'

Midir's eyes bored into Eochaid's. Eochaid was unnerved; thousands of winters lay behind those eyes. Yet he held Midir's gaze.

'Very well, then,' said Midir at last. 'On one condition. If I lose and must pay these stakes, they shall be met in one night. Yet no man must look over the walls of Tara until the sun has risen.'

Eochaid bowed. 'Very well.'

They parted.

Midir lost the wager.

'Confound this aged and addled mind of mine,' he said. 'Tomorrow the quilt of this land shall be rewoven. I have your word, do I not, that no man shall look over the walls of Tara tonight?'

'You have it. No man nor woman, no child nor hound.'

'Then we shall meet in the morning,' said Midir.

Eochaid could barely contain his excitement that day. He had seen conjurers and card-smiths at work, but this was real magic. Magic won by him and ordered by him. The landscape of Tara would change forever; he would be remembered as the man responsible for it.

Yet how would it be done?

He had to know.

That night, under Eochaid's orders, a black-clad guard peeped over Tara's ramparts.

He reported to Eochaid an hour before sunrise.

'I saw an army of men on the hills and fields around the fort,' he said by the dim light of a lamp. 'They worked in the fields, cutting rushes and clearing stones. They worked on the hills, carrying trees and thrusting them down into the ground. I never saw such strong men as these.'

'And what else did you see?'

'I saw a man directing them. He looked like a king, sire. Not as grand as you are, of course. But he carried a shining spear and there was... just something about him, if you take my meaning.'

Eochaid nodded. He took a bag of coins from beneath his own cloak and tossed it to the man.

'Spend them quietly, or you will pay in more than coin.'

The man bowed and hurried away.

Eochaid met Midir in their usual spot soon after.

'What wonder!' cried Eochaid as Midir strode towards him. 'I did not know if—'

'Be silent,' said Midir. 'You slug-tongued traitor. You false friend.'

'I...' Eochaid wilted before Midir's gaze. 'I am sorry.'

'How small a word that is for what you have done. When kings lie and play their friends for fools, what can we hope for from the common man? I can sense the land already sickening beneath our feet. Birds shall devour their own chicks thanks to this. Crops shall rot in the fields; the hind's milk turns to poison.'

The sidhe king's words had the weight of anvils.

'What can I do to make this right?' asked Eochaid.

'Game with me again. I decide the stakes and shall name them after we play.'

Eochaid tried not to laugh. 'Very well.'

They sat down and played. Eochaid was in no mood to be gentle; he would fall on Midir like an eagle upon a lamb.

Yet the game did not go as the others had. Midir seemed a different player altogether. He made of the board an indecipherable labyrinth; he surrounded and pounced on Eochaid's pieces, as relentless and merciless as the sea.

Eochaid lost the game.

The facade fell. Midir was no middling player, nor was he a friend.

Eochaid and Midir stood.

'Your winnings?' asked Eochaid.

'One kiss from your wife.'

Eochaid's mouth flapped like a flag in the wind.

'I will return in the evening, ten days from today. Have Étaín await me in the hall atop Tara. One kiss, and you will not see me again.'

ON THE PROMISED EVENING, Eochaid sat in the feasting hall, his wife at his side.

The tables had been cleared to make room for Eochaid's finest fighters. A forest of steel lay between Étaín and the doors.

Outside, not a blade of grass could be seen for Eochaid's warriors. They filled the fort; they filled the newly fertile plain beyond the fort.

All were silent. Alert.

Every fighter knew their orders. At the first sign of the sidhe-man, they were to attack. Eochaid had no interest in meeting the terms of the wager.

Étaín sat beside her husband on a throne draped with wolf-skins. At that moment, it was hard for her to say whom she scorned more; her husband or her lover of long ago. Eochaid had been tricked into giving away her kiss. Midir had schemed to win her kiss as if it were a trophy. They were as bad as each other.

No. Midir was the worse one. She saw his design; he was arrogant enough to think that one kiss would bring her back to him.

Sunlight stole in through the windows.

At the far end of the hall, the air shimmered and Midir appeared.

No one rushed at him nor drew their sword.

Étaín understood something in that moment. When Midir came to her on the hill, he had shown only a shade of himself. Now he revealed his full radiance. It was as if the sun and moon embraced within the hall, a being of fiery might and silver mystery that sang out to the ends of creation.

Midir strode forward and stood before Étaín. Eochaid found that he could not move; he could only watch as Étaín rose from her throne and descended the dais to stand before Midir.

This man had wronged her again and again.

She had suffered so much for his love. She hated him for it.

Yet standing there before the full brightness of his being, the stories she told herself scattered like shadows. As he lit up the throne room, so he illuminated the truth hidden in her heart.

She loved him.

For all his faults, despite all his mistakes, he had kindness and beauty in him, and she loved him.

Her arms entwined around his neck.

She kissed him.

Étaín slipped outside the halls of time. She went to another, far-off place. In that place, she knew without doubt that she could never be a Gael. She was a woman of the sidhe, and she belonged among them. She belonged with Midir.

In the hall at Tara, Midir and Étaín slipped off their human forms and became swans. They unwound their necks and took to the air. In a great rush of beating wings, they flew over the heads of the assembly, out of the gates which swung open for them, and across Eriu to Bri Leith.

They live there now.[1]

26

THE DREAM OF ANGUS

The Tuatha Dé Danaan never loved anyone so much as they loved Angus.

They loved him for his kindness, his generosity, the bounty of his feasts. Yet mostly they loved him for the way he made them feel. To stand in his presence, to look into his eyes, to hear him sing was to feel loved. To know that whatever troubles one had would soon pass. He made people feel loved and made people love one another, leaving a trail of happiness, friendship and new romance in his wake.

Hundreds of Tuatha were hopelessly in love with golden-haired Angus. Yet Angus had never been in love himself. That is not to say he never fancied a woman, or shared a kiss or a night of passion. Yet his heart had never opened so far as to fall in love.

That changed one night at Brú na Bóinne.

Angus was asleep in bed. He woke up to the sound of a harp

being plucked. He sat up and saw a woman sitting on the end of his bed. She wore a cloak of white feathers. Her hair was white, her skin pale, her eyes as black as a crow's wing.

She was the most beautiful woman Angus had ever seen.

He opened his mouth to greet her and found he could neither speak nor move. He could only lie still and listen. So he did.

He listened as she played and sang for him, gazing into his eyes all the while. It seemed like hours or even years passed in which she played. However long it was, it was more than long enough for Angus to finally fall in love.

Then he woke up.

Angus shot up in bed. It had been a dream. Yet she had seemed so real. And this awakening in his heart, how could he feel it if she had not been real?

He had to get back to her. That meant he had to get back to sleep.

Angus lay back and closed his eyes.

Sleep would not come.

Eventually Angus gave up trying to sleep. Instead he dressed and took his twin swords and spears to the practice yard. There he duelled all day with everyone who would face him, thinking to tire himself out and be sure of sound sleep that night.

It worked. Night fell, Angus went to bed and, despite his excitement, quickly fell asleep.

The white-cloaked woman was waiting for him.

Again she played and sang for him while he lay abed, entranced. When Angus finally woke up, it pained him to leave her, yet he was full of joy. He somehow knew he would see her again the coming night.

He was right. Angus saw her that night, and the night after that, and every night. It was always the same dream, and Angus never spoke a word to her. Yet he felt he came to know her all the same.

This went on until one night, a year and a night since the first visitation, Angus went to sleep and did not dream.

'It doesn't matter,' he told himself when he awoke. 'It's only one night. I will see her again tonight.' Yet she did not come that night, nor the night after. By that time, Angus knew in his heart that when he next dreamed, he would dream alone.

Angus plunged into despair. He stayed in bed day after day, scarcely rising to eat or bathe. His mother, Boann, grew greatly worried and asked him to tell her what was the matter. He could not even bring himself to speak. Boann sent for healers, but none who came found anything amiss with Angus.

THE DAGDA HAD BEEN on a tour of the country, visiting the halls of far-dwelling friends. He arrived at Brú na Bóinne, and Boann explained the situation to him. They talked at length before reaching a decision together.

They would summon Diancecht.

Neither of them had any great love for Diancecht. It was said that he had murdered his own son, and that he had fled the Well of Slaine when Bres attacked it at Moytura. Yet no healer in Eriu had more experience than him.

Diancecht no longer wandered the roads. He kept to his own hall, where he need not face the dark looks many sidhe would give him. Yet he could be lured from home with promises of coin. Thus, a messenger left Brú na Bóinne laden with silver and gold.

Several days later, the messenger returned, Diancecht walking behind him.

The white-bearded healer entered Brú na Bóinne. He met Boann and the Dagda and allowed them to guide him to Angus' bedchamber.

They entered. Angus was lying in bed. His skin was pale, his eyes empty of expression. He stared up at Diancecht, who studied him for a moment, then laughed.

'Why are you laughing?' asked Boann.

'I am laughing because you paid dearly for me to diagnose what should be obvious to everyone.'

'And what is that?'

'The lad is in love.'

'Don't be ridiculous!' said Boann. 'This is far more serious than lovesickness. I would know if my own son was in love—'

Angus interrupted her. 'He's right. I am in love. My lover has left me, and thus I have no will to live.'

Diancecht laughed and laughed until Boann ordered him out of the chamber.

'Now, son,' said the Dagda. 'You might have told us this sooner, but at least we know now. So give us the whole story.'

Angus relayed the tale of his dreams to his parents. When he was done, Boann said, 'It's clear what must be done. We must send scouts out across the country, to search every glen, hill and shore for this girl of yours.'

Angus nodded. 'Thank you,' he said.

Messengers left Brú na Bóinne soon afterwards, in search of the woman with the swan-feather cloak.

WEEKS LATER, THE DAGDA ENTERED ANGUS' bedchamber and said, 'I have good news for you, son.'

Angus sat up in bed, his malnourished bones creaking.

'One of our scouts went to Tipperary. She climbed into the high hills and reached the Lake of the Dragon Mouth. There she met the druid Bov, who claimed to have knowledge of your lover. Bov bids you go to him there.'

Angus leapt out of bed. Hurriedly he put on clean clothes and left Brú na Bóinne, shielding his eyes from the sun; he had not seen it for weeks.

He travelled south across the country. It was spring and Banba was coming alive all around him. Flowers bloomed in the meadows and red squirrels bounded through the trees. Angus swam in waterfall pools and ate fruits and berries off the branch. He waved greetings to strangers and felt his old spirits returning as Tipperary drew closer.

Finally Angus reached the Lake of the Dragon Mouth. It was a small, almost circular mountain lake, ringed by dark cliffs. Not far from the bank was a little hut, and in that hut Angus found Bov awaiting him.

Angus and the white-bearded druid sat down upon deer

hides. Bov poured ale for Angus, stoked his peat fire and said, 'I know the maiden you seek.

'Her name is Caer. She is the daughter of Ethel, a druid well-renowned in these parts. Yet as powerful as Ethel is, his daughter is more powerful.

'When Caer came of age, Ethel wished to see her married. She refused every man who courted her, which led her father to rage and threaten her.

'Caer took matters into her own hands. She came here to this lake, which has always been a favourite haunt of hers, and cast a spell.'

'What did this spell do?' asked Angus.

'Since the casting of the spell, Caer's life follows this order. Every first year, she is bound to the shores of this lake. She cannot leave it. Every second year, she takes the shape of a swan and flies across Eriu in a company of fifty swans. It is at Samhain that she turns.'

'So Caer believes that no man will wish to marry a woman who is either bound to a lake or flying free as a swan.'

Bov nodded. 'And I know what you're thinking, lad,' he said, his expression hardening.

'You're thinking that you're the famous Angus Óg. The man whom every maiden in Eriu swoons over. This woman went to the trouble of visiting you and singing to you in your dreams, every night for a year and a night. You're thinking that if you can only talk to her, she will change her mind. She'll break her own spell and go off with you as your bride.'

Angus nodded.

'I thought as much. You're wrong, son. So very wrong. That

might be what any other woman would do, but not this one. Not Caer. Her will is strong; she will not change her shape or her ways for you.'

Angus sat in silence for a while, searching the flames of the fire, before meeting Bov's gaze.

'We'll see,' he said.

SIX MONTHS REMAINED UNTIL SAMHAIN. During that time, Angus did not return to Brú na Bóinne. Instead he walked the length and breadth of Eriu. Wherever he went, people recognised him and asked him what business he was about. So the story soon spread that Angus Óg was gathering ingredients for a spell; one which would break Caer's enchantment and make her his.

Angus gathered quartz from the cliffs of Donegal. He hunted for owl feathers in the woods of Slieve Bloom. He filled his bag with bone, fur, stone, seed and claw, until Samhain drew near and he turned for Tipperary.

Angus approached the lake at sunset, beneath iron-dark clouds.

He was not alone there.

The cliffs surrounding the lake were packed with onlookers. Tuatha and even Gaels had come from across Tipperary and throughout Eriu to witness the working of Angus' spell.

Angus approached the water's edge. He waded in until he was knee-deep.

He waited.

Dusk inched towards night.

In the day's dying light, fifty-one swans flew towards the lake. They were bound in pairs by silver chains at their necks, and the lead swan wore a chain of gold.

They landed on the water. The swan with the gold chain paddled away from the others and towards Angus.

She cast off her swan form and became a woman with white hair, black eyes and a white, swan-feather cloak.

The watchers strained to hear as Angus cleared his throat and chose his words, which he found surprisingly difficult.

'I... er, I mean... I am Angus.'

'I know,' said Caer.

'Yes. Well... I am going to cast a spell.'

'Then cast it.'

Angus reached into his bag. Raising his trembling hand high, he scattered its contents over Caer, over himself and over the surrounding water.

Angus spoke the words of his spell, and became a swan.

Caer smiled. She spoke druid-words and became a swan again too. She and Angus beat their wings, rose into the sky and flew away into the night.

ANGUS HAD INDEED SET out to break Caer's spell. Yet as he walked the roads of Eriu, he came to realise that before he asked her to change her ways for him, he should learn her ways. If she wished to be a swan, he would be a swan too. If she wished to live by the lake, he would dwell there too, for a while at least.

Angus and Caer lived as swans for a time, and they lived by the Lake of the Dragon Mouth for a time. Eventually Caer tired of that life, and she and Angus left the lake, in their sidhe forms, as husband and wife. They dwell together now in Brú na Bóinne, but often leave home to fly as swans across the land they love.[1]

27

THE VOYAGE OF BRAN

There once lived among the Gaels a king named Bran. His hall was in Connacht, close to the ocean, and at his hall he once held a great feast.

Bran provided food, drink and entertainment. His guests came from many miles around. The sun shone each day, the night sky glittered and the feasters swore they never saw a better celebration.

It was late morning, the party four days deep. It might go on another four days, perhaps longer. A band was playing and nearly everybody was on their feet, clapping their hands and stamping in time to the music. Hounds and children ran among the dancers' feet; the air was moist with sweat and loud with laughter.

Bran could take it no more.

He rose from the high table. Seeing that for once nobody was watching him, he slipped out of a side door.

Bran sighed with relief as he closed the door behind him, muting the relentless music and merriment. He walked away across the green fields of his fort. Here, the only music was the music of birdsong. The light from the spring sun was near blinding after all those days cooped up in the hall. Why did people shut out the world for days on end? What were they hiding from?

Bran was tired of ruling. Winning the kingship had been thrilling, yes. The battles, the scheming, the political conniving, all leading to the moment when the crown found a home on his head. Then it was drinking, women, riches. Sitting above other men. Watching former enemies fawn at his feet as he plotted to enlarge his kingdom.

But no more. Nowadays he found simpering sycophants tedious; he could not be bothered to court a woman, let alone fight a battle. And then there was the administration. The settling of disputes, the angry farmers moaning about the placement of a boundary wall...

Even feasting bored him. He'd heard every song. Tasted every dish.

Bran had a very clear idea of what he didn't want.

So what did he want?

That was the question occupying his mind as he approached the outer wall of his fort and climbed the rampart. Slowly he walked its length, taking in the view of his kingdom. Tilled fields gave way to pasture, moor and meadow, while the sea glimmered on the blue horizon beyond.

Standing there on the rampart, listening to birds sing and searching for the point where the sea met the sky, Bran felt his tension easing. Indeed, it seemed to him that both time and tension slipped from his shoulders like a silken cloak, so perfect and peaceful was the scene. Looking out to the horizon and wondering what lay beyond had always soothed his heart. It stirred a part of him which he had almost lost.

Bran remained in that spot. He did not move.

The moment spread itself wide, like a butterfly emerging from a cocoon and unfolding its wings.

Bran heard on the wind a new music.

This was not the fierce and frenetic music of the feast. Nor was it the simple melody of birdsong. It was something else; something he had never heard before.

The music was faint. It kept disappearing from his hearing. Yet Bran found that if he remained still, and did not shift and strain or look this way and that, he could hear it clearly enough.

Then he remembered. A tale which an old woman working in the kitchens once told him. It claimed that on the ground where Bran had built his hall, there had once stood a fort of the Tuatha Dé Danaan. When the Gaels won Banba, the fort's occupants had burrowed underground, making a new home directly beneath the home they had lost.

Bran had always dismissed such tales as pure fancy. Yet what if the tales were true? What if a tribe of Tuatha Dé Danaan were feasting far beneath his feet, and it was their music that he heard? How else could any music be so beautiful?

Bran closed his eyes, the better to listen.

He lay down on the rampart and curled up on his side.

He fell asleep.

HOURS LATER, Bran woke up.

The sun hid behind clouds. His muscles ached from sleeping on hard wood.

That music... had he dreamed it? He must have. What a fool he was, disappearing from his own feast and falling asleep on the rampart. Had anyone seen him? They would all be laughing if so, saying the king had staggered away in his cups.

He rolled over.

A branch of glistening silver lay at his side.

At first Bran could only stare. Then he got to his knees, picked up the branch and held it before his eyes, full of wonder. A single apple blossom decorated the branch. He traced his finger across its length, holding it up to the sun. He knew the look and weight of silver in his hands. This was purest silver.

Even more wondrous, far more wondrous than the silver branch was what it told Bran: that he did not dream. Truly he had heard the music of the Tuatha Dé Danaan.

Bran turned and strode down the rampart steps, clutching the silver branch.

THE TIME for dancing had passed. The hall was quiet, the musicians filling their bellies while the feasters conversed at table.

Bran burst into the hall.

'Listen to me!' he roared as every eye turned towards him. 'Listen to me!'

Silence reigned as King Bran held the silver branch aloft.

'Only a few hours ago, I left this hall. I went out to take the air and find a little peace.

'I climbed the ramparts of my fort. I stood and enjoyed the view across the field and moors. And as I stood there... I heard music.'

'That was us,' said one of the musicians.

'No! It was not your music I heard. Your music is pleasant enough, of course. But this... this was music no Gael could make. This was the music of the sidhe.'

Bran observed a number of his subjects stealing glances at one another and covering their mouths.

'I know how it sounds,' he said. 'I know many of you think the sidhe are a children's tale. I thought so until today. But any of you who heard this music would think as I do.

'Anyway. I fell asleep. When I woke up, this branch lay beside me. A branch of pure silver! Where did it come from, what made it if not magic?'

Bran waited for an answer. None came. Silence as weighty as an anvil filled the hall. Bran saw that his guests avoided his eye; their amusement had turned to embarrassment.

'I know what I heard,' he said. 'I am not mad...'

'No, King Bran. You are not.'

The voice came from a shadowed corner of the hall. All eyes turned to watch as the one who had spoken stepped into the light.

The speaker was a woman. She was clearly no woman of

the Gaels, and she was surely a queen. She was taller than the tallest man there, with piercing grey eyes and hair bound in webs of woven silver. She walked with an unearthly grace as she approached Bran and said, 'Every word you have spoken is true. You did indeed hear music emanating from a hall of my people, the sidhe. But there is more that you must know.

'Many a Gael has stood on Eriu's western shore, wondering what other lands might lie between Eriu and the setting sun. I can tell you, Bran, and tell everyone assembled here, that there are other lands. Many of them.

Of all those lands, by far the loveliest is an island name Emain, the Land of Women. It is a land of green forests, tumbling waterfalls and sun-drenched meadows. Every fruit and flower grows there. Every pool and grove, every glen and dale is a sight for poets to sing of. And best of all,' and here she met the eyes of many a man listening, 'there are no men living there. Only women. Beautiful women who would eagerly take a man of the Gaels as husband, and live at his side for all the years of this world.'

She stepped forward and took the silver branch from Bran.

'This branch came from a tree upon Emain. Do not content yourself with but a branch, Bran. Assemble a crew. Launch a ship and cross the sea. Find your way to Emain and experience the island and her women in all their glory.'

With that, she turned and walked out of the hall. Bran ran outside after her, but she was nowhere to be seen.

He returned to the hall, where his guests still sat with wide eyes.

Bran's mind was already made up.

'You heard the woman of the sidhe,' said Bran. 'A call has been given. A call to adventure. A call to Emain, the Land of Women. That call shall be answered.

'Any man here who is not content with his lot. Any man who is content with his lot, but would still risk everything to know the truth of the sidhe woman's words. To see this land which already sings in my heart. I ask you to step forward now. Claim your seat upon my ship and sail west with me, into the unknown.'

Instantly a swarthy, red-bearded man stood up from his bench. He raised his cup, drank down the last of his ale and went to stand at Bran's side.

'I am Ronan,' he said, 'and I shall sail for the Land of Women.'

Another man rose from the benches and came to stand beside Bran and Ronan. He was tall and thin, with a pinched face that looked to have never known laughter.

'My name is Nechtan. I have always known that my life is not the life I was meant to live. I will sail for the Land of Women.'

'I'm Aidan. I lost my wife to sickness five winters past,' said another man. 'I thought I would never know happiness again. Perhaps happiness awaits me on Emain.'

'It's all very well dreaming of this Land of Women,' said a man with a lean, sea-weathered face, 'but you'll never get there without a good navigator. I'll see we get to Emain unscathed.'

'I've put in enough years at the plough,' said another man. 'I fancy spending the rest of my days—'

'Don't you even think about finishing that sentence!' said the woman sitting next to him, who was evidently his wife. But he stood up anyway and went to join Bran's crew.

Soon three nines of men had assembled beside Bran. They all looked ready to leave that instant.

'Go home and gather whatever you need for the journey,' said Bran. 'Sleep in your own beds for the last time. At noon tomorrow our voyage begins.'

AT NOON on the following day, Bran's ship left harbour and sailed for Emain.

The day was clear and bright, the sea calm. The men rowed out of the harbour then hoisted the sail, catching a wind that carried them west. The harbour was packed with friends and kinsfolk waving goodbye and cheering them on, though a few furious wives had stayed at home.

On board, the mood was good. Jests flew back and forth and many a song was sung. A few of the men cast guilty glances back towards Banba and the loved ones they had left behind.

Since his crew had assembled, Bran had worked to prepare them for their voyage. He had nominated his successor and formally handed over his kingship. He had purchased the ship they sailed on, and ordered his cooks to prepare three weeks' worth of food. Would it take that long to reach Emain, he wondered? Or would it take months? Years? Would they discover new lands on their voyage or simply die of thirst, a drifting crew of rotting corpses? Neither Bran nor any of his crew could guess, and that seemed right to them.

The first days of the voyage passed without incident. At times the sea swelled, demanding hard oar-work of every man; at other times it was as placid as a newborn calf. Gradually the songs and jests thinned out, giving way to periods of quiet. These seemed at times to stretch as wide as the horizon, as Bran's men gave their minds to questions which had never occupied them before.

MANY DAYS HAD PASSED since their departure. The day was utterly still, and the men utterly quiet, when the sea suddenly stirred and swelled before them.

Oars clattered to the hull. Jaws gaped as a mighty man, dressed in white armour and sitting upon a glistening white horse, rose out of the ocean.

None of Bran's crew had ever seen this man before. Yet they all knew who this was.

It could only be Manannán Mac Lir.

Manannán rode around the ship in a slow circle, Enbarr's hooves treading on the sea's surface as if it was firm soil.

'Men of Eriu,' he said. 'You have come far on your quest. Or so you think. You believe that you sail west upon the blue ocean. Is it not so?'

'It is so,' said Bran, gazing up in wonder at the Son of the Sea.

'You are mistaken,' said Manannán.

What appears to you as sun-speckled sea
Is in truth a green plain, bright with flowers.
Where you see waves breaking over the clear sea,
I see red-topped flowers without flaw.
Speckled salmon leap where you look;
I see lovely-coloured lambs at peace.

Manannán grinned at the sailors and, before they could question him, disappeared beneath the waves.

That was all they saw of Manannán, and all he told them. Yet they thought hard on his words, and counted themselves the luckiest of men to have heard them.

MANANNÁN'S VISITATION spurred the crew onwards. They rowed harder, new strength alive in their newly muscled arms. A few days later, they spied land.

The men cheered themselves hoarse, scarcely able to contain their delight and relief. They would not drift into death; they would not tumble from the rim of the world. Whether this was the Land of Women or not scarcely mattered.

Drawing closer, they saw an unremarkable coastline of small coves amid stretches of rock.

Sailing closer still, they learnt that the island was inhabited.

Every beach was as full of people as on a festival day. Bran's men expected the inhabitants of the island to spot their sails and shout out to them. But none did.

Coming even closer, they understood why.

The inhabitants of the cove were fully occupied with laughing. Every single man, woman and child was helpless with hilarity. They slapped their thighs, they wiped their eyes, they clung to one another lest they collapse. Bran's crew looked for the source of their laughter, but they looked in vain. They observed, too, that the people of the island were coarsely dressed, their hair wild, their skin sagging.

'I would like to hear the joke that made so many laugh so hard, and for so long,' said Nechtan.

'Then go ashore,' said Bran. 'Ask these ill-kempt people what land this is and why they laugh so hard.'

Nechtan kicked of his boots. He climbed onto the gunwale and dived into the water. Nobody on the shore spared him a glance as he swam to the beach and waded onto the sand.

Nechtan shook himself off then approached a group of men. He appeared to greet them and give his name.

Then he paused.

He looked about him.

Nechtan doubled over with laughter.

He fell to the ground; he pounded the sand with his fists. Eventually he got to his knees and tried to rise to his feet, but his hysteria was too much. He fell to the sand again, rolling over and waving his limbs like an upturned crab.

'I fear I should not have ordered Nechtan ashore,' said Bran. 'Nechtan!' he called out. 'Return to the ship! Leave these fools to their merriment!'

Yet Nechtan did not hear Bran. If he did, he ignored him.

'Nechtan!' called all the voyagers now. 'Nechtan, come back to us! We sail for Emain, the Land of Women!'

Nechtan only went on laughing.

'Are any of you here,' asked Bran, 'willing to go ashore and bring Nechtan back to us?'

No one answered Bran's request. Nor was he willing to go ashore himself.

'I name this place the Land of Joy,' said Bran. 'Though clearly such joy comes at a price. Put your oars in your hands, men. We sail onwards.'

THERE IS NOT much to tell of the next stage of their voyage. The sea was rough at times and calm at times. The men were quiet and times and loud at times, though they were mostly quiet and contemplative. They mourned the loss of Nechtan, and each man wondered if he too would fall prey to some strange danger.

This was the way of things until they again spied land on the horizon.

The crew leaned forward, forgetting to breathe. Was this it? Was this Emain?

The island lay directly in their path. Against a clear sky they saw tree-clad hills broken by rocky mountain peaks. Nearing the island, they saw shores of perfect white sand.

A few of them began to laugh. This drew wary glances from the others, but they did not laugh because of any enchantment. They laughed because their hearts told them that this was truly the Island of Emain.

In a horseshoe-shaped cove they docked their ship. As they did so, a line of women crested the sand dunes beyond the beach.

The women came down to meet them. One of them walked ahead of the others, and she had the bearing of a queen.

'Well met, King Bran and all you who sail with him,' she said. 'You are welcome to the Isle of Emain. Please, come ashore and let us make your acquaintance.'

Bran hesitated.

The woman frowned. 'You have come a long way, you men of Fodhla. Are you not keen to eat fresh food, drink fresh water and enjoy the other comforts we can offer you?'

Bran opened his mouth and closed it again.

'Come on, Bran,' hissed Ronan. 'What are you waiting for?'

'I've my eye on that redhead,' said Aidan. 'And she's looking at me too. Hurry up before she changes her mind.'

Yet something held Bran back. He didn't understand it. After coming all this way! He had persuaded his crew to give up homes and wives to join him. They had lost a dear friend on the way and now, finally, they had reached the Land of Women. From the look on the women's faces, it was clear that the warmest of welcomes awaited them.

These were all reasons to go ashore. Yet his hesitation came from a place beyond reason, a place deep beneath it.

Would his men mutiny if he told them to turn around and row away?

Before he could follow that thought further, the leader of the women pursed her lips. She reached into her cloak, took out a ball of yarn and threw it to Bran.

Without thinking, he caught it.

It stuck to his hand.

She pulled on the yarn. She had great strength, it seemed, for she reeled the ship into shore as if it were a child's plaything. Very soon the hull struck sand. There was to be no turning about for the men of Eriu.

They had no interest in doing so. As soon as the hull struck the sand, the crew forgot all decorum and leapt over the gunwale and onto the beach. The women came forward to greet them, each taking a man in her arms and kissing him deeply.

As for Bran, he accepted the way the wind was blowing. He stepped onto the beach, approached the leader and gave her what he hoped was a graceful bow.

She bowed to him, stepped forward and put her lips to his. It seemed she had forgiven his hesitation.

Bran had not come to Emain because it was full of women. He had come because the quest itself answered the deep need of his heart. Yet when he kissed that woman, he knew at once that the music of his heart was akin to the music of hers. He would remain with her, and only her, upon the Island of Women.

KING BRAN and his adventurers had finally reached Emain. Countless hours had they spent picturing a perfect land; none of their imaginings did it justice. Each day they went out together to explore. Every vista they encountered was lovelier than the last. Dragonflies made a chorus of colour by the rivers;

eagle-song scored snowy valleys; there were trees which stood taller than the highest hills of home.

It was good to spend time each day exploring the island. Yet most of their time was spent with the women. It turned out that there were a great many women on the island; far more than the small party which had greeted them. Each of Emain's women was hungry for male company, and firmly believed that their guests were duty-bound to keep them satisfied. The men went about their work without complaint, though they did get a little sore and tired at times.

This went on for... who can say how long? Time had ceased to matter to Bran's crew. Every day upon Emain was perfect. There was no reason to look back on any particular day with fondness, or to anticipate a day to come.

Yet Bran one day observed a strange longing in his heart.

He found himself thinking of Eriu.

Of course his old life drifted through his thoughts from time to time, though this happened less and less as time went by. He trusted his successor would rule well. And if that rule had been contested... well, it would probably be fine. What could he do about it now?

Yes, all was surely well in Eriu. He need not trouble himself with such worries.

Yet now he could not stop thinking of her. He pictured the view from the hills beyond his fort. He dredged dusty memories of friends and kinsfolk from forgotten corners of his mind. All was surely well in his kingdom. But wouldn't it be a fine thing to know that for sure? To look upon those hills and glens again, to surprise old friends and get their news?

These thoughts came to Bran more and more often until he scarcely thought of anything else. In time he spoke of it to the other men, and was surprised to learn that they had all been thinking similar things.

'It would be good to go back for a short while, at least,' said Ronan.

'I think I would appreciate these women better if I took a short break from them,' added Aidan.

So it was agreed. They would voyage home. Bran went to his beloved and told her of the plan.

She was horrified.

'You must not, Bran. You must not!'

'Why not?'

'Because...'

'Yes?'

'It is better not to say.'

'I will need more than that.'

'You do not like it here? You do not like me?'

'Not at all! I have never liked any place better than this. I have never liked any woman better than you. But... you must understand. Eriu was our home for many years. None of us expected to ever leave her. We will have no peace in our hearts if we do not see her again.'

'Very well,' she sighed. 'You are making a mistake, but it is yours to make. Go to Eriu, then. Leave us in want of your warmth and strength. But promise me one small thing.'

'Anything.'

'Do not step on Eriu's soil.'

Bran stared at her.

'You call that a small thing?' he said eventually. 'Sail all the way to Eriu and... what, stay on the ship?'

'Yes.'

'...Why?'

'Trust me, Bran. It is best if I do not tell you.'

He pressed her but she would reveal no more.

So Bran gathered his men together. He told them what had been said. Though it caused much consternation, he obtained an oath from each of them not to step on the soil of home. They would view Eriu from the water, and converse with their loved ones from the water, and that wouldn't be so bad.

THEY LEFT A FEW DAYS LATER. The sea sped them east, without incident, all the way to the Land of Joy.

There, they drew in close to shore and spied Nechtan. He still laughed amid the island's other inhabitants. While once he had been a splendid figure of a man, he was thin and wretched now. Without much hope of success, they called out to him, and were astonished when he looked up and recognised them.

'Come here, Nechtan! Come to your friends, your brothers!'

Shaking his head as if awakening from a dream, Nechtan waded out to sea. He swam to the ship and they hauled him aboard, slapping him on the back and hugging him fiercely, laughing nearly as hard as those on the shore.

NECHTAN'S successful retrieval galvanised the crew. Their ship galloped across the water, days and nights passing in a blur, until they spied Connacht ahead of them.

The men shouted themselves hoarse. All openly wept. They rowed harder than ever before until they neared the shore.

Before them lay a harbour, beyond it some village they did not recognise. The village looked pleasant enough... yet there seemed to be something wrong with its people.

As Bran's ship sailed into the harbour, the people of the village stopped what they were doing and went down to meet the boat. They stared at Bran and his men, who stared back at them.

'They are so small,' said Ronan. 'So weak and puny looking.'

'There is no colour to their skin, nor swagger to their step,' said Aidan. 'It is a wonder they have not suffered invasion.'

'Unless all the folk of Eriu are like this now,' said Bran.

'The others looked at him with shock. 'Do not even joke of such a thing,' said Aidan.

Yet at that moment, a woman called out from the shore.

'Strangers on your strange ship,' she said. 'How is that you sail here from the west, when it is known that there are no lands west of here? And how is it that you are so tall and fierce looking? Do you mean us harm?'

'Of course we do not,' said Bran. 'I am King Bran of Connacht. My men and I left Eriu perhaps a year or two ago, voyaging west in search of the Land of Women. I would know whether my court lies north or south of here, and what malady made your people shrink so small.'

The woman looked at those around her, then back at Bran.

'I never heard of a King Bran,' she said.

'I did,' said a small, hunched man who stepped forward to stand beside the woman. 'But only by the hearth, when tales were being told. The bards say that long ago, a king named Bran set out for this Land of Women you speak of. But this happened not a year ago, or so the tales tell. It happened five or six hundred years ago.'

Waves slapped the side of the ship.

Bran looked at his men. He waited for someone to say this was nonsense. But somehow he knew in his heart that it was true. He saw in the eyes of his men that they knew it too.

All but Nechtan.

'Lies!' he said. 'I don't feel six hundred years old. Do you? I will go ashore and get the truth from these charlatans.'

Before anyone could stop him, he climbed onto the gunwale and leapt onto the rocks.

Nechtan screamed. He bent double. There was a sickening sound as a hundred bones cracked, bent and wasted away. His skin sagged from his face; his hair greyed and fell to the ground.

Nechtan turned and reached out towards Bran and the ship. A moment later, a gust of wind turned him into dust.

Bran and his men remained on their boat after that. More and more of the small, strange people came to the shore throughout the day, gathering to listen as the crew took turns to tell of the lives they had lived, the battles they had fought, their meeting with Manannán Mac Lir and their time upon the Island of Women.

The people on the shore spoke in turn, telling the voyagers of things that had happened since their departure; of queens, battles and a strange new faith. This exchange went on all through the night. When dawn came, Bran thanked the villagers and told his men to set sail.

The voyagers turned their ship about and set off for the Isle of Women again. Whether they made it there or not, I do not know, but at least their tale lives on.[1]

28

THE CHILDREN OF LIR

There came a time when the sidhe had to choose a new king. Their leaders assembled at the Hill of Uisnech and spent three days debating who among them should rule.

Of all those nominated, it soon became clear that one of two would win: Bodb Dearg or Lir. Other candidates withdrew at this point, putting their weight behind whomever of the two they preferred. Those who backed Bodb Dearg pointed to his military prowess, his famed charge against Bres at the legendary battle of Eas Dara. Lir had never made his mark on the battlefield but was said to be wise and selfless.

Finally a vote was taken. The winner, the new king of the Tuatha Dé Danaan, was Bodb Dearg.

Bodb Dearg was overjoyed. In all his long years of life he had never expected to hold such a title. Yet he felt sorry for Lir, and wondered if the Tuatha had made the right decision. He himself had won renown on the battlefield, yes. But were the days of war not behind them?

Besides this, Bodb Dearg and Lir were friends. He knew that Lir greatly desired the kingship, not because he lusted for power but because he longed to serve his people. Lir had looked heartbroken when the vote went against him.

Bodb Dearg thought much on this matter after taking the throne. Eventually he decided to make Lir an offer, both to cheer up his friend and to ensure there was no bad blood between them. So he summoned Lir to the Hill of Uisnech.

LIR WENT to Uisnech and entered the hall beneath the hill. Bodb Dearg sat on his throne; his four daughters stood in a line before him.

'My friend,' said Bodb Dearg. 'Though you did not win the kingship, you are a great leader and a dear friend to me. My daughters have reached marrying age, and I think none of them could do better than to marry you. Please, pick whichever of my daughters most pleases you.'

Lir was stunned. He had expected a gesture of friendship from Bodb Dearg but not such generosity as this. Besides, he was a good deal older than each of Bodb Dearg's daughters.

Still, Lir thought to himself, *I am in need of a wife, and I would be a gentle husband. I should not refuse the daughter of a king.*

He looked the girls over for a while, then said to one, 'What is your name?'

'Aobh,' she said.

Aobh had flaxen hair and blue eyes. She was shorter than the others, with sun-kissed skin and a half-smile that made her look privy to a joke nobody else had heard.

'Would you consent to be my wife, Aobh?'

'I would.'

Lir searched Aobh's eyes. He would not accept marriage to a woman who did not truly desire him. Yet he saw no fear or discomfort there, only warmth and curiosity.

'Then my wife you shall be.'

LIR AND AOBH departed Uisnech the next day. They travelled to Lir's hall at Bri Leith and settled into life as a married couple.

Aobh swiftly won Lir's heart. She was quick-witted and full of life, always keen to go out riding or exploring. She could talk for hours with anyone and everyone. Though Lir was older than she, and did not always share her appetite for adventure, she loved to return to him and tell him all she had seen. He listened attentively to everything she said and never tried to restrict her.

Aodh had grown up as the daughter of a great lord. She had always known that when she married it would be for political advantage, not love. All she had ever hoped for was to marry a man who was kind and decent. She never felt any great passion for Lir, but she thought him a good man and, later, a good father.

Aobh became pregnant in the first year of her marriage. She

gave birth to a daughter, whom they named Finola. Lir and Aobh adored the child and spent their every moment with her. Though only an infant, Finola seemed to her parents to have a pensive, almost solemn nature, as if the most serious matters occupied her mind.

Two years after Finola's birth, Aobh birthed a boy named Aodh. Two years after that, she had twins: Conn and Fiachra.

It was in the birthing of Conn and Fiachra that tragedy struck Aobh. Their birth took a terrible toll on her, and she did not recover in the days that followed. Three weeks later, she died.

LIR WAS HEARTBROKEN. All of Bri Leith mourned Aobh, who had been a friend to one and all. Among the children, only Finola was old enough to have any comprehension of what had happened. While Conn and Fiachra were cared for by wet nurses, she sat on her father's lap and stared into his eyes as he wept over Aobh.

The world went on as it does. Finola, Aodh, Conn and Fiachra grew older and into good health. Though they had no mother, they did not want for attention. Lir made it his business to be two parents. He passed the care of his lands to his stewards and devoted himself utterly to his children. He personally taught them history and hunting, sword and spear, archery and argument. He took them into the forests and taught them the names of every herb; at feasts he would dance and dine with no one else. Some said that he gave too much time to parenting and not enough to the lordship of Bri Leith, but most believed his ways would change as his heart healed.

Bodb Dearg had other ideas.

THE KING of the sidhe visited Bri Leith regularly, both before and after Aobh's death. It was his duty as king to see that all was well in every part of the kingdom. After Aobh's death, he became increasingly concerned that Lir was in no fit state to rule. Yet he did not want to take the lordship from his friend, both for the strife that would cause and out of affection for Lir, who has been a good husband to Aobh.

Bodb Dearg thought long and hard before reaching a decision. He would invite Lir to choose another wife from among his daughters.

With this decided, Bodb Dearg gathered his daughters together and told them his intention. Two of his daughters thought that Lir was not yet ready to marry again, and were disinclined to take him as husband. But one of them, Aoife, was of a different mind. Of all the sisters, she had been closest to Aobh, though their natures were different.

'Lir has proved himself to be a good and kind man,' said Aoife. 'The years Aobh spent with him were her happiest. Though he grieves for her still, so do I, and I always shall. I would be happy to share my grief with him, and to raise my sister's children alongside him.'

Bodb Dearg was overjoyed. He summoned Lir to Uisnech and related to him what had passed.

'What do you think, old friend? Would you be happy to marry a daughter of mine again?' he asked.

Lir hesitated. Bodb Dearg frowned at that.

'You find some fault with Aoife?'

'No! No, not at all. I came to know Aoife through her many visits to Bri Leith. She was dear to Aobh and has a quick mind. But my heart is not mine to give; it belongs still to Aobh.'

'Your heart may belong to Aobh,' said Bodb Dearg, 'but your life belongs to your people. You are a lord, and must think of your duties above all else. I have been patient, friend, but my patience has its limits. Do you not think I grieve the death of my daughter? I do. But I place boundaries around my grief. It would be well for you to do the same.

'Give time to grief, Lir. Give time to fatherhood. But do your duty first.'

Lir wanted to argue with Bodb Dearg, but he understood that he had received an order, not a request.

'Very well. I will marry Aoife, gladly and gratefully.'

LIR AND AOIFE married at Uisnech and departed for Bri Leith. In the following weeks and months they learnt to live together. Though Lir had been hesitant to marry, he was not displeased with Aoife, at least not at first. She clearly admired him for his devotion to her sister and his children. She plied him with questions about the lands and people they ruled. Clearly she meant to be a ruler worthy of respect, and to repair any damage that had been done to his reign.

The Tuatha of Bri Leith and its surroundings quickly warmed to her. She was not as full of life and warmth as Aobh, but she cared for their wellbeing and never shirked her duties. Lir found himself being steadily less guarded with her, until a time came when he knew that, though he might not burn with love for Aoife, he did indeed love her. He was truly grateful to call her his wife.

Lir was content.

Aoife was not.

Aoife had always thought that as Lir's heart healed of its grief, he would grow to love her as he had loved Aobh. She had a persevering nature and was content to wait long years for this to happen. In truth, she had harboured a fondness for Lir even when he was married to her sister. Now he was her husband! It was a dream that she had never dared to dream, for she had loved Aobh. But now it was made true, and it only hurt her.

Lir had come to love her in all their years of marriage. The children were older now, able to run around and play together without need of a parent present. Yet Lir still spent every possible hour with them. She was allowed to join in, of course. They never purposefully excluded her. But never a single day did she spend with them in which she did not feel herself the outsider. A glass wall stood between Aoife and the rest of her family. No matter how she tried, she could not penetrate it.

Once the children had gone to bed, Lir would pay her all the attention she was due as his wife. But no more than that. He kissed her, but his kiss was cold. He listened to her, yet her words kindled no flame in his eyes. He held her at night the way a child holds a favourite doll.

Aoife held out for Lir's feelings to change. Yet there came a night when, just after waking in the dark, knowing pounced upon her before she could guard against it.

The man who slept beside her would never fall in love with her.

Aoife rose from bed. She wandered the lamplit corridors of Bri Leith while all others slept, feeling that she had finally, truly, awakened.

As things were now, so they would always be. While some kinds of love could be learnt, the kind she longed for could not. It struck suddenly, like lightning, or not at all. If Lir was going to fall in love with her, he would have done so by now.

Why could he not love her? Why could he not love the woman who stood before him, who ruled beside him, danced with him at feasts, wrapped her legs around him and made him moan in the deep night?

At that moment, Aoife emerged from her thoughts and took stock of her surroundings.

She stood outside the room where Lir's children slept.

The truth of things was plain to see.

Lir's heart had no room for that kind of love. The space in his heart which should have been hers, he gave to his children.

No. He gave it to Aobh, through his children. Their eyes were her eyes; in each of them lived some shard of her nature. And did others not say that Lir doted too much on them? Had her father not warned him to give less time to them, and more to his lordship?

Lir had obeyed her father, but only in deed. Not in his heart.

It was suddenly so clear what Aoife must do.

DAPPLED SUNLIGHT DANCED among the beech leaves where Finola watched her brothers play.

Aodh, Conn and Fiachra had risen early and were practising for an upcoming hurley game. The glade in which they sported lay deep in the forest, far from the prying eyes of any Gaels. All the same, Finola liked to keep watch. She did not enjoy games other than those which exercised the mind. Hurley bored her, yet she liked to watch her brothers play.

She enjoyed less the intricacies of the game – it mostly involved them hitting each other with their sticks then protesting innocence – and more what the game revealed in the players. Aodh loved to remind Conn and Fiachra that he was older than they, taking every opportunity to give instruction. Yet his authority quickly crumpled under pressure and he allowed them to push him this way and that, though he did not see it.

As for the twins, they dashed and passed and intercepted as if invisible threads bound their minds together. They would move from laughing to squabbling to scrapping almost faster than Finola could follow. Conn and Fiachra understood that it was hard for Aodh to stand outside of their fellowship, and Finola observed the many subtle ways in which they tried to include him, only to unwittingly exclude him a moment later.

Finola's thoughts drifted from the game. She noticed a subtle change in the shade of the late summer leaves. Autumn was not far off. Finola relished the time of turning and the colder months that followed. The long, bright days would give way to darkness and dreaming. Wandering bards would come in from the cold and take up residence at the hearths of Bri Leith, telling tales that could only be told at those times, unravelling them over many days and nights. Finola longed to hear of Lugh and Nuada, of the dreaded Fomorians who hung bodies from the masts of their ships...

'Children?'

A voice broke through Finola's thoughts. Their stepmother had come.

The game ceased as Aoife stepped into the sunlight. She must have some news to deliver if she had sought them out here. Finola had observed Aoife growing increasingly distant of late. She spoke less and less with the people of Bri Leith and with Lir, and hardly at all with Finola and her brothers. Finola had ransacked her memories of recent days, seeking some offence she might have given her stepmother, but found nothing.

'There you are. I have been looking for you all afternoon. Children, I need you to go home and pack your things.'

'Where are we going?' asked Conn.

'To Uisnech. I would like to visit my father, and for you to come with me. I know I have not found enough time for you recently. It will do us good to take a trip away together.'

'But we have a hurley game tomorrow,' said Fiachra. 'We've been practising every day.'

'You do little else besides playing hurley,' said Aoife. 'There will be other games. Come along now.'

'Now?' said Conn.

'Yes, now. I have a carriage ready and waiting for us.'

'But——'

'Do not test me,' said Aoife before Conn could finish. 'Come with me or you will not play hurley again until you have beards on your chins.'

Silently the boys acquiesced. Each was already rehearsing what they would say to their father about this. Finola walked between them and their stepmother as they made their way to Bri Leith, wondering why they must leave so urgently. She knew the business of the court well; she could discern no reason for hurrying away.

They each packed their things and gathered beside the carriage.

'Where is Father? Isn't he going to say goodbye to us?' asked Aodh.

'Your father is the lord of Bri Leith. A position which may be yours one day. You would do well to stop clinging to his coat-tails,' said Aoife. A strange look passed over her face. 'I'm sorry,' she said. 'I did not sleep well. Come, let us go or we shall lose the daylight.'

The children climbed into the carriage. Aoife followed and cracked the reins.

Heavy silence persisted as the hours passed. Aoife had described their outing as being for pleasure, yet she seemed to be far from at ease. Finola noticed that every time they passed a body of water, Aoife would study it as if trying to work something out in her mind. Grey clouds covered the sun and cast the landscape in gloom.

At length the road took them past Lough Derravaragh. As they passed the lake, Aoife called to the driver, 'Stop here.'

She climbed down and bade the children join her.

'Why are we stopping?' asked Finola. 'We don't seem to be taking the best road for Uisnech. There are far shorter routes we could have taken than this one.'

'And why must we take the shortest route? We are not Gaels, rushing to fit all we can into a brief span of years. I enjoy this route. The lake is fine for swimming. See for yourselves; take a swim and wash off the dust of the road.'

The boys did not hesitate. They leapt from the carriage and ran for the water, stripping off as they went. Finola remained in the carriage, though.

'What's wrong?' asked Aoife.

'Nothing. I just don't feel like swimming.'

'Your brothers are all swimming. You should join them.'

'I don't want to shiver all the way to Uisnech. We have still a long way to go.'

Aoife rolled her eyes. 'Do you wish it said that Finola is too scared of the cold to take a swim? Would you have people say that you are aloof, that you have no sense of fun?'

'I didn't know that you planned to spread tales about me.'

Aoife's mouth twisted into a snarl. 'Do not give me cheek. I am the Lady of Bri Leith and you will do as I say. I wish for some peace from whining children. Get into the water.'

Finola had never heard Aoife speak in such a tone. Stunned, she climbed down from the carriage and crossed the short expanse of grass that led from the road to the water's edge. She stripped off her clothes, slipped off her shoes and waded in.

Finola walked upon the lakebed, her feet finding purchase in the mud. Further out, her brothers shouted and splashed, oblivious to the strange words that had just passed between Finola and Aoife.

The water reached Finola's waist. Sharp cold made her gasp.

Yet it was not the cold that troubled her. It was not the cold that screamed in her mind, warning her that something was wrong. Very wrong.

Finola turned back to the shore.

Aoife stood at the water's edge. Her eyes were closed, her brow furrowed in concentration as she spoke rapid words which Finola could not hear but which felt like a sickness spreading through the air.

Aoife held a wand in her hand.

'Get out!' screamed Finola. 'Get out of the water!'

She ran for the shore then stopped and turned. Her brothers had ceased playing but had not obeyed her.

'We're in danger! Get out of the water now!'

Aodh began to swim towards her. Conn and Fiachra followed.

But it was too late.

'Hurry...'

Finola could no longer speak; her throat seemed to be caught in an invisible vice. Pain shot through her from head to toe and she collapsed into the water. She writhed in panic as water filled her lungs; she desperately tried to swim but the pain only grew worse. She shook and spasmed; it was as if every drop of her blood was on fire, her bones melting...

Finola's head broke the surface. She heaved water from her lungs and screamed out in rage at her stepmother and her magic.

Yet she did not scream.

She could give only a low, plaintive, trumpeting sound.

Finola looked herself over in horror. She had become a swan.

Finola looked back towards her brothers. They had met the same fate. They must have known the same pain, the same fear.

She turned back to Aoife.

Her stepmother stood still on the lakeshore.

Finola paddled towards her, not caring what danger that might put her in. She went on honking at Aoife as she did so, not caring whether Aoife understood her or not. Finola had known something was wrong. Why hadn't she listened to her own instincts? She had somehow known that Aoife meant them harm, even before they had set off for Uisnech.

Well, perhaps she could not speak her fury, but she could show it another way. She knew the strength that lay in a swan's wing.

Finola reached the edge of the water. She climbed out...

But could not.

Some invisible barrier held her back, binding her to the water.

Finola's wings and beak exploded into action. She battered at the barrier, enough strength in her swipes to break a man's arm, yet her raging did her no good.

After Finola had given up her struggle, Aoife spoke.

'Struggle and fight all you want,' she said. 'It shall make no difference. This is the form you shall live in, today and all your days.'

Finola regarded her stepmother. It seemed to her that doubt trembled in Aoife's eyes and voice. Instead of fighting, she simply watched Aoife.

'Do not look at me like that,' said Aoife. 'I do what any wife would do. I work to gain my husband's love, the love that is my right and due, clearing whatever obstacle stands in its way.'

Her lip trembled.

'We Tuatha Dé Danaan are immortal. Thus I must make my spell immortal. You shall never leave this lake, otherwise you would go to Lir and set him against me. I could have killed you; instead I have been merciful. Try to find peace with the forms you now wear. If you fail in that, the fault is not mine.'

Aoife turned away. She walked the short way to the carriage. Raising her leg to climb in, she stopped.

Turned back.

'For the sake of my sister,' she said.

Aoife took her wand from her cloak and spoke words of magic again.

Finola felt a loosening in her throat, as if a scab had been torn away.

She shrieked at Aoife as her brothers swam up beside her.

'You monster! You vile sorceress! We trusted you! You came into our home, you ate beside us, you lived all these years with us and now you do this to us—'

'I have been merciful! I told you my original intention, did I not? You would have lived as unspeaking swans forever, or until some man made you meat for his table. No more. I have changed my spell, and this shall be your fate.

'Three hundred years shall you spend upon Lough Derravaragh. When those years have passed, you shall fly to the Sea of Moyle, which lies between Eriu and Alba. Three hundred years shall you spend there. A further three hundred shall you spend upon the Isle of Inish Glora, where the waters are calm and peaceful. You shall take your original form again only when a king's son from the North marries a king's daughter from the South.

'In all that time, the use of your voices shall be yours. Speak, sing, curse me if you will. But I go now to live the life I am due; that would have been mine but for you. In my mercy I have honoured my sister, and I depart with my conscience clear.'

Those were the last words Aoife ever spoke to Finola, Aodh, Conn and Fiachra. She climbed into the carriage, cracked the reins and did not look back.

LIR'S CHILDREN spent the rest of the day and much of the night trying to break free of Lough Derravaragh. They could not. Eventually they succumbed to exhaustion and buried their heads in their necks, drifting on the water as the stars wheeled overhead.

In the morning they tried again, but only half-heartedly. Each of them sensed the iron power of Aoife's spell. It would not be broken.

They spoke among themselves, lamenting the dark turn their fates had taken. Then, around noon, they saw a woman of the Gaels walking past the lake.

None of them had ever spoken to a Gael before. Yet immediately Aodh called out, 'Hello! Come here and speak with us!'

The woman seemed stunned to be addressed by a swan. At further pressing from the siblings, she approached the water and conversed with them. They told their whole tale, and the woman saw no reason to disbelieve it.

'Go to your people and tell them this tale,' said Finola. 'Then leave your home and go abroad, telling this tale to all who will listen. It is bound to reach the ears of the Tuatha Dé Danaan in time, and our father will come to us.'

'What if my people wish to come and see you for themselves?' said the woman.

'Let them,' said Finola. 'Encourage them. What shall occupy us in the days to come, other than talking with whomever visits us?'

So the woman left. She did as instructed, telling the tale of the sidhe-turned-swans far and wide, while the siblings occupied themselves with foraging for food in the lake's murky waters.

It was only a day until their next visitors arrived.

A party from the woman's village arrived on the lakeshore.

It seemed to Finola that they came ready to mock the woman and her tale of talking swans. That changed when four swans paddled up to the water's edge and greeted them.

'Welcome to our waters,' said Finola. 'We are the Children of Lir. Please, sit, and we will tell you our tale.'

So those people heard the full story, each sibling taking a turn to tell part of it. Wonder and deep pity moved through the listeners. When the telling was over, one of them said, 'It is terrible what was done to you, but you have moved our hearts in sharing your tale. We will go now and leave you in peace.'

'No,' said Conn. 'Don't. Stay.'

'Yes,' said Fiachra. It's so dull to swim about here all day. We can't play hurley or any other games. Tell us about yourselves, or tell us a legend of the Gaels.'

The man who had spoken was willing. He told them every story he could think of, and his wife sang them songs. It was late evening when finally the Gaels left.

More visitors arrived the following day, and the day after. News of the strange fate of the Children of Lir spread like wild-fire across the land, and soon Gaelic people were travelling for many days to see them. People who had come so far did not want to immediately leave after meeting the swan children. They put up tents, and some took it upon themselves to distribute food, until the land around the lake was bright with firelight and lamplight each night. People sat pressed together upon the lakeshore as, each evening, the siblings told their tale. After it was told, other tales and songs came. None among Lir's children had been known for their singing prowess, but the song of any sidhe is marvellous to human ears, especially coming from the throat of a swan.

And it was not only Gaels who made the pilgrimage to Lough Derravaragh.

AS THE STORY spread among the Gaels, so it was heard in time by the Tuatha Dé Danaan.

Lir had not known anything was wrong. He believed his children were at Uisnech with his wife. Aoife told Bodb Dearg that the children were at home with their father, and he had no reason to doubt her. But there were some among the sidhe who conversed with Gaels from time to time, while others would spy on them for simple amusement.

So in time some Tuatha came to Lough Derravaragh. They walked among the Gaels, tall and shining and bright, and the Gaels stared at them in awe. Yet those Tuatha did not remain long by the lake.

They went to Lir's court. They found him there and told him when they had seen and heard. As strange as the story was, as much as Lir wished to dismiss it, he could not. He left his hall and rode at all speed for Lough Derravaragh.

Lir arrived just before sunset. Ignoring the crowds of gawping Gaels, he dismounted and walked to the water's edge just as the swans were preparing to tell their tale.

He knew them at once.

'My children,' he gasped.

The four children stared at him for a moment, then rushed

for the water's edge. It was the saddest thing the folk there ever saw, the way they flapped and beat their wings as they desperately tried to leave the water and go to him. Weeping, Lir waded into the water, and the swan-children swam in circles around him as he stroked their heads and necks.

Lir sat and listened to their tale alongside everyone else that evening. When it was finished, he left them, promising he would soon return. But he had business to attend to first.

Lir rode for the Hill of Uisnech. He arrived in the deep night, entered Bodb Dearg's hall and found his wife feasting with the High King and many guests.

'Aoife!' he called out, pointing a finger at her as he strode down the hall. 'Traitor! Liar! Dark druid who deceived me, I am deceived no more!'

Bodb Dearg did not know what had come over Lir. Nor did he like hearing his daughter described in such terms. He rose to his feet and put his hand on his sword hilt.

'Halt there, Lir, and remember to whom you speak,' he said.

Lir halted ten paces from where Aoife sat at her father's side. 'I know whom I address,' he said. 'My wife, my own wife, who told me that she was taking my children on a trip to visit Uisnech. Yet you never brought them here, did you, Aoife?'

'I said no such thing,' said Aoife. 'Perhaps you have drunk too much ale, husband.'

'You took them away with you in your carriage,' Lir continued as if she had not spoken. 'You led them to Lough Derravaragh and there you ordered them to enter the water. "For a swim," you said. And they are still there. Still swimming.

For as soon as they entered the water, you turned them into swans.'

Hubbub broke out at that. Aoife tried to laugh it off, but there was a redness to her cheeks, a shaking in her hand which was observed by many about her, including her father.

Bodb Dearg fixed his daughter with an icy stare.

'Aoife. This is a serious charge which has been brought against you. I am going to ask you a question. Bear in mind that if you deny this charge, I will ride straight from here to Lough Derravaragh and ascertain the truth of the matter myself.

'Did you do as your husband claims, and turn your own sister's children into swans?'

Aoife looked set to deny it, but then she lowered her eyes.

'Yes.'

'That is not all,' broke in Lir. 'Her spell is an elaborate one. Three hundred years, three hundred whole years, must they spend on those waters. Then another three hundred on the Sea of Moyle, and another on Inish Glora. They shall only be free when a king's son from the North marries a king's daughter from the South.'

'I was merciful!' snapped Aoife. 'I set the spell at first to last an eternity! I put limits on it for the love of my sister. And since all here must know it, let all here know why I did it. It is the fault of this man.' She got to her feet and pointed at Lir. 'All of us desire and deserve the love of our husband or wife, do we not? Yet I never had love from this man. Not true love. All he ever thought of was his children. He never—'

She got no further than that. Bodb Dearg made his own spell in that moment. He spoke dark, thunderous words which made of Aoife not a swan but a spirit, a spectral thing with no form, which blew away upon a sudden gust of wind.

IN TIME, Lir's children grew used to their life upon Lough Derravaragh. Though they sang mournful songs each night, they took pride in their growing skill at singing, and some measure of joy twined into their grief songs. They each came to know as many tales and songs as even the best bards. Indeed, no bard in Eriu would have dreamed of letting a year go by without spending a week or two camped at Lough Derravaragh, sharing tales and songs with the swan sidhe. The siblings also took joy in seeing sidhe and Gaels mingling happily on their shore.

Aodh once said to his siblings, 'Even though we sing of our fate each night, days now go by in which I do not remember the life we used to live.'

'It is the same for me,' said Conn, and the other two agreed.

So it was that the Lir's children found peace upon the lake for a time. But even a span of time so long as three hundred years must eventually end.

One day, the four swans found themselves compelled to take flight. With no control over their actions, they rose from the lake and flew northeast across Eriu, much to the shock of those camped by the lake.

All the way across the country they flew, until they came to the Sea of Moyle.

It was on that sea that their days of peace ended.

THE SEA of Moyle was a frightening sight to behold. Fierce winds flung foaming waves against the shore, sea-spray shooting far inland.

The four swans alighted upon the ocean. The sea did not seem to welcome them. It tossed them this way and that, sharp underwater rocks scraping their bellies, salty waves slapping and drenching them over and over again. The sky was darkening and they each feared their first night on the waves.

The harsh weather did not abate until the following afternoon. The children had been in swan form for three hundred years, so they were capable in those forms, and learnt soon enough how to ride the waves. Yet the worst thing was not navigating the sea; it was knowing that they would live this way for three hundred long years.

They gathered together as the sun rose behind grey-black clouds.

'I do not know if I can live like this,' said Aodh. 'I once thought it was a hard fate to swim upon Lough Derravaragh year after year. I laugh at that thought now.'

'If you can laugh at that twist in our fates, you can laugh at this one,' said Finola, though she sounded anything but sure of her words. 'We found our way through those days and we shall find our way through these. Last night was hard, but no sea is tempestuous all year round. We shall know days here where the sun shines down and the water is calm, when we can forage and feed with nothing to worry us. That is the best we can ask of our days now, and it is up to us to feel gratitude for such days when they come.'

Finola's brothers contemplated her words in silence. They each knew the truth of them. Each sibling had changed greatly since the time when they were children of the sidhe. That bond which Conn and Fiachra had shared belonged to all of them now. The twins' playfulness had receded. Where previously they would have played and pranked, they now spent days and even weeks in contemplation.

Only one thing remained the same: that Finola's brothers looked up to her and sought her guidance when times were hard.

If times had ever been hard, it was now. Though those quiet days Finola predicted did come, far more often came days of storm and tempest, days in which they could neither rest nor talk, but only occupy themselves with survival. They grew as adept at living upon that strait as any other bird.

But every now and then, a storm comes which makes all others look like its infant children.

One hundred years into their sojourn, such a storm came.

THE FOUR SWAN siblings were at the northwest of their range, some miles east of the Skerrie Islands, when they first caught sight of the storm.

It appeared to them as a curtain of darkness upon the western horizon. Conn noticed it first, and called out to his siblings. They bobbed upon the water for a time, simply watching it. Each of them knew that there was no escaping such a storm. It would come to them and they would ride it as best they could.

Yet they had never seen such a storm.

It stretched from one end of the horizon to the other, cloaking water and sky in a deep, tarry darkness. It seemed to be a living thing, a primeval being born to devour all in its path.

It would be upon them soon.

'Listen to me,' said Finola, breaking their reverie. 'Each one of us shall survive this storm. I swear it. Yet we shall not survive it together. The storm will cast us far across the sea. When it does, do not think of staying together. Think only of remaining afloat, and of watching for any rocks or skerries which the waves might skewer you upon.

'You each know the westernmost of the Skerrie Islands? When the storm has passed, we shall meet there. All of us.'

So the Children of Lir settled in to await the coming of the storm.

The wind struck them first. Then came the rising of the waves, and the hammering, horizontal rain, while thunder reverberated all around them and jagged spears of lightning smote the sea. The swelling waves were like enormous claws trying to pull them down; it took all their strength to stay afloat.

Soon their strength was exhausted. Yet still the storm hammered them, trying to force them down beneath the water. None of them had a thought of staying together. They each thought only of their next breath; of summoning some last reserve of strength to keep them from the depths, which grew ever more inviting.

Down there in the darkness was rest. Relief from struggle, relief from all their years of sorrow, the lingering lance of betrayal. The siren song of the deep grew ever louder as the storm sang on, day and night, until finally it dissipated.

The sea fell still. Sunlight shone through the clouds and danced on the water. It was as if the world had ended and now began again.

Each of Lir's children was desperate to be reunited with their siblings. Yet none of them could find the strength to make their way to the meeting place. Finola and Fiachra could each tell where they were by shape of the coastline; Aodh and Conn had been thrown far out to sea. Yet in time, they found the strength to flap their wings and find their way to the westernmost Skerrie Island. Aodh and Conn made use of that bone-knowledge which they had acquired as swans, which told them the way south and thus to Eriu. They each travelled along the coast and, in time, the four siblings gathered together again.

They celebrated their survival. Wings flapped furiously and necks intertwined as they greeted one another, honking wildly. Now they knew their own strength. Now they knew they would reach the end of their ordeal.

It is so much quicker to tell of how those three hundred years passed than to live them. Storm after storm came, but after the one just told of, none seemed formidable to Lir's children. Finally, the day came when without a word, they rose as one and flew inland. Over Eriu, all the way to the West Coast they flew, to Connacht and the Isle of Inish Glora.

The island was small, with gentle slopes and patches of verdant woodland. The autumn sun shone as the swans arrived at the lake and alighted upon the water. They swam a circuit around it, learning their new territory. The lake was much smaller than Lough Derravaragh and had an air of tranquility.

'I did not see any habitations upon the island,' said Aodh eventually. 'I think this final leg of our journey will be a quiet one.'

Aodh's words proved true. Though storms blew in from the west sometimes, they did little to disturb the lake water. Finally at peace, the siblings lapsed into long periods of quiet. They communicated less and less in speech, yet sang more than ever; somehow wordless song made more sense than speech in those years. If thoughts came to their minds, they were thoughts of food and shelter. Otherwise, their minds were like the sky above them, untroubled by the clouds that passed across it.

All that changed when a boat alighted upon the shore of Inish Glora.

It arrived on a summer's day. The boat docked in a bay on the island's east side, piloted by a man wearing a curious, drab garment. The styling of his hair was curious too; it was shaved at the front, revealing the dome of his scalp. His robe was bound by a length of rope.

The four swans looked up from their feeding and watched with intense curiosity as this man – the first man they had seen in over two hundred years – walked the length of the lakeshore.

His eyes returned over and over to a small island lying near the centre of the lake.

Eventually he halted, closed his eyes and put his hands together. The four swans watched him from nearby, but he paid them little heed.

'Jesus Christ, my lord and saviour,' he said. 'I believe I have found a place to make my quiet dwelling and live in contemplation of God's glory. If this is where you wish me to dwell, please grant me a sign.'

Whatever sign he might have had in mind, it was not for a swan to suddenly speak to him.

'Who are you?' asked Finola. 'What is your name, and who is this god you pray to?'

The man's eyes bulged.

The four swans swam closer.

'Your eyes and ears do not deceive you,' said Conn. 'We are swans, though we have not always been so, and my sister did indeed just address you.'

Eventually the man found his voice. 'My name is Malachi,' he said. 'I am a monk, and my god is the one true god, whose son is Jesus Christ, our saviour.'

'I am Finola. These are my brothers Aodh, Conn and Fiachra. Why have you come to Inish Glora, Malachi?'

'I wish to find a place where I can build a small and simple dwelling for myself. There I shall do nothing but see to my body's most basic needs and otherwise pray to God, night and day. You... you said you were not always swans?'

'We were once Tuatha Dé Danaan,' said Fiachra. 'Sit and we will tell you our tale.'

So the Children of Lir told their tale for the first time in hundreds of years. Malachi sat enrapt. When they had finished, he said, 'I sought a sign that I should dwell here. Though there is much in you tale that troubles me, our meeting is so strange that I believe it must be that sign. Would you consent for me to join you and live at your side here?'

The swans looked at one another.

'We would be glad of it,' said Finola.

MALACHI LABOURED for many days to build his dwelling upon the little island on the lake. The swans could not help him so they simply watched as his hut took shape. It was shaped like a beehive and formed from stones packed together without any binding substance. Malachi told them that he would install nothing inside it but a simple bench for sitting and sleeping upon.

'Why is it that you forgo comfort?' Finola asked him.

'God made this world, but he is not of this world,' answered Malachi. 'The pleasures which he made available to us are like spiderwebs in which we become stuck and entangled, unable to soar free into the realm of the spirit.'

'Where does your god dwell if he is not in the world?'

'He is beyond the world. He is everywhere and nowhere at once. It is a difficult thing to understand, I know. Like explaining colour to a man with no sight. That is why I wish to live in quiet contemplation. I hope that over many long, lonely days, the clouds of misunderstanding shall clear from my mind and the light of knowing shall shine through.'

'We have lived without comfort for years beyond count,' said Conn. 'Yet still we dream of the day when we shall take our natural shape again and return to our people. We shall not forgo dancing then, or rich food, or jesting or sport or any other pleasure. Such things are the very blood of life.'

'Your people may believe such things, and so do many of mine. Yet that is because you have not seen the light of truth. God has not graced you with his presence yet.'

'Why not?' asked Fiachra. 'Does he dislike us?'

Malachi seemed to wrestle for words. 'It is the teaching of the church that your kind... well, in truth, we are divided. Many say the Tuatha Dé Danaan,' and here he made a curious sign, 'do not exist at all, being but superstitions of the faithless and ignorant. Other say you are agents of the Devil.'

'Who?' asked Finola.

So Malachi explained that God had an eternal enemy, who lived for nothing but to spread wickedness in the world.

'Do *you* believe we are agents of this creature?' asked Aodh, his tone rank with offence.

Malachi hesitated. 'I... I do not know what I believe on this matter. I... I should get back to my building.'

Things were a little less cordial between Malachi and the Children of Lir after that. They were each stung by what the monk had said. But they lived close alongside one another, and in time they began to converse freely again. It seemed that Malachi had a subtle fear of them yet could not help seeking out their company. In time he began asking them to tell him tales of the Tuatha Dé Danaan. This was only that he might later record them for posterity, he said. But his eyes lit up when he pictured Lugh charging across the battlefield towards Balor, and he spoke little of heaven at such times.

Malachi and the Children of Lir lived alongside each other for years. Occasionally he would leave the island to spend time at his monastery. Once, he spoke with his abbot about the talking swans he had encountered. The abbot warned him to be wary of such creatures, saying that surely the Devil put them there to tempt him from his true path. Yet Malachi maintained his friendship with the Children of Lir.

WORD SPREAD through the monastery of Malachi and his friendship with the swans. It spread to laymen and spread across Eriu. So it was that Fiadh, the king of Munster's daughter, heard that Lir's children were alive and to be found on Inish Glora.

She could scarcely believe it. The tale of the four talking swans had been a favourite of hers since childhood. Her nursemaid had insisted it was a true tale, but she herself had harboured doubts. But now supposedly the swans had been found, alive and well.

Fiadh was due to be married at Beltane that year. She was to marry the king of Ulster's son, and now she knew exactly what she wanted for her wedding gift.

A new visitor arrived at Inish Glora one winter's day.

'Malachi,' the man called out from the lakeshore. 'I come on behalf of the king of Munster, carrying a message for you.'

Malachi emerged from his hut. He saw his swan friends paddling over from the far side of the lake.

He got into his little boat and rowed across the water. Soon he stood before the man and said, 'What message could the king of Munster have for a humble hermit such as I?'

'My king wishes you to know that his daughter will marry the king of Ulster's son this spring. As a wedding gift,' and here the man broke off to watch the four swans paddle up to him, 'she desires the four swans which are said to be the children of the sidhe-lord Lir.'

The man looked startled as Finola spoke. 'Do you mean to tell us,' she said, 'that a king's son from the North is set to marry a king's daughter from the South?'

'Er... well, yes, I suppose so,' said the messenger.

At that, a furious honking and splashing and beating of wings broke out among the four swans. They rubbed their necks together and swam around in circles.

'A king's daughter from the South... a king's son from the North,' said Malachi to himself, remembering the tale the swans had told him. A smile spread across his face. 'So, my friends, you are free.'

Malachi and the messenger watched in wonder as the four swans, one by one, approached the edge of the water.

Finola waded out first. As she did so, she fell to the grass. Feathers fell from her body. Her neck shrivelled, her beak fell from her face and she resumed her original form.

Aodh followed, then Conn, then Fiachra. They each become Tuatha Dé Danaan again.

But not as they once were.

The Children of Lir were children no more. They were four hunched and ancient grey-skins. What little hair they had blew away on the wind as they shivered on the lakeshore, their grey skin turning blue.

After a few moments, they could no longer stand. Malachi and the messenger helped each of them to lie down, wincing at the feel of their brittle bones beneath their sagging skin.

Malachi knelt down beside Finola. She reached out a hand to him, and the monk took her hand in his own.

Sensing that this was a moment not to intrude upon, the messenger retreated up the hillside.

'Malachi,' said Finola, her voice as dry as snakeskin. 'We are freed from our prison. But we will not live out the hour.'

'Let me leave you and your brothers in peace then,' said Malachi, a tear trailing down his cheek.

'No,' said Finola. 'You said... you said that your god would not allow us into heaven were we not baptised.'

'That... is true,' said Malachi, though it was hard to believe in that moment that such a kind, peaceful and wise being as Finola could ever be cast into Hell.

'I do not think Danu would mind,' said Finola, 'if you baptised us. Just to be sure. Though I have lived too long surrounded by water, I have no wish to see your Hell and its fires.'

Malachi nodded. 'What say the rest of you?'

Finola's brothers wearily nodded their assent.

So Malachi set to work. He called the messenger down to assist him and, one by one, he carried Lir's children into the water and baptised them.

Fiachra was the last. When it was done, Malachi lay him down beside his siblings and went to speak with Finola.

But she had closed her eyes for the last time.

So had all of the Children of Lir. They died there upon the lakeshore, side by side. And whether you believe they went to Heaven, or that their souls flew to Tir Nan Óg or some other place, it can be said for sure that Malachi missed them every day for as long as he lived. When his own death came, he greeted it happily, believing that wherever his swan friends had gone, he would go there too.[1]

THE END

AFTERWORD

In the introduction to his translation of the *Táin Bó Cúailnge*, that epic tale at the heart of the Ulster Cycle of Irish Mythology, Ciaran Carson writes:

The Táin might well be an archaeological site, but it need not be an appalling prospect. One could equally well see it as a magnificently ruined cathedral, whose fabric displays the ravages of war, fashion and liturgical expediency: a compendium of architectural interpolations, erasures, deliberate archaisms, renovations and restorations; a space inhabited by many generations, each commenting on their predecessors.

I love this quotation. For me it applies as much to the Mythological Cycle as it does to the Tain. The cycle is complex, dense and confusing. But we can choose to appreciate it for its very complexity, which reveals more to us the further we explore.

The same can be said of its principal characters, who refuse to fit into tidy categories. They're heroic one minute, conniving and cruel the next. I like this. A very reductive type of thinking is often applied to stories, in which we attempt to strip away every element of a tale to reveal the message lurking beneath. As if tone and texture, place and character, pacing, dialogue, simile, historical placement and everything else were but artifice to be surgically removed and discarded by the truly discerning reader. What is left is compared to contemporary values; if the two don't square up, we say the story should be remade or forgotten.

Myth encourages us to steer our thinking in the opposite direction. Instead of narrowing our vision, we open it wide. We explore the perspective of people whose worldview was vastly different from our own. We consider that a river can also be a woman, that a man can be a salmon and a stag. The Fomorians come from over and under the sea; they are monsters, magicians, pirates and Vikings. Our logical mind struggles to accept this; our dreaming, mythic mind has no problem with it. Manannán's meeting with Bran might be a Christian sermon, or maybe a pagan one, or maybe both. And where did the pre-Christian stories come from in the first place? Did the bards of old cleverly construct them, or did Ireland's hills and bogs somehow speak the stories into their dreams?

We'll never know, and it's good not to know. Myth multiplies our perspectives. It teaches shapeshifting; it's an incredible mental gym. We must attempt to hold polarised perspectives in our minds or else give up on these stories altogether. Myth, folk tale and pseudo-history. Towering gods, flawed humans, mischievous fairies. The language of crows and stones; the artifice of a medieval monk. Let the stories be all of the above. Let the Dagda be kind at times and cruel at times. Just like us.

My deep thanks for accompanying me on this journey. If you want it to continue, please go out and find other authors and storytellers – particularly Irish ones – to read and learn from. I want to recommend in particular the wonderful podcast *Candlelit Tales*, whose hosts have been such generous supports to me and one of whom, Aron Hegarty, was kind enough to read the audiobook version of this title.

This probably goes without saying, but if at all possible, get yourself to Ireland. There's something so incredibly special about walking the landscape of a story you have long been in love with. Walk the Boyne Valley while daydreaming about Boann. Gaze across the dark Atlantic, picturing Fomorians rising from the water. To do so is absolutely a pilgrimage, a stepping out of the ordinary and into the mythic. And that's something we all need.

If you'd like to hear more from me, take a listen to my *House of Legends* podcast or try some of my other books. *Finn & The Fianna* follows on from this title so that's a good next step; I've included the first chapter in this volume.

The bestselling *Scottish Myths & Legends* is there if you'd like to sample Scotland's stories; and fan-favourite *The Orkney*

Cycle beckons those who seeking total immersion in Pre-Christian Scotland. You can also train as a storyteller with me online or join one of my mythic immersion retreats in the Scottish Highlands. There's lots on offer; the best way to keep in touch is to join my mailing list at houseoflegends.me/landing-page, which gets you the Celtic Mythology Handbook. It's a free, full colour PDF and it's the guide I wish I'd had when I started out.

One last thing: if you enjoyed this book, please do leave a review. Reviews help me enormously and they help other readers.

Wishing you many good tales around many fires.

Daniel Allison

FINN & THE FIANNA: CHAPTER ONE

Long ago, in a time when the veils between the worlds were thinner than they are now, there lived in the wilds of Ireland and Scotland a band of warriors called the Fianna. It was their job to guard those lands against the men and monsters who would invade them. When the shores of their beloved homelands were safe, the Fianna would feast, fight and make their own trouble.

Coull was the leader of the Fianna. He was tall, fair, open-hearted and open-handed. His heart belonged to a maiden named Muirne, who loved him as he loved her.

Muirne was the daughter of Teig, Chief Druid to the High King of Ireland. You might have expected Teig to see Coull, the renowned Captain of the Fianna, as a fine match for his daughter. But it was not so. For the Fianna, admired as they were, were wild men. They lived their lives and made their beds beneath the boughs of trees, at the ocean's edge, in the high hill's shadow. They had dealings with the sidhe, whom some call the fairy folk; their trade was in battle, in blood and iron. In short, they did not always make good husbands.

Coull came to Teig's dwelling, a shining white fort on the Hill of Allen, and offered his suit. Teig refused him. Coull left and when Teig was next gone, he returned, climbing over the wall as the fort glistened in the moonlight. He found Muirne, kissed her and led her away into the wild woods.

Deep into the forest they went. By a waterfall pool they bound their hands together and exchanged vows of love. In beech-dappled light and to the blackbird's song they loved and laughed and fell into one another, knowing their time would be over soon.

Teig discovered his daughter had been taken. Storms shook Ireland as the druid raged. He went to Tara, seat of the High King, and demanded that the sword of justice strike Coull. The High King was reluctant.

'Coull is my friend,' he said, 'and the Fianna are a force to be feared.'

'If you do not move against Coull,' said Teig, 'I will speak druid-words against your name.'

The king quivered at that. Even he was not immune to a druid's curse. He called a meeting of his most trusted men, and set his power against the power of Coull.

War drums resounded at Tara. Battle-horns blew from east to west. Messengers crossed the country as fighting men took the road to Tara, where a great camp soon spread across the plain.

Among the king's forces were a group of Fianna disloyal to Coull. These were the Sons of Morna. Chief amongst them was Suchet, a tall, fierce and cunning warrior whom his brothers both loved and feared. His chief henchmen were bald-headed Conan and quick-tongued Black Gary. The High King promised Suchet that if he brought down Coull, he would be made Captain of the Fianna.

Coull and Muirne emerged from the forest. Around Coull the Fianna rallied and soon their army was ready to march. On the Plain of Cnuca, where the City of Dublin now sits, the two armies met.

For the first time, men of the Fianna faced one another across the battlefield.

It would not be the last time.

The sword-hour came. Spears were rattled, shields were beaten by grim-faced warriors ready for slaughter. Though the sun shone upon them, they knew this day was a dark one.

Ravens gathered in the air, hungry for the feast.

Coull took from his belt the Dord Fiann, the horn of the Fianna. He blew upon it; Suchet's horn answered and the battle began. Soon the grass was red and littered with corpses as the Fianna fought their brothers.

Amid the chaos of the battle, Suchet spied Coull. He called

to Black Gary and the two of them fought their way through the melee until no man stood between Suchet and Coull.

Coull attacked. Suchet answered his strike and the two greatest warriors of the Fianna fought.

For all Suchet's size, strength and cunning, he was not a match for Coull. The quick-armed captain slipped like a ghost through Suchet's attacks and lunged forward. Suchet pulled back but was not quick enough. Coull's sword pierced his eye. Suchet was thereafter known as 'Goll', or 'Blind', MacMorna.

Coull would have won then, but for Black Gary. As Suchet roared in pain, Black Gary threw himself against Coull from behind. Coull stumbled and it was all Suchet needed. He swung his sword and cut Coull's head from his body.

'Coull is dead!' went up the cry.

It carried across the plain, and soon Coull's forces were in rout, running for the forest that bordered the plain.

The king's forces cheered. Dark liquid streaming from his eye, Suchet laughed. The battle was won.

But what of Muirne?

Watching from the woods that bordered the battlefield, Muirne saw her lover slain. She retreated, heart-riven, into the forest. In a sunlit glade she fell to her knees and keened for Coull. Days and nights passed as she sang the death-song of the golden-haired, gentle-hearted warrior. Coull would never know his own child; the child growing within her.

When the first agonies of her grief had passed, Muirne

made her way home to the Hill of Allen. Teig would not open his gates to her. He came to the rampart and called her shameful names until she turned and walked away.

Muirne took another road. Travelling by night lest the Sons of Morna were after her, she made her way to the house of two druid-women, Liath Luachra and Bodhmall. These women were friends of hers, and they kept her hidden in their home until her son was born.

She named the boy Finn. Muirne was full of joy at her son's birth, but she was fearful too. Coull's son was a threat to Goll, and if Goll learnt of Finn's existence, he would surely kill him.

All night the three women talked as Muirne held her son to her chest. At last they came to an agreement. Muirne would leave her son with them and seek out a new life over the waves. Meanwhile, Liath Luachra and Bodhmall would take the boy into the wilds and raise him, keeping him hidden from those who would destroy him.

So it was that Muirne said goodbye to her son and left Ireland, a gown of grief heavy upon her shoulders. Finn's foster-mothers left their house and made for the deep, deep woods.

ACKNOWLEDGMENTS

Diving into Irish tradition is a daunting thing. My deepest thanks go to Mira, Maria, Frances, Paddy, Órla, Niceol, Mariam, Gráinne, Liz, Tim, Ali, Erin, Jenny, Eve, Aidan, Aron, Sorcha, Sandy and Jesse for hosting me, encouraging me and offered good craic as I traveled Ireland catching the scents of these stories and in the years that followed. Clare, thank you for going out your way to help me and believing I could do it.

Thank you to the Oak & Ash crew of Kirsten, Sorcha, Danica, Sam, John, Jake and Isa for helping me bring the stories off the page and back into the woods.

Fiona, thank you for ever-sharp editing.

Thank you to everyone who ever told these stories, wrote them down, listened to them, read them, loved them or otherwise kept them alive.

NOTES

Prologue: The Early Invasions

1. This short recounting is based upon the *Lebor Gabála Érenn*. So much of the narrative there is made up of biblical pseudo-history that is very hard to get a sense of how much (if any) older myth lies behind it.

   The shaman-like Fintan is, for many, the most appealing character of this era. His name may translate as 'white ancient' or 'white fire'; he is also referred to as Fintan Mac Bochra though the identity of 'Bochra' is unknown. In a later story, he has a dialogue with the ancient Hawk of Achill. The two of them discuss the events they have witnessed over the ages, from the death of Cesaire to the wars of the Tuatha Dé Danaan and the deeds of Cuchulainn, before dying together.

   I've removed the references to Noah and other biblical characters as I've aimed to depict a pre-Christian world, at least until the final stories of the cycle. If you're curious about the source material, you can access the *Lebor Gabála Érenn* online. I'd also highly recommend the retelling and discussion of these invasion tales on episodes 105–112 of Candlelit Tales podcast.

1. The Landing

1. The question of why the Tuatha Dé Danaan came to Ireland at this time is not resolved in the source texts. They make no speeches about reclaiming their lost homeland. I've heard some storytellers describe this as a return long in the planning, while others will depict them as having forgotten where they came from. I chose to depict the Tuatha Dé Danaan as having lingered so long in the North that they forgot their homeland, so that she in time (perhaps impatiently) called them home.

   I have talked with Irish tradition-bearers who dislike the popular contemporary notion of the Morrigan as a bloodthirsty badass. They tell me that she and her sisters were once known more as mothers and wisdom-keepers than warriors. This is fascinating, but difficult to reconcile with the events of the narrative (as you will soon see) and those of the Ulster Cycle. I tried to find a compromise by suggesting that while the sisters recognise the grim certainty of war, and excel at the practice of it, they do not thirst for it (at least in this cycle). I've taken other opportunities to flesh out the Morrigan where possible.

I refer to the Tuatha Dé Danaan sometimes by that title, sometimes in translation as the Children of Danu, and sometimes as the sidhe. The latter title derives from their association with hills and mounds, which comes about later in the narrative, but I've started using it here in order to have a snappier name to use at times. The former title refers to the goddess Danu, an early Indo-European mother goddess who gave her name to the river Danube. Despite the prominence of her name, which suggests her great significance, she is very rarely mentioned in the sources.

The descendants of the culture known as Indo-European covered a vast area, with its last cultural remnants surviving in the far west of Eurasia in Irish language and myth, and as far east as Bali, where we find the water goddess Dewi Danu. Peter Berresford Ellis includes a fascinating passage on this in the introduction to *The Mammoth Book of Celtic Myths & Legends*.

One last issue was what to call Ireland! The word Ireland is derived from Eriu, which becomes a name for the island in a pivotal moment later in the cycle. To avoid confusion when that moment comes, I chose to have the Tuatha Dé Danaan refer to Ireland as the Isle of Destiny for now.

2. Fire in the Sky

1. This chapter expands upon a short passage in the *Cath Maige Tuired*, taking further inspiration from Lady Gregory's retelling. The three sisters' methods might well remind you of Tolkien's Nazgul, whom they doubtless inspired.

3. The First Battle of Moytura

1. The first thing to clarify here is that Moytura is not a place. The word can be translated as 'The Plain of the Pillars'. To further confuse things, there is a Second Battle of Moytura, taking place in a different location. Nobody said Irish mythology was straightforward.

There is believed to have existed an 8th century text, now lost, describing the second battle. The *Cath Maige Tuired* is thought to relate the events of the 8th century text with a good level of accuracy. So we can think of the second battle (in which the Tuatha Dé Danaan fight the Fomorians) as a more ancient, authentically mythic text.

However, the medieval writers wished to create a history for the Tuatha Dé Danaan in which they fought and displaced an earlier race: the Firbolgs. Thus, according to Ó hOgáin, the second battle was more or less duplicated to create the first battle. The title, Moytura, was even borrowed, though the two battles take place in different locations; this one takes place near Cong in County Mayo. Thus you may notice, once you reach the second battle, a fair degree of similarity between the two events, although I have tried to make their atmospheres distinct.

Do bear in mind, then, that much of what you are reading here can be described as 'mythic pseudo-history'. But that needn't stop us enjoying it.

I chose to depict the Tuatha Dé Danaan as having superior military tactics to the Firbolgs. This is alluded to in the *Lebor Gabála Érenn*; I've leaned into it in order to clearly demarcate the Tuatha Dé Danaan from their foes. I emphasised the mental and physical toughness of the Firbolgs as this fits with what we come to know of them later in the narrative, and hopefully creates a sense of sympathy for them in the reader.

Corpre's speech is my own invention, taking inspiration from Amergin's poem in Part III and from the mythical Welsh poet Taliesin.

The important events of the battle are more or less as given in the *Lebor Gabála Érenn*, condensed to lend momentum to the narrative. Though Nuada gives Connacht to Sreng, we hear very little of the Firbolgs from this point onwards. I like to imagine that they were eventually assimilated into the Tuatha Dé Danaan through war, intermarriage or both.

4. A New King

1. Reading this chapter, you might wonder whether Nuada had a son and if so, why he did not become king. In ancient Ireland and many other societies, kingship was not conferred through parentage. When a king died, it was customary for his successor to be elected from among his chief followers, as we see happening here.

   On the subject of family relations, I chose to depict who is related to whom only when necessary. Many of the principal characters are listed as being kin in the medieval texts, yet these relationships often feel crudely forced and rarely have any bearing on events.

   The Dagda is believed to have been the principal deity in ancient Ireland. His name derives from the Celtic *dago-Dewios,* the second part of which means 'sky' and links him to the Latin *Deus* and Greek *Zeus*. He is often referred to as the Good God, with 'good' in this case referring to ability rather than character. Linked with the sun in particular as well as the sky, he is strongly associated with fertility, farming and brewing, which led some Christian writers to portray him as a grotesque glutton with an enormous stomach and member.

   Some readers might feel uncomfortable with the Dagda's exclusion of

Bres on the basis of race. Bear in mind that the word 'race' is closer here to 'species' than our own definition of the word, and is located within a cosmology which includes supernatural creatures whose very nature is death and destruction.

5. The Spoils of War

1. The idea that the king and the land are one may seem strange to us. It is reflective of an ancient belief now known as animism, which appears to have been almost universal until the advent of monotheism. Animism tells us that all things are ensouled, alive and conscious.

    Nuada's advice to Bres, and the law that the king must be whole, is founded on the idea that there is a kind of sacred relationship, sometimes expressed as a marriage, between a sovereign and the land they rule. This idea was once widespread and can be seen expressed in numerous rituals and myths.

    In the Gaelic kingdom of Dalriada in Scotland, the king placed his foot into a footprint carved into the stone. In the Sumerian city of Uruk, a young man representing the mythic shepherd Dumuzid would couple with a priestess of the fertility goddess Inanna in her temple. Back in Ireland, historical kings would marry the land in a ritual known as *banais ríghe*.

    A well-known known folk tale motif deriving from this concept is that of the loathly lady. In these stories, a male hero kisses an ugly woman only for her to transform into a beautiful young woman, who reveals she has been under a curse and bestows gifts upon the hero. Examples include the Fianna tale of 'The Daughter of King Under Wave' and the Arthurian story of 'The Wedding of Sir Gawain & Dame Ragnelle', which appears in another guise as 'The Wife of Bath's Tale'.

6. A Time of Chains

1. Manannán is something of an enigma even among the Tuatha Dé Danaan (who are all pretty enigmatic). He was known in Wales as Manawydan and appears in that guise in the Welsh legendary collection *The Mabinogion*. In some stories he is said to live upon the Isle of Man (a place with strong otherworld associations) and in others he is said to live beneath the sea. His title 'Mac Lir' translates as 'Son of the Sea'.

    In many stories we see him using magic, while in some later narratives he is depicted as a shapeshifting trickster figure. In the *Lebor Gabála Érenn*, his appearances are relatively rare; he seems to stand apart from the

Tuatha Dé Danaan. Yet when he does ride in on his shining white steed, we get the impression he is greatly respected, able to advise the entire race of the Tuatha Dé Danaan. Tolkien's Gandalf is known to be based on Odin, but perhaps Tolkien took some inspiration from Manannán as well?

Morgan Daimler's *Pagan Portals – Manannán Mac Lir* is an excellent resource on Manannán.

This chapter is an exciting one as we finally meet our first Fomorians since the prologue. As mentioned in the introduction, the Fomorians went from being seen as something like 'underworld phantoms' to pirates and even Vikings. They might have been a real historical people, demonised by their enemies. In the *Lebor Gabála Érenn* various individual Fomorians are described as dog-headed, or having one arm, one tooth and one leg. At other times, they are alike to the Tuatha Dé Danaan in appearance.

It is common for mythological figures to become smaller in stature over time. Gods becomes legendary heroes then folk tale tricksters and end up as mascots and fridge magnets. An obvious example of this is Lugh; though this is by no means certain, this towering god of Celtic myth may be the origin of the leprechaun. Ó hOgáin suggests that the sometimes human, sometimes monstrous Fomorians might once have been awesome, primeval beings, perhaps akin to the Vanir of Norse myth or the Asuras of India. Their fight with the Tuatha Dé Danaan might once have been a clash of cosmic, elemental forces, a battle between night, day, life and death.

Thus there exists a spectrum of representations on which a teller must plant themselves. I've depicted the Fomorians as monstrous and other-worldly but with some human characteristics; more earthy representations are no less valid.

7. The Silver Hand

1. The dynamic between the family of healers depicted here is an enjoyable (at least for now) dimension of the mythological cycle. Diancecht was a god of healing, his name meaning 'Swift Traveller', who becomes a more earthly doctor or physician in our source texts. He is sometimes presented as having other children beyond Miach and Airmed, but they are the two with the most agency. They are appealing characters – Airmed is particularly popular with modern followers of Irish Paganism – but the texts tell us very little about them.

Diancecht is sometimes said in the texts to have a well of healing, at other times a cauldron. I chose the association with wells to avoid him lugging a cauldron around on the road. Wells are also a bit bigger than cauldrons, and thus better for healing entire armies.

Goibniu, whose name means 'smith', was certainly a pagan deity. He is sometimes given as the owner of the Cow of Plenty; some stories have the cow belonging to his friend Cian, whom we will meet later. The Cow of Plenty (in Irish, *Glas Gaibhnenn,*) is discussed in the notes to 'The Birth of Angus'.

8. A King Reforged

1. One of the major differences between stories as they were written in the early Middle Ages, and stories as they are written now, is that the emotions of characters was very little discussed. There were no inner monologues as typically found in modern novels. Generally speaking, we know what a character feels because they tell us so in words or because we infer it from their actions or their literal description.

   We might then interpret Nuada's metal hand as telling us that he is cold, rigid, unfeeling. I chose to make him somewhat stubborn, hard when he needs to be, but showing tenderness in his relationship with Bres.

   The hero who loses their hand is a theme that has been picked up in modern stories, with two obvious examples being Luke Skywalker and Jaime Lannister. George Lucas is widely believed to have drawn inspiration from Irish mythology; fans have conjectured that George R.R. Martin did the same, but (as far as I know) this hasn't been confirmed either way.

9. A Cloak of Flowers

1. For many readers, this is the most heartbreaking episode of the cycle. In order to make Diancecht's actions here more believable, I've emphasised the conflict between him and his son in this chapter and the previous ones, making Miach the more skilled healer of the two.

   Despite Diancecht's actions here, there is little in the texts to suggest that his people blamed him for his son's murder, and he appears to have remained a popular deity in Ireland. Miach's death in this chapter doesn't stop him from appearing later on in the *Lebor Gabála Érenn*, working alongside his father and sister at the Second Battle of Moytura. This doesn't fit with the tone of my narrative so I chose to have him remain dead.

10. The Flight of Bres

1. The Fomorians are nowadays strongly associated with Tory Island, a small island off the coast of Donegal, where Balor is said to have his hall. They are also said to come from below the sea and below the earth.

   I chose not to make Tory Island the Fomorian homeland in part because it is too small to raise an army capable of threatening the entire population of Ireland. I also wanted to depict a more liminal Fomorian realm, one in line with their casting as otherworldly, primeval entities.

   I've thus depicted their realm as lying across the sea, though a veil, though they can appear at times from beneath the sea and beneath Ireland itself. Their realm intersects with ours but not in a way that you could plot on a map, rather like the nine realms of Norse myth.

   This doesn't make logical sense, but myth isn't always meant to make logical sense! At times, myth will depict things that logic can grasp; at other times it speaks a language that only makes sense to the subconscious, dreaming mind. Much of myth's value lies in training us to hold both modes of perception at once, like a Fianna warrior dancing on the tips of spears.

11. The Coming of Lugh

1. Lugh is the central character in this story and throughout the second part of the cycle. Though well-known as an Irish deity, Lugh also turns up in Welsh myth, where he appears as Llew Llaw Gyffes, nephew of the magician Gwydion, in the fabulous story of the Fourth Branch of *The Mabinogion*. Over on the continent, he was known to the Gauls as Lugos. His Irish name of Lugh Lamhfada translates as 'Lugh of the Long Arm', as he is sometimes referred to here. He is also known as the Ildánach, or many-skilled.

   Nowadays, Lugh lives on in the Lughnasa Festival. Taking place on 1st August, midway between the summer solstice and autumn equinox, the festival celebrates the beginning of the harvest and can feature games, athletic contests, feasting and the dressing of holy wells. The festival is still widely celebrated in Ireland, and to a lesser extent on Man and in Scotland, and by pagans worldwide. There are several stories of the festival's origins. One comes from the *Lebor Gabála Érenn* and tells us that Lugh himself started the festival in honour of his mother, Tailtu, who died after clearing for agriculture the plain known by her name.

   You can hear me tell this story on episode 70 of *House of Legends* podcast.

12. The Birth of Lugh

1. This version of Lugh's origin is based on the work of Lady Gregory. Gregory (1852–1932) was a writer, playwright and translator and, alongside W. B. Yeats, a major figure in the Irish literary renaissance. She is best known for *Cuchulain of Muirthemne* and *Gods and Fighting Men*, which retold the stories of the Mythological Cycle, the Ulster Cycle and the Fenian Cycle. Though her work has been widely praised, including by Thomas Kinsella, translator of *The Táin*, she has also been criticised for censoring her work to suit Victorian tastes.

   Gregory put together her version of this story using a number of different folk tales, which is why the story strikes a different tone to others in this volume. This version of Lugh's origin is thus fairly recent but has become very prominent.

   Stories about Balor are particularly popular in Donegal, with some casting him as a wily trickster rather than a dark lord. In Gregory's version, Balor holds his daughter captive in his glass tower on Tory Island.

13. A Gathering of Strength

1. Horses appear often in the Ulster Cycle, in which they draw chariots, though there is no evidence that chariots were ever used for warfare in Ireland. They appear less often in the Fianna Cycle, and even less often in the Mythological Cycle. The overall impression one gets of the Tuatha Dé Danaan at war is that of a force fighting on foot. I have incorporated Gregory's fleeting description of the Riders of the Sidhe into my telling as I found it an interesting counterpoint to the typical Tuatha Dé Danaan fighting style.

14. The Battle of Eas Dara

1. This chapter is based upon some short passages by Gregory, which I enlarged upon in order to give time for momentum towards the Great Battle of Moytura to build.

   Concurrent to these events in Gregory's text is a tale known as 'The Sons of Tuireann'. In this story, Cian (who made it home after his journey to retrieve the Cow of Plenty) is murdered by three brothers who are then ordered by Lugh to go on a quest of atonement. It's a reasonably entertaining story but long, discordant and largely irrelevant to our main narrative, so I've left it out, and left open the question of whether Cian survived his quest to retrieve the Cow of Plenty.

We will see a little more of Bodb Dearg in the coming chapters, though sadly the source texts tell us little about him. His name 'Bodb' can be translated as 'fighting man', with the epithet 'Dearg' meaning 'red' in Irish. He is sometimes given as a son of the Dagda.

15. The Muster of Lugh's Army

1. The names of Balor's generals and magic-workers given here come from the source texts. The texts give few hints as to their appearance, personality and distinctive roles, however, so these are my own invention. I've elevated Lobais to a prominent role as I felt the Fomorians needed a powerful sorcerer on their side, given the magical firepower the Tuatha Dé Danaan will bring to the party.

I've deviated from the sources in describing how the Dagda delays the Fomorians. The Dagda is commonly depicted in medieval texts as an oafish glutton, his belly and behind bulging out from his clothes, with uncontrollable appetites for food, drink and sex. There is good reason to believe that this was a character assassination by Christian writers, intended to turn the revered god into a figure of fun. Normally, we see the Fomorians mock the Dagda when he visits them by filling an enormous cauldron with food and forcing him to eat it, which he happily does. I had no desire to perpetuate this image of the Dagda, so instead created a scene in which he used his magical harp to delay the enemy.

The following scene between the Morrigan and the Dagda originates in the *Cath Maige Tuired* and gives us a chance to see her more peaceful and sensual aspects. We can also see this as her bestowing through sex her blessing upon the Tuatha Dé Danaan fighters, mirroring the kind of sovereignty ritual mentioned in the footnotes to 'The Spoils of War'.

16. The Second Battle of Moytura

1. These next few chapters necessitated a fair bit of creativity on my part, as the sources don't get into the nitty gritty of battlefield action. The framework given by the sources is that Lugh gathers his chiefs and champions, asking how they will serve, which they answer as you have seen. He is informed of their decision not to let him fight, as his loss would be too great a blow. We learn that Diancecht heals fallen Tuatha at the Well of Slaine, and that Bres helps the Fomorians concoct a plan to weaken their enemies by taking out Goibniu and destroying the well. Otherwise, the

details of the fighting, the parts played by Liath, the exact words of Corpre's speech and Lugh's flashback are my own invention.

You will recall that the Second Battle of Moytura takes place in a different location to the first, as explained in the footnotes to that chapter. This battle is said to have taken place by Lough Arrow in County Sligo.

Caitlín's name may appear discordant as it is a form of the French name Catherine. She is sometimes called Caitlín of the Crooked Tooth, suggesting an unattractive appearance, but other than this and her gift of prophecy, we know very little of her.

17. Three Blows

1. The scenes at the well and the forge are elaborations upon scenes in the *Cath Maige Tuired*. Ruadan is given there as Bres' son by Brigid; I omitted this detail as foreshadowing this would have required more invention and distraction from the main narrative than I felt was appropriate. In the *Cath Maige Tuired*, Brigid finds her son dead and sings a grief song over his body, which is said to be the first keening heard in Ireland.

On the subject of Brigid, she was a pagan goddess who was amalgamated over time with a historical saint. The goddess appears to have come to Ireland via the powerful British tribe of the Briganti who moved into Ireland in the 1st century. She is mentioned in the *Lebor Gabála Érenn* but takes little action other than in the scene mentioned above.

The saint Brigid lived in the 5th–6th centuries and is considered one of the three patron saints of Ireland. She founded a famous monastery in Kildare and is well-loved in Ireland, appearing in numerous folk tales and giving her name to the feast of St Brigid's day (1st February) which subsumed the pagan festival of Imbolc.

I have given Airmed a prominent role in the scene at the well. We know from the *Cath Maige Tuired* that she was present but the text does not mention her in this particular scene.

18. The Eye of Balor

1. These events again follow the basic pattern laid out in the *Cath Maige Tuired*. Balor kills Nuada; Lugh enters the fray and kills Balor as his eye opens.

In the *Cath Maige Tuired* Lugh uses his slingshot rather than the Spear of Victory. The biblical story of David and Goliath very likely influenced this.

19. The Aftermath

1. Tethra may have been a divinity related to the sea. He is said in other stories to have been reborn as a ruler of Mag Mell, an island far to the west of Ireland which can be seen as an afterlife paradise, a literal place which intrepid voyagers can reach, or both. The scene between Oghma and Tethra is tantalising in its brevity and has inspired modern video game designers, with the sword appearing as a rare magical item in *The Mabinogi* online role-playing game.

   The scene in which Bres escapes execution by imparting knowledge relating to farming is very important. It echoes back to the time when this story was a cosmic clash between the forces of night and day, underlining the association between the Fomorians and the earth and reminding us of the victory of the Aesir (warlike sky-gods) over the Vanir (a group of fertility gods) in Norse myth.

20. Enter the Gaels

1. We now enter Part III, in which the Gaels or Milesians, supposedly the ancestors of the modern-day Irish, win Ireland from the Tuatha Dé Danaan.

   The narrative given here and continued in the following chapter originates in the *Lebor Gabála Érenn*. The text gives an incredibly complex and confusing backstory to these people, tying them to Moses, the Israelites, the pharaoh of Egypt and the king of Scythia, with their ultimate origins lying in Scythia.

   I've offered here a massively simplified backstory, forgoing the biblical associations of the *Lebor Gabála Érenn* in favour of a narrative centred on Amergin, whom I find the most interesting and fleshed-out character of the invading Gaels. Once his force reaches Ireland, I've followed the narrative of the *Lebor Gabála Érenn*, with the three queens (or earth goddesses) blessing the invasion, followed by a negotiation with the three Tuatha Dé Danaan kings which leads to the contest described in the following chapter.

   Though this story is for the most part a medieval fabrication, it reflects the historical reality of Ireland being successfully settled by waves of incomers. However, unlike in these tales, the Celtic tribes who arrived from around 500 BC probably arrived in a steady stream rather than a great invasion fleet. Upon entering a land already occupied – for Ireland had been settled since at least 7000 BC – they likely did their best to assimilate themselves to the existing culture. The writers of the *Lebor Gabála*

Érenn may have had a different view of the past, imagining waves of violent conquest.

21. The Song of Amergin

1. This battle for Ireland centres on a spell-poem which has become known far beyond those who read Irish myth. Though the exact words were probably the invention of the author of the *Lebor Gabála Érenn*, it likely reflects ancient animistic beliefs in which spiritual practitioners could reach beyond their own consciousness and into the souls of animals, celestial bodies and the universe itself. I added the final line 'It is I'.

   Rees and Rees in *Celtic Heritage* note the similarity between Amergin's poem and Krishna's words in the *Bhagavad Gita*: 'I am the radiant sun... I am the moon... I am the spirit of fire, I am Meru among the mountain peaks'. This reinforces the idea that such spell-poetry echoes back to ancient, Indo-European origins.

   We can assume that to speak such words in poetry was not done to relay information but rather as a performative act, reinforcing connections through which a practitioner could channel divine power.

   The source texts do not go into any detail about the wars of succession following the Gaels' successful invasion, so I've given these only a brief mention before moving onto the more colourful post-invasion tales of the cycle.

   On their collaborative album *Immortal Memory*, Lisa Gerrard and Patrick Cassidy created a stunningly atmospheric piece of music, entitled 'The Song of Amergin', in which Gerrard sings the poem in Irish. It's a wonderful way to experience the poem in a different form.

22. The Birth of Angus

1. As well as giving us the origins of Angus Óg, this story acts as a prelude to the much larger following tale: 'Midir & Étaín'. In the sources they are one story, which has its own peculiar origin tale. 'The Wooing of Étaín' was recorded in the 12th century *Book of the Dun Cow*, but was incomplete until two missing sections turned up in the Phillips Collection in Cheltenham, England, in 1935.

   I find this story particularly interesting as it allows us to explore the Dagda's character, and the trouble his appetites can cause, without going so far as to lampoon him. Angus will go on to be a recurring character, not only in this cycle but in the Fianna Cycle, where he acts as a foster parent and guide to Diarmuid.

It should be noted that Elcmar may have been another name for Nuada, who is named at times as Boann's husband yet has no agency in that role. I omitted this relationship in Nuada's chapters as it wouldn't work to have her present but never speaking or taking action.

The earlier form of Boann's name was Bouvinda, which can be translated as 'white cow' or 'illuminated cow', with the second translation suggesting wisdom as well as literal brightness. We can thus see a connection between her and the Cow of Plenty, which is mirrored in Vedic belief.

Irish and Vedic mythology are believed to have derived from a common Indo-European ancestor. The Vedic name Govinda is an epithet for Vishnu and his avatar Krishna, both of whom are strongly associated with cows. This leads us to an association between Boann, the Cow of Plenty and Danu.

As mentioned previously, Danu is likely an early Celtic mother goddess who gave her name to the river Danube. She survived as the mother of the Tuatha Dé Danaan in Irish myth, and as the goddess Danu in Hindu myth, where she appears as the embodiment of the primeval waters in the famous story of 'The Churning of the Ocean'. Rivers are associated with the milk of cows in Vedic myth.

Thus we have a tantalising web of associations between Boann, the Cow of Plenty and Danu. None of this can tell us exactly how the ancient Irish saw these figures, of course, but it gives our imaginations plenty to go on.

25. Midir & Étaín: Part III

1. As mentioned previously, this strange and beautiful story was recorded in the 12th century *Book of the Dun Cow*. The story is very popular today and has inspired numerous retellings and artworks. Many modern retellers have Étaín turning into a butterfly or dragonfly rather than a fly, but the scholarly consensus seems to be that she became a (possibly purple) fly. Étaín's name has been said to translate as 'one who provokes envy'.

There is a further section of the story in which Eochaid sets out to recover Étaín. The narrative becomes quite confusing and loses impetus at this point, so some storytellers will end the story with the two swans flying away together, as I've done here. You can read Jeffrey Gantz's translation of the original story 'The Wooing of Étaín' in his excellent *Early Irish Myths & Sagas*.

26. The Dream of Angus

1. This version of Angus's story was inspired by a telling by Aron Hegarty on *Candlelit Tales* podcast. Aron heard it from a teller named Brendan Nolan.

   The story was found in a 15th century manuscript and is mentioned in the 1160 *Book of Leinster*. It is a well-known one and may have inspired Yeats' poem 'The Song of Wandering Aengus'. In the better-known version of this story, Angus enlists the help of Bodb Dearg, as well as King Ailil and Queen Maeve of the Ulster Cycle, to help him find his lost love.

27. The Voyage of Bran

1. This very early story dates back to between the 7th and mid-8th centuries. Its gentle, dreamy tone may give it the feel of a classic, almost textbook Celtic voyaging tale. But there is a lot more going on beneath the surface.

   Mark Williams includes a fascinating study of this story in *Ireland's Immortals*, in which he argues that the story is almost a parody of pagan belief. Williams points out that divinisation, the idea that humans could become gods through the word of God, was central to early Gaelic Christianity. To this end, the tale's author puts Ireland's pagan gods to work as metaphors for redeemed souls who can lead a hero to salvation.

   Thus when Bran encounters Manannán, Manannán (in the first literary appearance of a pagan Irish god) tells Bran that while Bran sees a plain of water, he sees a flowery plain. Williams argues that this is Manannán standing in for God himself, telling Bran that what appears temporary is in truth eternal. Saying that the sea is a flowery plain, that one thing is another, may be intended to act like a Zen koan, breaking down the limiting, logical structures of the human mind.

   While this may well be true, it does not mean that the pre-Christian Irish did not also recognise and interpret the dynamic between the temporal and eternal, as we considered in the notes to 'The Song of Amergin'.

28. The Children of Lir

1. We close with probably the most famous Irish story. It's a fairly recent narrative, possibly 14th century, and is likely related to the European stories of 'The Six Swans' and 'The Seven Ravens' recorded by the Brothers Grimm. The presence of the new faith in the story makes it a fitting place to close this cycle.

Aoife is sometimes painted as a typical wicked stepmother; I wanted to explore a more sympathetic take on her. The swan children are usually portrayed as converting to Christianity without reservation, with their baptism assuring entry to heaven, while other tellings will have the swans return to the Tuatha Dé Danaan. I wanted to portray an ambivalent set of relationships between Malachi, the swans and the new faith, along with a more open-ended conclusion.

The story has inspired a huge amount of music, literature and art. It also inspired a very moving statue in the Garden of Remembrance in Dublin, commemorating those who gave their lives in the centuries of struggle for Irish freedom.

ALSO BY DANIEL ALLISON

Scottish Myths & Legends

Scottish Myths & Legends Volume II (coming soon)

Finn & The Fianna

The Orkney Cycle: The Shattering Sea

Silverborn & Other Tales

HOUSE OF LEGENDS PODCAST

House of Legends is a podcast focused on deep and powerful stories told by storytellers from across the world. Stories are told alternately by Daniel and his guests, and Daniel also regularly shares readings from his books.

Listen on Apple Podcasts, Spotify or wherever you get your podcasts.

FREE DOWNLOAD OFFER

The Celtic Mythology Handbook is an accessible and entertaining introduction to Celtic Mythology. I've drawn on my extensive experience as an author and teacher to create the guide I once looked for but never found.

I'm offering the Celtic Mythology Handbook as a FREE full colour PDF download exclusively to members of the House of Legends Clan.

Get my FREE full colour PDF at www.houseoflegend-s.me/landing-page

ABOUT THE AUTHOR

Daniel Allison is a *USA Today* bestselling author, oral storyteller, podcaster and storytelling coach from Scotland. He hosts the *House of Legends* podcast and is the author of *Scottish Myths & Legends, Irish Mythology, Finn & The Fianna* and *The Orkney Cycle*, as well as the forthcoming *Scottish Myths & Legends Vol. II*.

Myth Singers, Daniel's online Celtic Storytelling Apprenticeship, provides a unique training platform for emerging storytellers throughout the world. He leads annual mythic immersion retreats in the Scottish Highlands which support participants to create a living relationship with traditional stories.

Daniel has performed throughout the world, from the jungles of Peru to Thai villages, Hebridean hilltops, Indian theatres, Arabian markets and global festivals. He divides his time between Scotland and Thailand.

Made in the USA
Columbia, SC
26 October 2024

45112508R00239